3D Fraud Risk Assessment Model

Dinev's SMARTGuide

IEPI - Institute of Expert Fraud Examiners

FIRST EDITION - 2012

From The Experts

"Dr. Dimiter Dinev is one of Europe's most progressive anti-fraud thinkers, whom I have known personally for more than a decade.

He is founder and chairman of the Association for Counteraction to Economic Fraud and an accomplished researcher.

The 3D Model of Fraud Risk Assessment (Dinev's SMARTGuide) is a revolutionary new approach to fighting fraud, which could be of untold benefit to organisations."

Dr. Joseph T. Wells, CFE, CPA
Founder and Chairman
Association of Certified Fraud Examiners

April 18, 2012

Foreword

The more money you are waiting to get it - the higher is the risk that you will not get it!

The Author

Dear Reader,

Dinev's SmartGuide was developed as a result of the recently performed research and my own experience as a Founder and Chairman of The Association for Counteraction to Economic Fraud and it presents "The 3D Fraud Risk Assessment Model" (3D FRAM)!

For the first time you will be introduced to the originally developed Fraud Risk Assessment Model created in 3 Dimensions: Functional, Methodological and Timing Dimensions!

You maybe already have heard about " The Dinev's Compass for Fraud Detection" published in Fraud Magazine, ACFE, 1/2009, and "The Puzzle for Fraud Investigation" presented first at The IX PIKW Congress in Krakow, Poland in 2010.

For the first time my "3D Fraud Risk Assessment Model" was presented in Krakow in 2011 and in Internet trough LinkedIn but its detailed description is before you now.

All of my current and future publications will be available and found on the Internet Web pages of www.iepinet.eu in BG and/or USA sections!

I would like to dedicate this publication to my friend Dr. Joseph T. Wells, The Founder and Chairman of ACFE (Association of Certified Fraud Examiners) for his enormous and valuable support and for his help as to make me able to continue my work in the sphere of fighting fraud.

I would like to thank all the members of The Association for Counteraction to Economic Fraud for their support and efforts to help me as to develop this "3D Fraud Risk Assessment Model"!

Dr. Dimiter Dinev, CFE, EFE

Founder & Chairman of ACEF

April 18, 2012

Sofia, Bulgaria

How To Use Dinev's SMARTGuide?

The Dinev's SmartGuide is divided into the following parts:

Part I: Navigating Fraud Risk Assessment Terminology

Dinev's SMARTGuide provides a range of terminology, semantics, corruption and fraud taxonomy and samples applied to the 3D FRAM. This part shows you the classical and modern approaches and uses of Risk, Chance, Fraud, Fraud Risk Appetite and Tolerance, Corruption, Perception to Detection, Fraud Resistance, The Limitations of the current COSO Internal Control Framework and the Glossary of terms.

Part II: 3D FRAM

Dinev's SMARTGuide covers the chapters about what 3D Fraud Risk Assessment (3D FRAM) does best. This part will help governmental entities and businesses of all sizes, from sole proprietorships, non-for-profit organizations to large corporations learn how to help themselves using 3D FRAM. The Model is developed and presented in 3 dimensions: Functional, Methodological and Timing Dimensions. This part covers its goals, actors and the knowledge needed as to provide this new business opportunity. Where it is you're going you will be using Dinev's SMARTGuide in .pdf, .ePub and .MOBI formats with your tablet, reader and/or smart phone.

Part III: 3D FRAM - Functional Dimension

"The Functional Dimension" encompasses all functions of the systematic fraud risk assessment process. This part presents "What To Do" and also reveals the detailed description of the fraud scenarios and their variations, ranging the fraud risk and recommends the measures if necessary. You also learn about The Fraud Scenario and how to create the 13 (8W+5H) fatal for the fraudster questions looking for the reliable data and information.

Part IV: 3D FRAM - Methodological Dimension

This part will learn you "How To Do" or to apply different methods and techniques for conducting all the functions necessary for the 3D FRAM. The methods and techniques like data mining, discovery sampling, Internet search engines, specialized software, what-if-analysis, cost benefit and sensitivity analysis will help you to receive and analyze quantitate and qualitative data as to reach the final conclusion.

Part V: 3D FRAM - Timing Dimension

Time is money! As any other business engagement the 3D FRAM is limited in time and depends on the other two dimensions the 3D FRAM - Functional and Methodical Dimensions. Proper planning and organizing the conduct of the 3D FRAM is the prerequisite for a successful finalizing of the engagement.

Part VI: 3D FRAM as a Part of Experts' Responsibilities following the ISA 240 and SAS 99

Find out about how 3D FRAM could be used and applied as a part of the financial statement audit following the requirements of ISA 240 and SAS 99.

Part I: Navigating Fraud Risk Assessment Terminology

In this part:

- What The Dinev's SMARTGuide Isn't and Is?
- Fraud And Corruption Terminology
- Fraud Risk Assessment Framework

1.1. WHAT THE DINEV'S SMARTGUIDE ISN'T AND IS?

First of all, the title of this Guide - "Dinev's SMARTGuide" presumes a pool of ideas, assumptions, references, samples and comments which will be filled and expanded continuously with new ideas, comments, recommendations and guidelines.

Second, the author of the SMARGuide, Dr. Dimiter Petrov Dinev, is the Founder and Chairman of The Association for Counteraction to Economic Fraud and Certified Fraud Examiner with knowledge, expertise and experience in the field of for more than 26 years.

1.1.1. The Dinev's SMARTGuide Isn't ...

- The Dinev's SMARTGuide is not a Fraud Risk Assessment Bible. The Bible metaphor presupposes so many things as a central source for resource information, a paid staff dutifully indexing new material as it comes in, a well understood and rigorously adhered-to ontology - that trying to think of the SMARTGuide as a Bible can be misleading.

- Dinev's SMARTGuide is a snapshot of all that there is recently developed and applied. Nobody - not even Wikipedia - knows everything. There's simply too much and its all flowing too fast to keep up.

- Everything in The Dinev's SMARTGuide is credible. It's not. There are presumptions and things in it that are biased, or maybe just wrong—whether intentional or not. Watch out!

- Using your own knowledge and experience and content filtering will protect you from offensive ideas and recommendations. While the author's knowledge and experience about the matter and his content filtering is good, it's certainly not perfect.

- Dinev's SMARTGuide covers all the areas and terminology of the risk management and respectively fraud risk assessment. It simply cannot be so. It presents a model which could be applied only with regard of the specifics of each organization.

1.1.2. The Dinev's SMARTGuide Is ...

- Dinev's SMARTGuide is a methodology which provides a range of terminology, semantics, fraud and corruption taxonomy and samples applied to the 3D Fraud Risk Assessment Model (3D FRAM). It shows you new approaches and uses of Risk, Fraud, Fraud Risk Appetite and Tolerance, Perception of Detection, Fraud Resistance, Fraud Risk Assessment.

- Dinev's SMARTGuide covers the chapters about what 3D Fraud Risk Assessment (3D FRAM) does best. It will help governmental entities and businesses of all sizes, from sole proprietorships, non-for-profit organizations to large corporations learn how to help themselves using 3D FRAM. developed and presented in 3 dimensions: Functional, Methodological and Timing Dimensions.

- You're not stuck to your desk with Dinev's SMART Guide. When you're on the go, find out where it is you're going using Dinev's SMARTGuide in .pdf, .ePub and .MOBI formats with your tablet, reader and/or smart phone. It also helps you get the most from the different approaches underlying the systematic process of fraud risk assessment.

- You also learn about applying the 3D FRAM as a responsibility following ISA 240 or SAS 99 during an financial statement audit.

- Dinev's SMARTGuide could be dealt as "The New Kid On The Anti-Fraud Wall" providing insights of this new study and the approaches associating the fraud risk assessment!

Let's dive in the ocean of the fraud risk assessment taxonomy and terminology!

1.2. FRAUD AND CORRUPTION TAXONOMY

3D FRAM develops a Fraud and Corruption Taxonomy of different types of fraud and abuse with their definitions, directions and specifics which could be practically used for the fraud risk assessment engagement regarding their significance in quantitative and qualitative impacts.

1.2.1. Risk, Chance, Fraud and Corruption

There is a diversity of definitions of terms like risk, risk management and risk assessment but there are not so many studies and practical applications of the fraud risk, fraud risk assessment and fraud risk management! You are reading one of the few ones!

The risk is usually associated with the likelihood of some irregular, wrong, undesired or non-prestigious event to occur now or in the future. For example, the more money you are waiting to get in, the higher is the risk that you won't get in. Risk is widely used in the terminology of banking, insurance and investing industries and especially recently with introducing the corporate risk management approaches.

The chance, from another point of view, usually presents the likelihood that something desired, intended and prestigious (lotto winner, for example) would be happened. Another example, the use of the Dinev's SMARTGuide for 3D FRAM will enhance the chance to mitigate the fraud risk and to strengthen the whole organizational resistance to fraud.

There are many definitions of *fraud* and for purposes of this SMARTGuide we will use the definition already applied by the authors of "Managing the Business Risk of Fraud: A Practical Guide": *"Fraud is any intentional act or omission designed to deceive others, resulting in the victim suffering a loss and/or the perpetrator achieving a gain."*[1]

For the definition of corruption we are using the following definition: *"The abuse of public or private occupation for personal gain"*.

Before starting the discussion of the taxonomy of fraud and fraud scams which covers as many forms of inappropriate commercial behavior as possible, our compound definition of fraud and corruption will be:

"Any form of theft, embezzlement and abuse in the widest sense, deception in financial and non financial reporting, bribery and illegal gifts in the widest sense and any other form of dishonest or unethical activity which eats into profits or harms reputation or the organizational culture."

Of course, this is just a working definition and it is not perfect. Maybe, it will take years to reach international agreement on the definitions of fraud and corruption and on what it costs organizations and economies. Rather than waiting for precise international definitions to materialize the Dinev's SMARTGuide proposes that organizations start gaining a better understanding of the fraud and corruption risks that they face and then developing a much greater level of chance to deter and resist to them.

Whether you are an owner, a manager, or an executive director or an employee, it makes sense to pay more attention to the behavioral aspects of fraudsters, corrupt public or private employees, rather than being blinded by accounting, legal or procedural risk issues.

There are currently different approaches existed addressing the research issues of risk in the context of internal control systems involving its assessment, appetite, tolerance, velocity, ranging and management as a whole. The risk assessment and risk management concepts are widely applied not only in banking, insurance and investing activities but as in all internal controls systems worldwide.

While the fraud risk assessment is conducted traditionally as a part of the "inherent", "strategic" or "operational" risks, this type of risk has its specifics merely because fraud is a crime everywhere in the world, fraud has multiple facets and is usually a part of the most known crimes. The main goal of this publication is to develop a methodology covering the *fraud universe* which would be used for conducting further studies and developing more effective and practical tools for fraud resistance in all organizations.

Before focusing on the specific process of fraud risk assessment we will show you why we already use the term "fraud universe" describing below our try to the taxonomy of corruption, fraud and fraud scams.

And after highlighting this endless and continually expended universe of possible fraudulent acts and scams we will continue with the underlying assumptions of our 3D Fraud Risk Assessment Model and our "ZERO" tolerance to fraud.

Let's continue with the taxonomy of fraud, fraudulent activities and corruption activities now!

1.2.2. Classifications of Fraud and Corruption

There are not so many classifications of the different types and facets of fraud and all the attempts usually have a common goal - to make clearer and understandable this phenomenon called fraud. For the purposes of Dinev's SMARTGuide we use main three classifications referencing to WIKIPEDIA, to ACFE (The Association of Certified Fraud Examiners) and to ACEF (The Association for Counteraction to Economic Fraud). The types of fraud grouped in these classifications will present the fraud universe, whose risks will be assessed for each type and in total.

1.2.2.1 WIKIPEDIA CLASSIFICATION OF FRAUD AND CORRUPTION

How WIKIPEDIA defines the different types of fraud in an alphabetical order you could see visiting the link: http://en.wikipedia.org/wiki/Fraud, about the corruption the link is: http://en.wikipedia.org/wiki/Corruption and all other associated links as references.

This Internet source is free and worldwide accessible!

Let's look at it!

"...FRAUD

In criminal law, a **fraud** is an intentional deception made for personal gain or to damage another individual; the related adjective is fraudulent. The specific legal definition varies by legal jurisdiction. Fraud is a crime, and also a civil law violation. Defrauding people or entities of money or valuables is a common purpose of fraud, but there have also been fraudulent "discoveries", e.g., in science, to gain prestige rather than immediate monetary gain.

Types of fraudulent acts

Fraud can be committed through many media, including mail, wire, phone, and the Internet (computer crime and Internet fraud). The international dimensions of the web and ease with which users can hide their location, the difficulty of checking identity and legitimacy online, and the simplicity with which hackers can divert browsers to dishonest sites and steal credit card details have all contributed to the very rapid growth of Internet fraud.

Types of criminal fraud include:

Advance-fee fraud - a confidence trick in which the target is persuaded to advance sums of money in the hope of realizing a significantly larger gain.

Bait and switch - a form of fraud, most commonly used in retail sales but also applicable to other contexts. First, customers are "baited" by advertising for a product or service at a low price; second, the customers discover that the advertised good is not available and are "switched" to a costlier product.

Bank fraud to obtain money, assets, or other property owned or held by a financial institution

Bankruptcy fraud - Bankruptcy fraud is a white-collar crime. While difficult to generalise across jurisdictions, common criminal acts under bankruptcy statutes typically involve concealment of assets, concealment or destruction of documents, conflicts of interest, fraudulent claims, false statements or declarations, and fee fixing or redistribution arrangements. Falsifications on bankruptcy forms often constitute perjury. Multiple filings are not in and of themselves criminal, but they may violate provisions of bankruptcy law. In the U.S., bankruptcy fraud statutes are particularly focused on the mental state of particular actions.[7][8

Benefit fraud, when someone obtains governmental benefit they are not entitled to or deliberately fails to report a change in their personal circumstances.

Counterfeiting of currency, documents or valuable goods

Charlatanism - A charlatan (also called swindler or mountebank) is a person practicing quackery or some similar confidence trick in order to obtain money, fame or other advantages via some form of pretense or deception. Charles Ponzi, for whom the "Ponzi scheme" is named, a scam that relies on a "pyramid" of "investors" who contribute money to a fraudulent programme.

Bernard Madoff, an American stockbroker who ran the world's largest Ponzi scheme, defrauding investors out of $18 billion.

Confidence tricks such as the 419 fraud and Spanish Prisoner creation of false companies or "long firms"

Diploma Mills - As qualifications become increasingly important in gaining employment, "diploma mills" (usually online sites that sell degree and diploma certificates) and unaccredited colleges are proliferating around the world. Most use traditional and respectable-sounding names (many of which are very similar to legitimate institutions) and many claim accreditation by bogus accreditation bodies, making the identification of such entities very problematic.

Embezzlement, taking money which one has been entrusted with on behalf of another party

False advertising - False advertising or deceptive advertising is the use of false or misleading statements in advertising. As advertising has the potential to persuade people into commercial transactions that they might otherwise avoid, many governments around the world use regulations to control false, deceptive or misleading advertising.

False billing - is a fraudulent act of invoicing or otherwise requesting funds from an individual or firm without showing obligation to pay. Such notices are often sent to owners of domain names, purporting to be legitimate renewal notices, although not originating from the owner's own registrar.

False insurance claims - are insurance claims filed with the intent to defraud an insurance provider.

Forgery of documents or signatures,

Franchise fraud where the real profit is earned, not by the sale of the product, but by the sale of new franchise licenses.

Fraud upon the court - "Fraud upon the court" has been defined by the 7th Circuit Court of Appeals to "embrace that species of fraud which does, or attempts to, defile the court itself, or is a fraud perpetrated by officers of the court so that the judicial machinery can not perform in the usual manner its impartial task of adjudging cases that are presented for adjudication".

Health fraud, for example selling of products known not to be effective, such as quack medicines,

Identity theft - Insurance fraud or false insurance claims are insurance claims filed with the intent to defraud an insurance provider.

Insurance fraud - Insurance fraud occurs when any act committed with the intent to fraudulently obtain some benefit or advantage to which they are not otherwise entitled or someone knowingly denies some benefit that is due and to which someone is entitled.

Investment frauds - Securities fraud, also known as stock fraud and investment fraud, is a practice that induces investors to make purchase or sale decisions on the basis of false information, frequently resulting in losses, in violation of the securities laws.

Generally speaking, securities fraud consists of deceptive practices in the stock and commodity markets, and occurs when investors are enticed to part with their money based on untrue statements.[1]

According to the FBI, securities fraud includes false information on a company's financial statement and Securities and Exchange Commission (SEC) filings; lying to corporate experts; insider trading; stock manipulation schemes, and embezzlement by stockbrokers.[4]

Ponzi schemes A Ponzi scheme is a fraudulent investment operation that pays returns to its investors from their own money or the money paid by subsequent investors, rather than from any actual profit earned by the individual or organization running the operation. The Ponzi scheme usually entices new investors by offering higher returns than other investments, in the form of short-term returns that are either abnormally high or unusually consistent. Perpetuation of the high returns requires an ever-increasing flow of money from new investors to keep the scheme going.

The system is destined to collapse because the earnings, if any, are less than the payments to investors. Usually, the scheme is interrupted by legal authorities before it collapses because a Ponzi scheme is suspected or because the promoter is selling unregistered securities. As more investors become involved, the likelihood of the scheme coming to the attention of authorities increases.

Pyramid schemes - A pyramid scheme is a non-sustainable business model that involves promising participants payment or services, primarily for enrolling other people into the scheme, rather than supplying any real investment or sale of products or services to the public. [1][2]

Pyramid schemes are illegal in many countries including Albania, Australia,[3] Brazil, Bulgaria, Canada, China,[4] Colombia,[5] Denmark, the Dominican Republic,[6] Estonia,[7] France, Germany, Hungary, Iceland, Iran,[8] Italy,[9] Japan,[10] Malaysia, Mexico, Nepal, The Netherlands,[11] New Zealand,[12] Norway,[13] the Philippines,[14] Poland, Portugal, Romania, [15] South Africa,[16] Spain, Sri Lanka,[17] Sweden,[18] Switzerland, Taiwan, Thailand,[19] Turkey,[20] the United Kingdom, and the United States.[21]

These types of schemes have existed for at least a century, some with variations to hide their true nature, and many people believe that multilevel marketing is also a pyramid scheme.[22][23][24][25]

Marriage fraud to obtain immigration rights without entitlement

Moving scam - A moving scam is a scam by a moving company in which company provides an estimate, loads the goods, then states a much higher price to deliver the goods, effectively holding the goods hostage.

Religious fraud - A term used for civil[1][2] or criminal fraud carried out in the name of a religion[3][4] or within a religion, e.g. false claims to being Kosher[5][6] or tax fraud.[7]

Rigged gambling games such as the shell game - The shell game (also known as *Thimblerig, Three shells and a pea, the old army game*) is portrayed as a gambling game, but in reality, when a wager for money is made, it is a confidence trick used to perpetrate fraud. In confidence trick slang, this swindle is referred to as a *short-con* because it is quick and easy to pull off.

Securities frauds - Securities fraud includes outright theft from investors and misstatements on a public company's financial reports. The term also encompasses a wide range of other actions, including insider trading, front running and other illegal acts on the trading floor of a stock or commodity exchange.[2][

Pump and dump - "Pump and dump" is a form of microcap stock fraud that involves artificially inflating the price of an owned stock through false and misleading positive statements, in order to sell the cheaply purchased stock at a higher price. Once the operators of the scheme "dump" their overvalued shares, the price falls and investors lose their money. Stocks that are the subject of pump-and-dump schemes are sometimes called "chop stocks".[1]

Tax fraud, not reporting revenue or illegally avoiding taxes. In some countries, tax fraud is also prosecuted under false billing or tax forgery[2]

United States

Common law fraud has nine elements:[3][4]

1. a representation of an existing fact;
2. its materiality;
3. its falsity;
4. the speaker's knowledge of its falsity;
5. the speaker's intent that it shall be acted upon by the plaintiff;
6. plaintiff's ignorance of its falsity;
7. plaintiff's reliance on the truth of the representation;
8. plaintiff's right to rely upon it; and
9. consequent damages suffered by plaintiff.

Most jurisdictions in the United States require that each element be pled with particularity and be proved with clear, cogent, and convincing evidence (very probable evidence) to establish a claim of fraud. The measure of damages in fraud cases is to be computed by the "benefit of bargain" rule, which is the difference between the value of the property had it been as represented, and its actual value. Special damages may be allowed if shown proximately caused by defendant's fraud and the damage amounts are proved with specificity.

CORRUPTION

Political corruption is the use of power by government officials for illegitimate private gain. Misuse of government power for other purposes, such as repression of political opponents and general police brutality, is not considered political corruption. Neither are illegal acts by private persons or corporations not directly involved with the government. An illegal act by an officeholder constitutes political corruption only if the act is directly related to their official duties, is done under color of law or involves trading in influence.

SYSTEMATIC CORRUPTION

Systemic corruption (or endemic corruption[5]) is corruption which is primarily due to a weaknesses of an organization or process. It can be contrasted with individual officials or agents who act corruptly within the system.

Factors which encourage systemic corruption include conflicting incentives, discretionary powers; monopolistic powers; lack of transparency; low pay; and a culture of impunity.[6] Specific acts of corruption include "bribery, extortion, and embezzlement" in a system where "corruption becomes the rule rather than the exception."[7] Scholars distinguish between centralized and decentralized systemic corruption, depending on which level of state or government corruption takes place; in countries such as the Post-Soviet states both types occur.[8]

Forms of corruption vary, but include bribery, extortion, cronyism, nepotism, patronage, graft, and embezzlement. Corruption may facilitate criminal enterprise such as drug trafficking, money laundering, and human trafficking, though is not restricted to these activities.

The activities that constitute illegal corruption differ depending on the country or jurisdiction. For instance, some political funding practices that are legal in one place may be illegal in another. In some cases, government officials have broad or ill-defined powers, which make it difficult to distinguish between legal and illegal actions. Worldwide, bribery alone is estimated to involve over 1 trillion US dollars annually.[1] A state of unrestrained political corruption is known as a kleptocracy, literally meaning "rule by thieves".

Types
Bribery

A bribe is a payment given personally to a government official in exchange of his use of official powers. Bribery requires two participants: one to give the bribe, and one to take it. Either may initiate the corrupt offering; for example, a customs official may demand bribes to let through allowed (or disallowed) goods, or a smuggler might offer bribes to gain passage. In some countries the culture of corruption extends to every aspect of public life, making it extremely difficult for individuals to stay in business without resorting to bribes. Bribes may be demanded in order for an official to do something he is already paid to do. They may also be demanded in order to bypass laws and regulations. In addition to using bribery for private financial gain, they are also used to intentionally and maliciously cause harm to another (i.e. no financial incentive). In some developing nations, up to half of the population has paid bribes during the past 12 months.[2]

In recent years, efforts have been made by the international community to encourage countries to dissociate and incriminate as separate offences, active and passive bribery. Active bribery can be defined for instance as *the promising, offering or giving by any person, directly or indirectly, of any undue advantage [to any public official], for himself or herself or for anyone else, for him or her to act or refrain from acting in the exercise of his or her functions.* (article 2 of the Criminal Law Convention on Corruption (ETS 173) of the Council of Europe). Passive bribery can be defined as *the request or receipt [by any public official], directly or indirectly, of any undue advantage, for himself or herself or for anyone else, or the acceptance of an offer or a promise of such an advantage, to act or refrain from acting in the exercise of his or her functions* (article 3 of the Criminal Law Convention on Corruption (ETS 173)). The reason for this dissociation is to make the early steps (offering, promising, requesting an advantage) of a corrupt deal already an offence and, thus, to give a clear signal (from a criminal policy point of view) that bribery is not acceptable. Furthermore, such a dissociation makes the prosecution of bribery offences easier since it can be very difficult to prove that two parties (the bribe-giver and the bribe-taker) have formally agreed upon a corrupt deal. In addition, there is often no such formal deal but only a mutual understanding, for instance when it is common knowledge in a municipality that to obtain a building permit one has to pay a "fee" to the decision maker to obtain a favourable decision. A working definition of corruption is also provided as follows in article 3 of the Civil Law Convention on Corruption (ETS 174): *For the purpose of this Convention, "corruption" means requesting, offering, giving or accepting, directly or indirectly, a bribe or any other undue advantage or prospect thereof, which distorts the proper performance of any duty or behavior required of the recipient of the bribe, the undue advantage or the prospect thereof.*

Trading in influence

Trading in influence, or influence peddling in some countries, refers to the situation where a person is selling his/her influence over the decision process involving a third party (person or institution). The difference with bribery is that this is a trilateral relation. From a legal point of view, the role of the third party (who is the target of the influence) does not really matter although he/she can be an accessory in some instances. It can be difficult to make a distinction between this form of corruption and some forms of extreme and loosely regulated lobbying where for instance law- or decision-makers can freely "sell" their vote, decision power or influence to those lobbyists who offer the highest compensation, including where for instance the latter act on behalf of powerful clients such as industrial groups who want to avoid the passing of specific environmental, social, or other regulations perceived as too stringent, etc. Where lobbying is (sufficiently) regulated, it becomes possible to provide for a distinctive criteria and to consider that trading in influence involves the use of "improper influence", as in article 12 of the Criminal Law Convention on Corruption (ETS 173) of the Council of Europe.

Patronage

Patronage refers to favoring supporters, for example with government employment. This may be legitimate, as when a newly elected government changes the top officials in the administration in order to effectively implement its policy. It can be seen as corruption if this means that incompetent persons, as a payment for supporting the regime, are selected before more able ones. In nondemocracies many government officials are often selected for loyalty rather than ability. They may be almost exclusively selected from a particular group (for example, Sunni Arabs in Saddam Hussein's Iraq, the nomenklatura in the Soviet Union, or the Junkers in Imperial Germany) that support the regime in return for such favors. A similar problem can also be seen in Eastern Europe, for example in Romania, where the government is often accused of patronage (when a new government comes to power it rapidly changes most of the officials in the public sector).

Nepotism and cronyism

Favoring relatives (nepotism) or personal friends (cronyism) of an official is a form of illegitimate private gain. This may be combined with bribery, for example demanding that a business should employ a relative of an official controlling regulations affecting the business. The most extreme example is when the entire state is inherited, as in North Korea or Syria. A milder form of cronyism is a "Good ol' boy network", in which appointees to official positions are selected only from a closed and exclusive social network – such as the alumni of particular universities – instead of appointing the most competent candidate.

Seeking to harm enemies becomes corruption when official powers are illegitimately used as means to this end. For example, trumped-up charges are often brought up against journalists or writers who bring up politically sensitive issues, such as a politician's acceptance of bribes.

Electoral fraud

Electoral fraud is illegal interference with the process of an election. Acts of fraud affect vote counts to bring about an election result, whether by increasing the vote share of the favored candidate, depressing the vote share of the rival candidates, or both. Also called **voter fraud**, the mechanisms involved include illegal voter registration, intimidation at polls, and improper vote counting.

Embezzlement

Embezzlement is outright theft of entrusted funds. It is political when it involves public money taken by a responsible public official. A common type of embezzlement is that of personal use of entrusted government resources; for example, when an official assigns public employees to renovate his own house.

Kickbacks

See also: Anti-competitive practices

A kickback is an official's share of misappropriated funds allocated from his or her organization to an organization involved in corrupt bidding. For example, suppose that a politician is in charge of choosing how to spend some public funds. He can give a contract to a company that is not the best bidder, or allocate more than they deserve. In this case, the company benefits, and in exchange for betraying the public, the official receives a kickback payment, which is a portion of the sum the company received. This sum itself may be all or a portion of the difference between the actual (inflated) payment to the company and the (lower) market-based price that would have been paid had the bidding been competitive. Kickbacks are not limited to government officials; any situation in which people are entrusted to spend funds that do not belong to them are susceptible to this kind of corruption.

Bid rigging - **Bid rigging** is a form of fraud in which a commercial contract is promised to one party even though for the sake of appearance several other parties also present a bid. This form of collusion is illegal in most countries. It is a form of price fixing and market allocation, often practiced where contracts are determined by a call for bids, for example in the case of government construction contracts.

Bid rigging almost always results in economic harm to the agency which is seeking the bids, and to the public, who ultimately bear the costs as taxpayers or consumers.

Types of Bid Rigging

There are some very common bid rigging practices:

- **Subcontract bid rigging** occurs where some of the conspirators agree not to submit bids, or to submit cover bids that are intended not to be successful, on the condition that some parts of the successful bidder's contract will be subcontracted to them. In this way, they "share the spoils" among themselves.
- **Bid suppression** occurs where some of the conspirators agree not to submit a bid so that another conspirator can successfully win the contract.

- **Complementary bidding**, also known as **cover bidding** or **courtesy bidding**, occurs where some of the bidders bid an amount knowing that it is too high or contains conditions that they know to be unacceptable to the agency calling for the bids. Complementary bidding, however, is not always a corrupt practice. A contractor that is too busy to complete the work will often place a high bid simply to maintain a relationship with government agencies.
- **Bid rotation** occurs where the bidders take turns being the designated successful bidder, for example, each conspirator is designated to be the successful bidder on certain contracts, with conspirators designated to win other contracts. This is a form of market allocation, where the conspirators allocate or apportion markets, products, customers or geographic territories among themselves, so that each will get a "fair share" of the total business, without having to truly compete with the others for that business.

These forms of bid rigging are not mutually exclusive of one another, and two or more of these practices could occur at the same time. For example, if one member of the bidding ring is designated to win a particular contract, that bidder's conspirators could avoid winning either by not bidding ("bid suppression"), or by submitting a high bid ("cover bidding").

North America

In the United States, bid rigging is a criminal offense under Section 1 of the Sherman Act. In Canada, it is a criminal offense under Section 47 of the Competition Act.

United Kingdom

In the United Kingdom, individuals can be prosecuted criminally under the Enterprise Act 2002.

Japan

Although both a violation of Japanese criminal law and the Japan Anti-Monopoly Law, bid rigging is still a habitual practice of the Japanese construction industry. It has been shown by a number of academic studies both in Japan and in the USA to be a system which considerably inflates the cost of construction projects, and in the Japanese public sector, considerably wasteful of annual tax money amounting to billions of Japanese yen. The US Government, specifically the United States Trade Representative Office and Department of Commerce, made fierce efforts[1] [2] in the late 1980s and early 1990s to urge the Japanese government to scrap "Dango" as a de facto non-tariff barrier to foreign firms in the Japanese construction market. Despite years of negotiations, including promises by the Japanese government in the S.I.I. (Structural Impediment Initiative)[3] trade talks, the practice was never fully stamped out and continued to flourish.

Unholy alliance

An unholy alliance is a coalition among seemingly antagonistic groups for ad hoc or hidden gain. Like patronage, unholy alliances are not necessarily illegal, but unlike patronage, by its deceptive nature and often great financial resources, an unholy alliance can be much more dangerous to the public interest. An early, well-known use of the term was by Theodore Roosevelt (TR):

Involvement in organized crime

An illustrative example of official involvement in organized crime can be found from 1920s and 1930s Shanghai, where Huang Jinrong was a police chief in the French concession, while simultaneously being a gang boss and co-operating with Du Yuesheng, the local gang ringleader. The relationship kept the flow of profits from the gang's gambling dens, prostitution, and protection rackets undisturbed.

The United States accused Manuel Noriega's government in Panama of being a "narcokleptocracy", a corrupt government profiting on illegal drug trade. Later the U.S. invaded Panama and captured Noriega.

Conditions favorable for corruption

It is argued that the following conditions are favorable for corruption:

- Information deficits
  - Lacking freedom of information legislation. For example: The Indian Right to Information Act 2005 is perceived to have "already engendered mass movements in the country that is bringing the lethargic, often corrupt bureaucracy to its knees and changing power equations completely."[12]
  - Lack of investigative reporting in the local media.
  - Contempt for or negligence of exercising freedom of speech and freedom of the press.
  - Weak accounting practices, including lack of timely financial management.
  - Lack of measurement of corruption. For example, using regular surveys of households and businesses in order to quantify the degree of perception of corruption in different parts of a nation or in different government institutions may increase awareness of corruption and create pressure to combat it. This will also enable an evaluation of the officials who are fighting corruption and the methods used.
  - Tax havens which tax their own citizens and companies but not those from other nations and refuse to disclose information necessary for foreign taxation. This enables large scale political corruption in the foreign nations.[13][citation needed]
- Lacking control of the government.
  - Lacking civic society and non-governmental organizations which monitor the government.
  - An individual voter may have a rational ignorance regarding politics, especially in nationwide elections, since each vote has little weight.

- o Weak civil service, and slow pace of reform.
- o Weak rule of law.
- o Weak legal profession.
- o Weak judicial independence.
- o Lacking protection of whistleblowers.

  Government Accountability Project

- o Lack of benchmarking, that is continual detailed evaluation of procedures and comparison to others who do similar things, in the same government or others, in particular comparison to those who do the best work. The Peruvian organization Ciudadanos al Dia has started to measure and compare transparency, costs, and efficiency in different government departments in Peru. It annually awards the best practices which has received widespread media attention. This has created competition among government agencies in order to improve.[14]

- Opportunities and incentives

  - o Individual officials routinely handle cash, instead of handling payments by giro or on a separate cash desk—illegitimate withdrawals from supervised bank accounts are much more difficult to conceal.

  - o Public funds are centralized rather than distributed. For example, if $1,000 is embezzled from a local agency that has $2,000 funds, it is easier to notice than from a national agency with $2,000,000 funds. See the principle of subsidiarity.

  - o Large, unsupervised public investments.

  - o Sale of state-owned property and privatization.[citation needed]

  - o Poorly-paid government officials.

  - o Government licenses needed to conduct business, e.g., import licenses, encourage bribing and kickbacks.

  - o Long-time work in the same position may create relationships inside and outside the government which encourage and help conceal corruption and favoritism. Rotating government officials to different positions and geographic areas may help prevent this; for instance certain high rank officials in French government services (e.g. treasurer-paymasters general) must rotate every few years.

  - o Costly political campaigns, with expenses exceeding normal sources of political funding, especially when funded with taxpayer money.

  - o Less interaction with officials reduces the opportunities for corruption. For example, using the Internet for sending in required information, like applications and tax forms, and then processing this with automated computer systems. This may also speed up the processing and reduce unintentional human errors. See e-Government.

- o   A windfall from exporting abundant natural resources may encourage corruption. [15] *(See Resource curse)*
- o   War and other forms of conflict correlate with a breakdown of public security.
- • Social conditions
  - o   Self-interested closed cliques and "Good ol' boy networks".
  - o   Family-, and clan-centered social structure, with a tradition of nepotism/ favouritism being acceptable.
  - o   A gift economy, such as the Soviet blat system, emerges in a Communist centrally planned economy.
  - o   Lacking literacy and education among the population.
  - o   Frequent discrimination and bullying among the population.
  - o   Tribal solidarity, giving benefits to certain ethnic groups

In the Indian political system, for example, it has become usual that the leadership of national and regional parties are passed from generation to generation[16][17] creating a system in which a family holds the center of power. Some examples are most of the Dravidian parties of south India and also the Congress party, which is one of the two major political parties in India.

Types of Corruption Found in Local Government

There are several types of political corruption that occur in local government. Some are more common than others, and some are more prevalent to local governments than to larger segments of government. Local governments may be more susceptible to corruption because interactions between private individuals and officials happen at greater levels of intimacy and with more frequency at more decentralized levels.

Forms of corruption pertaining to money like bribery, extortion, embezzlement, and graft are found in local government systems. Other forms of political corruption are nepotism and patronage systems. One historical example was the Black Horse Cavalry a group of New York state legislators accused of blackmailing corporations.

Bribery is the offering of something which is most often money but can also be goods or services in order to gain an unfair advantage. Common advantages can be to sway a person's opinion, action, or decision, reduce amounts fees collected, speed up a government grants, or change outcomes of legal processes.

Extortion is threatening or inflicting harm to a person, their reputation, or their property in order to unjustly obtain money, actions, services, or other goods from that person. Blackmail is a form of extortion.

Embezzlement is the illegal taking or appropriation of money or property that has been entrusted to a person but is actually owned by another. In political terms this is called graft which is when a political office holder unlawfully uses public funds for personal purposes.

Nepotism is the practice or inclination to favor a group or person who is a relative when giving promotions, jobs, raises, and other benefits to employees. This is often based on the concept of familism which is believing that a person must always respect and favor family in all situations including those pertaining to politics and business. This leads some political officials to give privileges and positions of authority to relatives based on relationships and regardless of their actual abilities.

Patronage systems consist of the granting favors, contracts, or appointments to positions by a local public office holder or candidate for a political office in return for political support. Many times patronage is used to gain support and votes in elections or in passing legislation. Patronage systems disregard the formal rules of a local government and use personal instead of formalized channels to gain an advantage…."

Everybody will be more aware of fraud and corruption after using WIKIPADIA but more specific knowledge about fraud could obtain from the works of Dr. Joseph T. Wells, Founder & Chairman of ACFE (Association of Certified Fraud Examiners). His bestseller-books and especially "Encyclopedia of Fraud" will help you to better to understand what **the fraud universe** consists of!

1.2.2.2. THE ACFE CLASSIFICATION OF FRAUD AND CORRUPTION

In its "2010 REPORT TO THE NATIONS On Occupational Fraud And Abuse" The Association of Certified Fraud Examiners (ACFE) defines the occupational fraud as:

"The use of one's occupation for personal enrichment through the deliberate misuse or misapplication of the employing organization's resources or assets."

This definition is very broad, encompassing a wide range of misconduct by employees at every organizational level.

Occupational fraud schemes can be as simple as pilferage of company supplies or manipulation of timesheets, or as complex as sophisticated financial statement frauds.[2]"

The ACFE Fraud Tree[3] classification presented on the Exhibit 1.1 covers different types of Occupational Fraud and Abuse.

1.2.2.3. THE ACEF CLASSIFICATIONS OF FRAUD

For example, according the current Bulgarian Penal Code fraud is a crime and has its types covered in different clauses:

- Ordinary Fraud
- Documentary Fraud
- Insurance Fraud
- Computer Fraud
- Accountant Fraud

- Business Evaluator Fraud
- Certified Public Accountant Fraud

Of course, it is difficult to embrace all the facets of fraud only with the shown above breakdown and for the purposes of the Dinev's SMARTGuide we will use the following classifications:

- **A) According to the ownership and the occupational position in the managerial hierarchy fraud is conducted by:**
- Owners
- Directors
- Managers
- Employees
- Non-employees
- Organized criminals

B) According the place of occurrence:
- Internal fraud
- External fraud

C) According its directions fraud is classified as:
- Against the entity or organization - embezzlement, insider trading, bribery
- In the name of the entity or organization but against a third party - financial statement fraud,
- Through the entity or organization and for its own benefit but against a third party - tax fraud, computer and Internet fraud,
- For the benefit of the entity or organization but against third parties - project fraud, customer fraud, bribes and kickbacks

The most common classification of the fraud universe regarding the directions could be:

- Fraud against the organization, and
- Fraud perpetrated in the name, through and/or for the benefit of the organization.

Occupational Fraud and Abuse Classification System

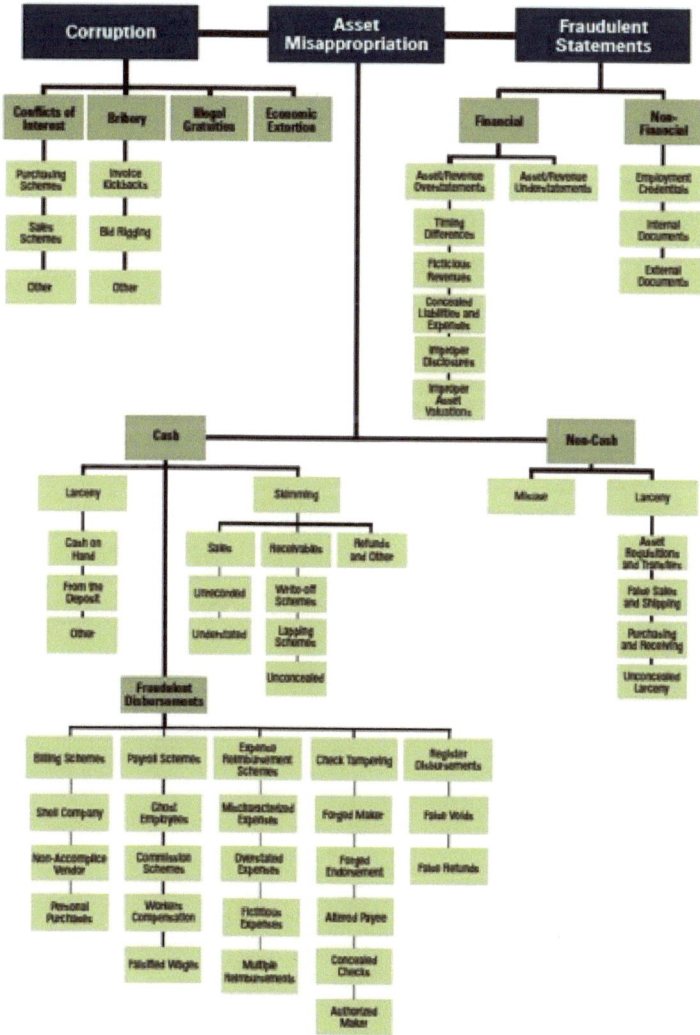

Corruption	Asset Misappropriation	Fraudulent Statements

Corruption
- Conflicts of Interest
  - Purchasing Schemes
  - Sales Schemes
  - Other
- Bribery
  - Invoice Kickbacks
  - Bid Rigging
  - Other
- Illegal Gratuities
- Economic Extortion

Fraudulent Statements
- Financial
  - Asset/Revenue Overstatements
    - Timing Differences
    - Fictitious Revenues
    - Concealed Liabilities and Expenses
    - Improper Disclosures
    - Improper Asset Valuations
  - Asset/Revenue Understatements
- Non-Financial
  - Employment Credentials
  - Internal Documents
  - External Documents

Asset Misappropriation
- Cash
  - Larceny
    - Cash on Hand
    - From the Deposit
    - Other
  - Skimming
    - Sales
      - Unrecorded
      - Understated
    - Receivables
      - Write-off Schemes
      - Lapping Schemes
      - Unconcealed
    - Refunds and Other
  - Fraudulent Disbursements
    - Billing Schemes
      - Shell Company
      - Non-Accomplice Vendor
      - Personal Purchases
    - Payroll Schemes
      - Ghost Employees
      - Commission Schemes
      - Workers Compensation
      - Falsified Wages
    - Expense Reimbursement Schemes
      - Mischaracterized Expenses
      - Overstated Expenses
      - Fictitious Expenses
      - Multiple Reimbursements
    - Check Tampering
      - Forged Maker
      - Forged Endorsement
      - Altered Payee
      - Concealed Checks
      - Authorized Maker
    - Register Disbursements
      - False Voids
      - False Refunds
- Non-Cash
  - Misuse
  - Larceny
    - Asset Requisitions and Transfers
    - False Sales and Shipping
    - Purchasing and Receiving
    - Unconcealed Larceny

Exhibit 1.1 ACFE's Occupational Fraud and Abuse Classification System

D) According the specifics in the organization fraud could occur in the following activities and processes:

- Bidding, contracting and contractor performance
- Finance and credit activities
- Project funding
- Investing and reporting the operating expenses and capital expenditures
- Insurance and claims reimbursement
- Health Care and Social Security
- Procurement of goods and services
- E-commerce and Internet banking
- Taxation and tax evasion
- Money and securities counterfeiting
- Education and Research (Academic Fraud)
- Charities and non for profit organizations activities
- Church and its charity activities
- Other "galaxies" in the fraud universe.

1.2.2.4. OTHER CLASSIFICATIONS OF TYPES OF FRAUD

The classification presented at Exhibit 1.2. will help you to be acquainted with other creative approaches and studies of other authors such Zabihollah Rezaee and Richard Riley.

According to these authors fraud is defined as:

„....1) management fraud and

2) employee fraud"[4]

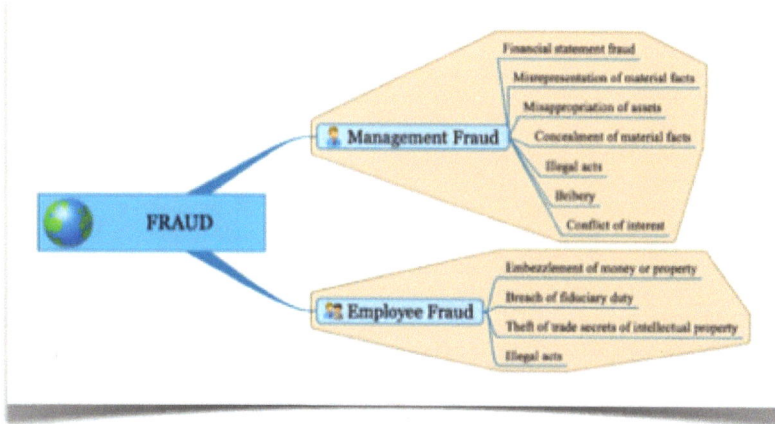

Exhibit (Adapted) 1.2. Types of fraud

In their book the management fraud includes: financial statement fraud, misrepresentation of material facts, misappropriation of assets, concealment of material facts, illegal acts, bribery, conflict of interest and the employee fraud involving embezzlement of money or property, breach of fiduciary duty, theft of trade secrets of intellectual property, illegal acts.

In another classification[5] published by a UK non-for-profit organization CIFAS in March 2012 the fraud by fraud types is as follows:

- Identity Fraud
- Facility Takeover Fraud
- Misuse of Facility Fraud
- Application Fraud
- Asset Conversion
- False Insurance Claims

Just before publishing this SMARTGuide there was revealed a new information about annual fraud indicators in U.K. National Fraud Authority[6] titled "ANNUAL FRAUD INDICATOR" which presented the following classification of fraud:

Fraud by victim

- Public sector

- Private sector
- Not-for-Profit sector
- Individuals

Fraud by enabler

- Insider-enabled fraud
- Identity fraud
- Cyber enabled fraud
- Fraud perpetrated by Organized Crime Groups

Fraud by type

- Benefit fraud
- Blue badge scheme abuse
- Council tax fraud
- Electricity scams
- Grant fraud
- Housing tenancy fraud
- Insurance fraud
    - Staged motor vehicle accidents
- Mass marketing fraud
- Mortgage fraud
- Motor finance fraud
- National Savings and Investments fraud
- Online ticket fraud
- Patient charges fraud
- Payroll fraud
  - Expenses fraud
- Pension fraud
- Private rental property fraud
- Procurement fraud
- Recruitment fraud

- Retail Banking fraud
  - Cheque fraud
  - Online banking fraud
  - Plastic card fraud
- Telephone banking fraud
  - Student finance fraud
  - Tax Credits fraud
  - Tax fraud
  - Telecommunications fraud
  - Television licence fee evasion
  - Transport fare evasion
  - Vehicle excise duty evasion

In all of its 3 dimensions our "3D Fraud Risk Assessment Model" requires revealing the potential or possible patterns, types and schemes of fraud and corruption to the potential clients who should be informed about the variations and the facets of fraud in their organizations.

One of the specifics of the legislations of different countries (Eastern European countries, for example!) is that fraud could be a part of another type of crime - for example, money laundering and/or tax evasion and not to be treated as a separate economic crime.

Of course, each case should be dealt separately and the experts should be very careful about the difference between fraud and error!

Based on the presented above classifications, 3D Fraud Risk Assessment Model is supposed to encourage a further development of new and more effective strategies, methods and techniques as to make it possible every organization worldwide to establish its own strong fraud resistance to fraud and corruption!

1.3. FRAUD RISK ASSESSMENT FRAMEWORK

1.3.1. Contemporary Fraud Risk Assessment Developments
For the description of the recent developments included in this SMARTGuide we use the following sources:

- The COSO 2012 Exposure Draft of Internal Control - Integrated Framework - www.coso.org

- The Dinev's Myths about Fraud and Corruption - presented at the 10th PIKW Congress in Krakow, Poland - 2011
- The Fraud Risk Assessment Terminology - used in the 3D FRAM

Let's describe all of them below!

The recent COSO 2012 Version of the Internal Control— Integrated Framework:

- Enhances consideration of anti-fraud expectations
- Contains the term "fraud" 38 times and the term "fraudulent"- 17 times. **The 1992 version** respectively contained these terms 1 and 18 times
- Considers the potential for fraud as a principle of internal control
- Introduces corruption as a category of fraud
- Introduces the concepts of fraud risk assessment
- Considers fraud risk relating to material misstatement of reporting, inadequate safeguarding of assets, and corruption as part of the risk assessment process
- Defines fraud risk assessment - management's assessment of the fraud risks relating to the safeguarding of the entity's assets, fraudulent reporting and management consideration of possible acts of corruption
- Contains the same or similar internal control limitations as in the 1992 version described as "reasonable assurance", "deficiencies" and a chapter with "limitations of internal control"
- Misses the definitions of corruption, fraud, fraud risk, fraud risk appetite, fraud risk assessment etc. in the Glossary of Terms

We would like to remind you here that the above comments are made based on the Exposure Draft of COSO 2012 Version of The Internal Control - Integrated Framework and we reserve the right to update our comments after receiving the final COSO publication!

The Dinev's 10 Myths about Fraud and Corruption - revealed and presented at the 9th PIKW International Congress in Krakow, Poland - 2010*

1. Corruption is something good!
2. Corruption is a crime!
3. The terminology of management control, controlling, internal control, financial control, internal fraud risk assessment has uniform understanding by the management
4. Risk management is the favorite process/activity of the management, especially the fraud risk assessment

5. There is no fraud but only errors, irregularities and abuse

6. Fraud Risk Assessment is focused on indicators of errors, irregularities and fraud

7. Internal experts are independent on the management

8. Internal experts are communicative and the management hear their proposals

9. External experts are independent on the requirements of their clients

10. Fraud Risk Assessment committees are the panacea for curbing fraud

The Myths are statements which are believed to be true BUT they are NOT!

Let's comment the statements above!

1. Corruption is something good!

Corruption is a human condition and an ancient phenomenon. From Mesopotamian times, if not before, public notables have abused their offices for personal gain; both well-born and common citizens have sought advantage by corrupting those holding power or controlling access to perquisites. The exercise of discretion, especially forms of discretion that facilitate or bar entry to opportunity, is a magnetic impulse that invariably attracts potential abusers.

Moreover, since nearly all tangible opportunities are potentially zero-sum in their impact on individuals or classes of individuals, it is almost inevitable that claimants will seek favors from authorities and that authorities, in turn, appreciating the strength of their positions, will welcome inducements.

Until avarice and ambition cease to be human traits, corruption will continue to flourish. Self-interest dictates the using and granting of favors. Merit will determine outcomes and advancement only in a minority of nations, and the riptide of corruption—even in the most abstemious nations and societies— always exists as an undertow to be resisted. Indeed, in many nations, obtaining even rightful entitlements in a timely fashion, or at all, is characteristically subject to inducement. Almost everywhere, and from time immemorial, there is a presumption that most desirable outcomes are secured through illicitly pressed influence or hard-bought gains.

More research, studies and education in the universities are needed!

2. Corruption is a crime!

Huge amounts of money, political speeches, efforts of non-for-profit organizations are aimed at curbing corruption worldwide but in fact, corruption is not treated as a crime and is not punished as a crime anywhere. A good example for directing the anti-corruption efforts in Europe is The UK Bribery Act 2010!

3. The terminology of management control, controlling, internal control, financial control, internal fraud risk assessment has uniform understanding by the management

Unfortunately there is not an uniform understanding! There are often significant misunderstandings in the application to such terms between the countries according the specifics of their national legislations and educational and training programs.

4. Risk management is the favorite process/activity of the management, especially the fraud risk assessment

It is hard to say so far! The situation could be changed after a while applying "The COSO 2010 Internal Control - Integrated Framework" and especially at its Section "Fraud Risk Assessment".

5. There is no fraud but only errors, irregularities and abuse

The terminology used mostly in the accounting profession has concerned deficiencies, irregularities, errors but the terms fraud, corruption and fraudulent reporting in this combination began to be used just recently. Why so late? The answer could be: Time has told it!

6. Fraud Risk Assessment is focused on indicators of errors, irregularities and fraud

Since 1990 the discussion about why the focus of the financial fraud risk assessments was aimed only to systems, processes and checklists and not to fraud and abuse is still continuing.

7. Internal experts are independent on the management

It is difficult to set a clear border between the auditing and consulting functions services provided by definition to the bosses who appointed the internal experts! If the internal expert detects fraud perpetrated by the top management he or she has usually two alternatives - to report it and then to quit or to cover it and stay in "the play"!

8. Internal experts are communicative and the management hear their proposals

Yes, mostly the internal experts posses adequate communication skills but if there are negative reports they are blamed being not communicative and the management don't take seriously their recommendations. There are exceptions too, of course, but they usually confirm the statement.

9. External experts are independent on the requirements of their clients

Unfortunately, the rule "The customer has always right!"is still prevailing!

10. Fraud Risk Assessment committees are the panacea for curbing fraud

There where audit committees exist the professional society very often meets incompetent members, low remuneration or very rarely meetings held. The panacea for curbing fraud should be build based on all pieces of The Dinev's Fraud Resistance Cube - Ethics, Compliance, Fraud Risk Assessment, Fraud Detection, Fraud Investigation!

1.3.2. Dinev's SMARTGuide and Fraud Risk Assessment Terminology

The Dinev's SMARTGuide will use the terminology presented below.

Dinev's Compass for Fraud Detection - a methodology for systematic description of the fraud detection process

Fraud Detection - a systematic process for revealing the patterns or the indicators of fraud

Perception of Detection - the established atmosphere and organizational environment where the owners, management and employees are able to reveal the patterns of fraud and to respond adequately

Fraud Investigation - a systematic process for objectively collecting, obtaining and analysis of sufficient evidence as to determine the truth and to take the proper corrective measures

Fraud Investigation Puzzle - includes 12 questions (12 pieces of the puzzle) and answering them makes it possible to see the whole picture of the crime

Fraud Pattern - (Red flag, Indicator), A **pattern**, from the French *patron*, is a type of theme of recurring events or objects, sometimes referred to as elements of a set of objects. The most basic patterns, called Tessellations, are based on repetition and periodicity

Fraud Risk - the likelihood that a fraud has been occurring, is occurring or/and will be occurring

Fraud Risk Assessment (3D FRAM) - systematic and iterative process of assessment of the risks relating to the safeguarding of the entity's assets and fraudulent reporting and management consideration of possible acts of corruption

Fraud Risk Management - includes fraud risk identification, analysis, assessment, response

Reasonable Assurance - concept applied mostly as not for focusing on fraud and abuse

Professional skepticism - concept applied mostly for suspecting errors, irregularities, fraud

Fraud Risk Pool - the myriad of risks of corruption, misappropriation of assets and fraudulent reporting which the organization faces daily

Risk Analysis - assessing the likelihood of the risk occurring and estimating its impact

Fraud Risk Analysis - assessing the level of the likelihood of fraud occurring and type of response

Inherent Risk - the risk to an entity in the absence of any actions management might take to alter either the risk's likelihood or impact

Inherent Fraud Risk - the likelihood of existence of a fraud before applying of a fraud risk assessment process

Risk - the possibility that an event will occur and adversely affect the achievement of objectives

Risk Appetite - the broad-based amount of risk an entity is willing to accept in pursuit of value

Risk Assessment - a dynamic and iterative process for identifying and assessing risks to the achievement of objectives

Risk Impact - the effect of the negative event

Fraud Risk Impact - the effect of fraud

Risk Pool - the myriad of risks which the organization faces daily

Risk Response - includes acceptance, avoidance, reduction, sharing

Fraud Risk Response - includes fraud detection, fraud investigation, legal prosecution, elimination

Risk Tolerance - the acceptable level of variation relative to achievement of a specific objective, and often is best measured in the same units as those used to measure the relative objective

Fraud Risk Tolerance - normally should be accepted as "ZERO"

Risk Velocity - refers to the pace with which the entity is expected to experience the impact of risk

Fraud Risk Velocity - refers to the pace with which the entity is expected to detect fraud occurrence

Risk Appetite - the broad-based amount of risk an entity is willing to accept in pursuit of its mission/vision

Fraud Risk Appetite - if used and applied it would be a nonsense. It would be a dangerous affair to being "hungry" or "greedy" for fraud. Fraud is a crime!

Fraud Scenario - the story of how a fraud is carried out

Dinev's Fraud Scenario - 13 (8W+5H) fatal for the potential fraudster descriptive questions

Risk - the likelihood that an event will occur and adversely affect the achievement of objectives

Expert's Fraud Risk - the likelihood that the expert will collude or cover a fraud concerning the financial or nonfinancial statements

Risk Significance - depends on likelihood of risk occurring and impact, velocity or speed to impact upon occurrence of the risk, persistence or duration of time of impact after occurrence of the risk

Fraud Risk Significance - depends on the type of fraud, detection lag, activities, processes, ownership, impact, managerial judgement

Fraud Deterrence - the proactive identification and removal of the causal and enabling factors of fraud

Fraud Triangle - The Donald R. Cressey's idea for describing three factors that are present in every situation of fraud: motive (or pressure) , rationalization and opportunity

Fraud Risk Assessment (COSO 2012) - management's assessment of the risks relating to the safeguarding of the entity's assets and fraudulent reporting and management consideration of possible acts of corruption, both by entity personnel and by external parties directly impacting the entity's ability to achieve its objectives.

Fraud Resistance - the proactive approach, tone on the top, anti-fraud activities, procedures and legal prosecution against fraud in the organization

Fraud Universe - the totality of fraud that could exist or the whole myriad of fraud and abuse which could occur in an organization. As a little humor, for example: The "galaxies" include corruption, misappropriation of assets, fraudulent reporting, money laundering etc. "The planets" could be the countries, "the stars" - the potential fraudsters etc.

Dinev's Fraud Resistance Cube - Ethics, Compliance, Fraud Risk Assessment, Fraud Detection, Fraud Investigation, Legal Prosecution!

Part II. 3D Fraud Risk Assessment Model (3D FRAM)

In this part:

- Characteristics of the Fraud Risk Assessment Process
- Fraud Risk Assessment Models
- Why 3D Fraud Risk Assessment Model (3D FRAM)?

- Who will be the 3D FRAM actors?
- All 3D FRAM experts with proper knowledge, skills and experience!

This part would help governmental entities and businesses of all sizes, from sole proprietorships and non-for-profit organizations to large corporations learn how to help themselves using 3D FRAM. The Model is developed and described in 3 dimensions: Functional, Methodological and Timing Dimensions. This part covers its goals, actors and the knowledge needed as to provide this new business opportunity.

2.1. Characteristics of the Fraud Risk Assessment Process

It is a common story that when you ask different managers about fraud occurrence in their organizations they will often respond to this observation with comments like 'that is not true, we have done a scorecard analysis of the risks', 'fraud is not possible because we have not had any incidents', or 'we have expended a great deal of effort in implementing controls to prevent fraud and both internal and external fraud risk assessment have checked the controls and are satisfied with them'.

There was a case when somebody called me and recommended me to change the title of our training course "Procurement Fraud - Detection and Prevention" with another one - "How to comply with the new Procurement Act?". And when I asked him why he answered me in the similar way mentioned above: 'If I send my employees to your training seminar I will confess that we have fraud in our organization!'

However, when the question is asked of senior management 'can you test what frauds your controls are trying to prevent', they often do not have an answer. Yet they firmly believe that they have good controls in place to prevent fraud. That is because they are focussed on controls, not on the fraudsters.

As to make clearer the specifics of the fraud risk assessment process we provide you with the following statements:

- There can also be a big difference between having what appears to be an effective risk management strategy on paper and really understanding the risks of fraud and corruption.
- There is a potential for fraud risk in every organization - whether not material or significant - but it always exists and the purpose of Dinev's SMARTGuide is to demonstrate our "ZERO" tolerance to it.

- The category of fraud risk differs significantly regarding other traditional types of risks - operational, financial, technological etc. There is a big difference between error and fraud and then - between risk of fraud and risk of error. The intent creates this difference and during the fraud risk assessment this difference should be taken in account.

- The intent to deceit is a critical component of the fraud and it should be identified and recognized during the fraud risk assessment. Hence, the fraud risk assessment process should be prepared and accomplished based on this premise.

- It always should be taken into account that everybody employed or associated with the organization could perpetrate a fraud if there are opportunities for that.

- Fraud could be also used for achieving the organizational objectives. For example, after providing fraudulent financial statements the company's offer wins the project funding by European Union.

- Everyone has their own individual perception of honesty and level of how far they are willing to bend the rules.

- An organization has little control over someone's personal life outside of work, and over the factors which might motivate a person to consider fraud or corrupt behavior.

- An ethical culture in an organization can be rapidly undermined if the executive directors do not follow their own company code.

- Creating new laws, regulations, documentation and controls have greatly increased the compliance burden on organizations, but appears to have done little to decrease the incidence of fraud and corruption.

- Fraud and corruption could exist without being recognized or detected. They are a common part of the business somewhere in the world!

- A route to greatly improved profitability, stronger reputation and competitive advantage is to set a clear, visible and credible tone at the top, obtain a detailed understanding of the fraud and corruption risks and then measure the organizational resistance to them.

- Whether you are an employee, a manager or an executive director it makes sense to pay more attention to the behavioral aspects of fraudsters, corrupt employees or corporate psychopaths, rather than being blinded by accounting, legal or procedural issues.

- Before the risk assessment is carried out, the owner(s) and management should agree the impacts which the organization and other stakeholders are going to worry about. Typically these can include:
  - Direct or indirect financial loss
  - Damage to reputation and loss of market share

- Erosion of the organizational culture
- Risk of legal and regulatory actions
- Negative effect on employee morale.

With this in mind, according the already referenced publication of "Managing the Business Risk of Fraud: Practical Guide" a fraud risk assessment process generally includes three key elements:

"• *Identify inherent fraud risk* — Gather information to obtain the population of fraud risks that could apply to the organization. Included in this process is the explicit consideration of all types of fraud schemes and scenarios; incentives, pressures, and opportunities to commit fraud; and IT fraud risks specific to the organization.

• *Assess likelihood and significance of inherent fraud risk* — Assess the relative likelihood and potential significance of identified fraud risks based on historical information, known fraud schemes, and interviews with staff, including business process owners.

• *Respond to reasonably likely and significant inherent and residual fraud risks* — Decide what the response should be to address the identified risks and perform a cost-benefit analysis of fraud risks over which the organization wants to implement controls or specific fraud detection procedures."[7]

Let's continue with the fraud risk assessment models now!

2.2. FRAUD RISK ASSESSMENT MODELS

The use of fraud risk assessment models will be very common in all industries soon. (In some cases of risk assessment, managers know they should be using them but aren't quite sure how!) Many applications like those for response or mitigation are quite straightforward. But as companies attempt to model more complex issues, such as resistance to fraud, clearly and specifically defining the goals and the process to achieve them is of critical importance. Risk models are unique to certain industries that assume the potential for loss when offering a product or service, especially in the banking and insurance industries.

Banks assume a financial risk when they grant loans. In general, these risk models attempt to predict the probability that a prospect will default or fail to pay back the borrowed amount. While risk models are used for all types of loans, they are used extensively for credit cards. Some banks develop their own risk models and others banks purchase standard or custom risk scores from any of the several companies that specialize in risk score development.

For the insurance industry, the risk is that of a customer filing a claim. The basic concept of insurance is to pool risk.

Insurance companies have experience in managing risk because life, auto, health, accident, casualty, and liability are all types of insurance that use risk models to manage pricing and reserves. Due to heavy government regulation of pricing in the insurance industry, managing risk is a critical task for insurance companies to maintain profitability.

Many other industries incur risk by offering a product or service with the promise of future payment. This category includes telecommunications companies, energy providers, retailers, and many others. The type of risk is similar to that of the banking industry in that it reflects the probability of a customer defaulting on the payment for a good or service.

The risk of fraud is another area of concern for many companies but especially banks and insurance companies. If a credit card is lost or stolen, banks generally assume liability and absorb a portion of the charged amounts as a loss. Fraud detection models are assisting banks in reducing losses by learning the typical spending behavior of their customers. If a customer's spending habits change drastically, the approval process is halted or monitored until the situation can be evaluated.

It is a common practice, where the response of the organizations regarding changes, restructuring, employee promotions etc. are initiated based on some of applied by them *passive, reactive and/or proactive approaches*.

Then, there will be a a very logical situation where the initiative for and conducting of a fraud risk assessment engagement will be a logically consistent with of one of these approaches.

Passive approach is in the case, for example, when the auditor has made tests during a regular fraud risk assessment and has revealed significant weaknesses in the control system. After assessing the inherent and control risk the auditor makes conclusions that there is a potential risk of fraud and abuse. Following the ISA 240 or SAS 99 the auditor should include the findings in the audit report and present them to the client for a response.

Reactive approach applies usually when there are tips, claims and/or consequences of detected fraud and abuse and although it is already late, there are internal investigations initiated, involving the police and law enforcement. Time tells that a perceived need for a fraud risk assessment has been available. Unfortunately, such situation is very common currently in the practice worldwide.

Proactive approach is the most efficient and smart approach and proposes an accomplishment of a fraud risk assessment engagement without waiting for tips, claims or detected cases of fraud and abuse in the organization..

This is the smart approach because it demonstrates a strategic thinking and the tone of the management regarding the prevention and clever treatment of the risk of fraud and abuse and we use this approach as a starting point for our model described in Dinev's SMARTGuide.

Our 3D FRAM is based on the design of a fraud risk assessment process which encompasses eight elements:

1. The kind of information about fraud to be acquired,

2. The sources of information (for example, documents, types of respondents),

3. The methods to be used for sampling sources (for example, discovery sampling),

4. Methods of collecting information (for example, Internet search, interviews, questionnaires, specialized software),

5. The timing and frequency of information collection,

6. The analysis of the data,

7. The ranging the risk comparing outcomes with and without a fraud (what-if, cause-and-effect questions), and

8. The conclusions and response recommendations.

Dinev's SMARTGuide proposed you two basic models which you could use applying the fraud risk assessment process.

The first model, already called 3D Fraud Risk Assessment Model (3D FRAM) includes the basic principles, phases and procedures applied by the assessment of corruption, fraud and abuse. It could be used as a stand-alone engagement provided by internal and external experts, fraud examiners and other professionals with appropriate knowledge, skills and experience.

The second model (Part VI) is based on the requirements of the International Standard on Auditing 240 "The Expert's Responsibilities Relating to Fraud in an Fraud Risk Assessment of Financial Statements" and covers the required phases and procedures mandatory for complying with this important standard worldwide.

2.3. WHY 3D FRAUD RISK ASSESSMENT MODEL (3D FRAM)?

After watching an fabulous concert on my new 3D TV set I realized that my idea of developing a methodological model for a fraud risk assessment will be very productive if this model is created and presented in 3 dimensions: functional, methodological and timing nonoverlapping dimensions. Shortly, this is the answer to the question above.

Let's continue first, with our definition of the fraud risk assessment process, namely:

The fraud risk assessment is a systematic iterative process of collecting, receiving, analyzing and evaluating data as to determine the likelihood of a occurrence, detection and prevention of fraud in the organization and an adequate response and timely decisions to be taken by the stakeholders as to enhance the resistance to fraud.

A systematic process means step-by-step conducting preliminary established, adequately planned and organized activities and procedures, carried out by professionally trained experts.

Collecting, receiving, analyzing and evaluating data about the organization - about bylaws, business cycle, activities, processes, transactions, the existing internal controls and those applied for fraud deterrence (if any) - require a possession of different knowledge and skills needed for understanding the types of fraud and fraud schemes, the pattern and red flags of fraud and corruption and the risks of their occurrence in the organization.

This model is designed to improve the efficiency of actions based on specific activities and/ or risk. But before this activities are conducted, it is important to get a good understanding of current customer status and activities.

The determination of the likelihood of an occurrence, detection and prevention of fraud in the organization includes the analysis of date collected, the assessment of the opportunities for fraud occurrence - ineffective controls, controls to be overridden, no detection and anti-fraud controls - and a description of the possible fraud scenarios, the types of fraud and schemes specific for the organization and possible for occurrence at the different levels, processes and activities of the organization.

Ranging the impacts of different types of fraud occurrence for the organization is the next phase of the process of fraud risk assessment. The measures are quantitative - usually money and qualitative - spoiled image or moral, for example.

Development of proposal for adequate response and timely measures, if necessary, is *the output* of this engagement.

The stakeholders, such as the owner(s), management, directors, employees, vendors, government regulators should take active part in applying the measures undertaken for developing and/or enhancing the resistance to fraud, which is *the outcome* of this engagement.

The outcome of the fraud risk assessment mainly depends on the established environment of perception of fraud detection and resistance to fraud. It depends on the stakeholders too - especially on who pays for the engagement and who accepts the arguments for the scope defined and types of fraud occurrence assessed. The different levels of ownership and management will influence the scope of the engagement and, hence, the types of fraud, corruption and schemes assessed.

Therefore, the normally desired outcome for the stakeholders is increasing the chance for fraud detection and prevention and enhancing the resistance to fraud with due care to the people and the organization.

The main intent for the development of 3D FRAM is presented through its goals at the Fig. 2-1:

Fig. 2-1 The main goals of the 3D FRAM

The main goals of the The 3D Fraud Risk Assessment Model (3D FRAM) are the underlying fraud risk assessment process to become:

- A New Business Opportunity
- A Stand-Alone Engagement
- A Part of ERM (Enterprise Risk Management)
- A Fraud Risk Assessment Responsibility under ISA 240 and SAS 99
- Simple and Understandable
- Worldwide Applicable
- Cost Effective
- Periodic
- Practical, and
- Actually Usable

All the goals are targeted at achieving better resistance to fraud in the organization using three dimensions: functional, methodological and timing dimensions.

Let's continue with whom such an engagement will be conducted!

2.4. WHO WILL BE THE 3D FRAM ACTORS?

The proactive approach for undertaking such an engagement presumes the actors to be independent experts, who could carry out the fraud risk assessment at or under the management level depending on who initiates and pays for such engagement - the owner(s), the principal, the audit committee etc.

The actors (the expert team) should consist at least of two persons possessing different expertise in risk assessment management but having common knowledge and skills of fraud examination.

The list of the professionals who could be engaged in the fraud risk assessment is not exhaustive and you could add somebody else if missed below! The list is as follows:

- Anti-Fraud and Corruption Specialists
- Risk Managers
- Risk Analysts
- Internal Experts
- National Fraud Risk Assessment (Accountability) Experts and Evaluators
- Certified Public Accountants as a responsibility according ISA 240 or SAS 99 and/or as a stand-alone engagement
- Certified Management Accountants
- IT, CISM and ISACA Specialists
- Financial Controllers
- Fraud Prevention Specialists
- Certified Financial Services Experts
- Certified in Financial Forensics Specialists
- Forensic Accountants
- Compliance Officers
- Certified Fraud Examiners
- Expert Fraud Examiners
- Certified Internal Control Experts/ Specialists
- External Experts

The list could be expanded with...

2.5. ALL 3D FRAM EXPERTS WITH PROPER KNOWLEDGE, SKILLS AND EXPERIENCE!

What scope and kind of expertise the mentioned above specialists should possess? The answer is - the following:

- Knowledge
- Skills
- Training and education
- Experience
- Personal characteristics

Knowledge About:

- Specialized knowledge about the industries will also be necessary in order to provide service to those industries.
- Banking procedures, restaurant operations, or bankruptcy laws would be required to investigate bank, restaurant, or bankruptcy fraud.
- Technological subjects, such as computer technology, in order to identify and recognize different fraud patterns.
- Accounting, controls, and auditing matters that are the traditional purview of CPAs and internal auditors and that can be expected to be used in most fraud examinations.
- Matters not typically included in undergraduate or graduate accounting and business degree programs. Such matters include
  - The numerous different types of fraud schemes and how they can be perpetrated, concealed, detected, and prevented;
  - Criminology and civil and criminal legal concepts such as how to gather information within the constraints of the legal system,
  - Legal rights of suspects, attorney/client/work product privilege,
  - Civil and criminal rules of evidence and procedure, etc.

Some of these matters are more relevant to expert witness services than to expert consultant services.

Skills Required:

- Strong analytical skills, including skills in analyzing financial statements and other financial information for trends and anomalies,

- Examining and tracing great quantities of documents and data for telltale details and patterns without being overwhelmed by the quantity,
- Researching public records and electronic databases for information.
- Good written and oral communication skills, including
  - Skill in questioning people at all levels of an organization and
  - Eliciting information from reluctant witnesses or suspects,
  - Skill in explaining often complex transactions or schemes to managements, attorneys, and
  - Skill in presenting findings and recommendations accurately, clearly, and completely in written reports.

Training and Education Needed:

- The knowledge and skills necessary for fraud risk assessment engagements can be obtained in numerous ways through
  - Association of Certified Fraud Examiners (ACFE)
  - American Institute of Certified Public Accountants (AICPA)
  - Institute of Internal Experts (IIA),
  - Association for Counteraction to Economic Fraud (www.acefraud.org), and
  - The Institute of Expert Fraud Examiners which provide conferences, seminars, self-study courses, books, and e-journals on fraud matters that are available to their members and to nonmembers as well.
- Numerous books have been written about fraud matters. (for example, "Economic Fraud - Parts I & II" - www.iepinet.eu - in the Bookstore!
- Dinev's SMARTGuide provides information about fraud matters, including reprints of selected documents, lists of sources of information about fraud risk assessment process
- The organizations mentioned above provide certification programs leading to a professional designation.

Experience Obtained:

- The best fraud risk assessment experience is gained by providing more and more engagements to working under the direction of an experienced professional expert.
- The inexperienced expert can learn valuable information from conversations with experienced colleagues and
  - from reading any available fraud cases manuals and handbooks.

Personal Characteristics as a Must:

- Analytical ability to accept and apply modern analytical technologies and methods
- Ability to work with a lack of structure that is common in traditional accounting, audit, and tax engagements
- An inquiring, observant, and alert attitude, and a high degree of intuition, professional skepticism, attention to detail, and judgment
- Ability to work with the client's attorney and to follow the requirements of the applicable legal jurisdictions
- Willingness to work on short deadlines and unpredictable schedules at irregular intervals
- Frame of mind - There is something out there for him/her to find-he/she just need to find it
- Instinct or Nose - He/she can see "the forest and the trees", fraud patterns and/or indicators
- Experience if already obtained - Experience will teach you when to go down a certain path or change the direction of an fraud risk assessment, and it will tell you where to look and the right questions to ask
- Confidence - Not only believing in yourself; it's also being able to admit that you don't know everything.

It is just time to dive deeper in the fraud risk assessment methodology now! Let's do it now!

Part III: 3D FRAM - Functional Dimension

In this part:

- The Characteristics of the Functional Dimension
- The Functions of 3D FRAM Functional Dimension:
  - Fraud Exposure, Awareness, Recognition
  - Fraud Risk Data Analysis
  - Fraud Risk Data Assessment
  - Fraud Risk Response

3.1. The Characteristics of the Functional Dimension

"The Functional Dimension" encompasses all functions of the systematic fraud risk assessment process. This part presents "What To Do" functions and also reveals the detailed description of the fraud scenarios and their variations, ranging the fraud risk and recommend the measures if necessary. You also learn about "Dinev's Fraud Scenario" and how to create the 13 (8W+5H) fatal for the potential fraudster questions looking for the reliable data and information.

Fraud is a very dynamic entity and is constantly changing, adapting, and morphing itself to take advantage of vulnerabilities and flaws within the oversight and control systems that are established to minimize their presence.

These types of situations are prevalent throughout many systems and processes. Ultimately, their detection, interpretation, and resolution are up to the client; they are the ones that determine the tolerance on how much fraud is acceptable and eventually bear additional costs in trying to minimize their losses. Approaching the problem space from different angles, from new starting points, and with nontraditional methods will most likely yield a better return on investment. Additionally, applying analytical techniques from different industries (in Part IV) can help increase yields. The trick is in recognizing where and when they should apply!

Let's think, for example, about a situation where you have received an anonymous tip about a possible embezzlement or misuse of company's assets perpetrated by your partner and the company accountant both in collusion. This fact could urge you, of course, immediately to initiate a fraud risk assessment engagement conducted by an independent expert.

3D Fraud Risk Assessment Model describes this professionally conducted process as a stand-alone engagement and in our SMARTGuide it could be presented with three dimensions - functional (this Part), methodological (Part IV) and timing (Part V).

Let's remind you that fraud risk could exist in every organization and the main goal of the 3D FRAM is not to be the next exercise but if there is a significant fraud risk identified the adequate and timely measures to be taken by the stakeholders as to develop or to increase the existing resistance to fraud in the organization.

In defining this goal, you must first decide what types of fraud and relevant risks of fraud you are trying to measure, assess or predict. Failure to correctly define the goals of the fraud risk assessment process can result in wasted money and lost opportunity.

The Functional Dimension comprises of activities which will be grouped and conducted in the following sequence (iteration):

• Fraud Exposure, Awareness and Recognition

• Fraud Risk Data Analysis

- Fraud Risk Data Assessment

- Fraud Risk Response

The initial assessment of fraud risk should consider the inherent risk of particular frauds occurring in the absence or the existence of internal controls. After all relevant fraud risks have been identified, they are assessed, ranged and the total fraud risk is calculated. Fraud risks that remain unaddressed by appropriate measures could comprise the pool of residual fraud risks. The fraud response is the final logical step concerning all done before.

But let's describe the phases of "3D FRAM - Functional Dimension - What to Do?" bellow.

3.2. THE FUNCTIONS OF "3D FRAM-FUNCTIONAL DIMENSION ?"

The all 10 functions of this dimension described below are grouped in 4 phases presenting the cycle of the fraud risk management process and are depicted at Fig. 3-1 below.

FRAUD EXPOSURE, AWARENESS AND RECOGNITION PHASE

1. Providing awareness to the client about the nature, scope, fraud exposure and specifics of the fraud risk assessment process

2. Collecting, obtaining and developing of external and internal information to get understanding of the legal status and business of the organization

3. Identification of the possible exposure of fraud types, corruption and fraud schemes at different levels, processes and activities of the organization.

4. Recognition of a fraud scenario and its variations, concerning different levels, processes and activities of the organization.

5. Collecting and obtaining external and internal information about the existing controls, applied for detection and prevention fraud in the organization, if any.

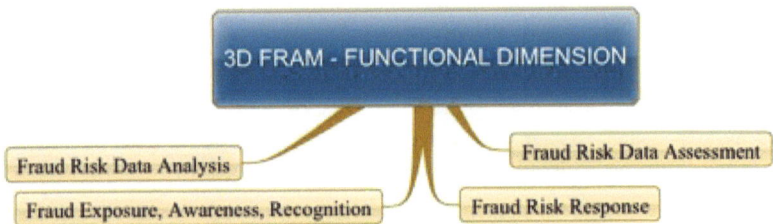

Fig. 3-1 3D FRAM - Functional Dimension Phases

FRAUD RISK ANALYSIS

6. Identification of the opportunities for occurrence of fraud and abuse and for their concealment.

7. Analysis of the data available for patterns of fraud, corruption, abuse, errors, intent, irregularities

FRAUD RISK ASSESSMENT PHASE

8. Ranging the fraud risks according their source, ownership level and significance using two measures - quantitative and qualitative

9. Determination of the fraud risk in two rages - significant or nonsignificant.

FRAUD RISK RESPONSE

10. Development of recommendations for an adequate response and timely measures according the significance of the assessed fraud risk as to develop and/or to enhance the resistance to fraud.

3.2.1. Fraud Exposure, Awareness and Recognition Phase

Function 1. Providing awareness to the client about the nature, scope, fraud exposure and specifics of the fraud risk assessment process

Providing awareness to the client about the nature, scope, fraud exposure and specifics of the fraud risk assessment process includes a precise explanation about the differences between fraud risk and other types of risk and between the methodologies of this engagement with the traditional audit.

The entrance interviews with the client should provide him/her with the awareness about the concepts of fraud prevention, types of fraud and corruption, fraud and corruption patterns or indicators as like, for example, "This engagement is not an fraud risk assessment, the types of fraud specific for your organization could be…, There would be a significant fraud risk here, because…, Have you heard about the following terms!…".

You could read more about conducting an interview in Parts IV and V.

As to provide an independent and unbiased fraud risk assessment engagement the experts should not forget and be aware of the following events impairing their independence:

- Who is the client and who pays for this engagement?
- The client is always right - a informal "rule" for the external experts conducting audit!

- The boss is always right - a "rule" for the internal experts conducting audit!
- The choice of the methodology should not be made according the client's desire!

The good starting point for the interview could be the explanation of a possible fraud scenario and then an information to be obtained about the client's view about the possible fraud scenarios and anti-fraud controls, established and applied for a deterrence of fraud in the organization.

Of course, if there is no the case when an proactive approach is undertaken in the organization, the potential client's reaction would be: 'No, there is no any fraud risk here', 'Our employees are honest and we trust them etc.'

During this phase the expert should concentrate its efforts for focusing the attention of the client - the owner, the audit committee, the management - to the following points:

- Not to be blinded by the beauty of a theoretical risk management model: aim to obtain a practical understanding of the fraud and corruption risks.
- To make sure everyone involved in fraud and corruption risk management is aware of the tools which fraudsters use.
- To identify the areas in the organization where technology could be misused.
- To obtain top management approval to first understand the fraud and corruption risks which the organization faces before looking at countermeasures.
- To conduct fraud and corruption risk profiling exercises right across the organization.
- To provide specialist resources to assist employees identify potential methods.
- To include the board in the profiling exercise.
- To implement a process to record fraud and corruption risks and follow up the treatment of them.
- To provide a route for line managers to report whenever a change initiative creates new fraud and corruption risks.

The terminology used for this engagement should be included in the program where the definitions of possible fraud and abuse to be an indispensable part of the working papers and the process documentation.

Function 2. Collecting, obtaining and developing of external and internal information to get understanding of the legal status and the business of the organization

The expert team conducting the fraud risk assessment should obtain an understanding of the company's industry, operations, and controls to determine whether fraud might be occurring and to identify where it might be occurring or concealed. Matters the expert team might obtain an understanding of include the following:

- The nature of the organization/company's business, industry, competition, market share, and major suppliers and customers
- The company's legal and financing structure (bank accounts maintained and how and for what purpose they are used, information about investment accounts, etc.)
- The flow of funds through the business (sources of funds, such as from cash sales or sales on account, loans, asset sales, or supplier rebates; how funds are disbursed; bank accounts used; etc.)
- The signed contracts with vendors and related parties
- Pending claims and legal issues
- Production methods
- Purchasing methods (contract, bidding, etc.)
- Employee compensation methods (salary, hourly, commission, etc.)
- Accounting and control system and procedures, and accounting records maintained and
- Political influence, if any and
- Other - all external and internal factors which could influence significantly the activities of the organization during the engagement.

This understanding of the business will provide the expert team with valuable knowledge as to make possible to differ between the common business practices and the exceptions, irregularities, errors, mistakes, fraud patterns, indicators or red flags, suspicious activities etc.

Function 3. Identification of the possible exposure of fraud types, corruption and fraud schemes at different levels, processes and activities of the organization.

The fraud risk identification process requires an understanding of fraud risks and the subset of risks specific to the agency. This involves understanding the agency's business processes and gathering information about potential fraud universe from internal or external sources by interviewing personnel and suppliers, brainstorming with them and performing analytical procedures. Let's discuss the fraud universe below.

Fraud Universe is Typical For Any Organization

Fraud has many different names, including embezzlement, bribery, kickbacks, forgery, falsification, and conflicts of interest, to name a few as shown in the Part I. One particular conflict of interest comes in the form of procurement fraud, where purchasing agents earmark contracts for a favored or preferred vendor without requiring competitive bids. This situation can also manifest itself in a pattern of employees also acting as vendors of the organization - where they might have inside knowledge regarding the budgets, specifications, or competition bidding for the work.

In the commercial world as well as in the noncommercial one, there are innumerable ways in which to conduct internal frauds against a company/organization, including improper billing practices, padding expense reports, filing duplicate invoices, submitting fictitious receipts, tampering with checks, or voiding cash entries—the list is virtually endless. Frauds can be perpetrated throughout the corporate hierarchy, from top management officials involved in complicated investment scams all the way down to the mailroom clerk stealing from the petty cash drawer.

Sometime, without completely realizing it, management and employees convince themselves that certain frauds are in fact beneficial for the company. In addition to the payment of bribes to win contracts, common examples include:

- Smoothing or the inflation of sales figures and assets, often justified as necessary so as not to destabilize the market;
- Hiding bad debts or obsolete stock;
- Price fixing or the establishment of cartels;
- Circumventing export embargoes;
- Submitting lower valuations to avoid customs duties;
- Avoiding VAT and other taxes;
- Overcharging of clients;
- Obtaining subsidies and grants on false or partly false premises;
- Moving funds into and around offshore destinations to avoid taxes, smooth profits and
- More.

All of the above increase profits and shareholder value, and are sometimes seen as justifiable frauds which need to be perpetrated in the best interests of the company, its shareholders and employees.

'Transactional red flags' is the name for patterns or indicators which are buried within transactions, held on computer systems, or on paper documents or reports. Employees in risk

areas such as procurement or payroll should receive specific training in recognizing transactional pattern/red flags.

Depending on the profile of the organization, there are usually hundreds of transactional red flags (patterns). Some typical ones include:

- Unusual supplier relationships
- Business partners, intermediaries and so on, which are in effect front companies
- Non-transparent counter parties where indications of criminal association exist
- Payments for goods and services where the description is unduly vague
- Preferential supplier treatment and/or a lack of competitive tendering
- Payments to offshore or tax-haven-based companies or bank accounts
- Preferential customer treatment in terms of service, prices and so on
- Receipt of potentially 'dirty money' payments
- Hidden salaries or other employee benefits
- Private expenses processed through expense claims
- Poorly monitored profit and loss and balance sheet accounts.

Arguably the single largest red flag of fraud and corruption is where a company or bank account located in a tax haven is involved as some sort of vehicle. While the misuses can range from terrorist and arms financing to tax evasion, the more common fraud patterns include:

- Kickbacks paid to the management on the acquisition or disposal of a subsidiary using a tax haven vehicle
- Company-controlled 'slush funds' and the payments of bribes to and from offshore companies (bribes are often politely referred to as 'marketing commissions')
- Secret bonuses to top managers and executives which are most commonly paid into such accounts
- Money ostensibly for bribes paid instead into executive and employee-controlled accounts (this is much more common than one would expect)
- Tax evasion in the form of split salaries (for employees, consultants and sometimes also the company)
- Hiding a conflicting ownership interest in suppliers, customers and business partners using a cascade of offshore companies to disguise the ownership.

By identifying red flags (fraud patterns) in a process, it is possible to put in place early warning systems about the use of a particular method of fraud. For example, a number of financial institutions, which have been the victims of unauthorized transfers from corporate accounts, now monitor all employee requests to view account details – in order to detect someone who may be identifying potential high value accounts for fraudsters to target.

Patterns/Red flags in a process arise from anomalies on documents or transactions. For example, red flags on payment instructions being processed through a bank payment centre include:

- Unusual delivery of instruction, for example through the mail or by courier with an urgent processing request
- Photocopied document or attachment
- Unnecessary words or explanations on the instruction to try to make it seem more plausible
- Appearance or style not consistent with normal transactions
- Beneficiary name spelt incorrectly, mismatching with account number
- Payment not consistent with the normal business of the customer.

Potential corporate patterns/red flags indicating fraud, which we have regularly seen in organizations where we have subsequently uncovered senior management frauds, include:

- Over-zealous acquisition strategies (without proper screening and due diligence)
- Autocratic management decisions around business relationships, such as a refusal to change a major supplier
- Losses and declining margins on sales
- Artificial barriers put up by directors to avoid answering questions
- Excessive secrecy
- Rumors and low morale
- Complacent finance director
- Overriding of budgetary controls
- Discrepancies and deviations
- Missing records or lack of detail
- Unusual manual payments or adjustments
- Consultants given a free rein.

Some patterns/red flags could be indicative of an impending organizational collapse; this should trigger concerns that there may be some fraud associated with the decline in business. However, a pattern/red flag is not firm evidence that a fraud is occurring. Once a series of patterns/red flags have been identified, specific detection tests will still need to be designed as a response and implemented to gather enough evidence to warrant a full-scale examination. This is relatively straightforward if the problem lies at the employee level and the internal audit department has the charter to add detection tests to its normal audit.

Fraud and Corruption Schemes Typical For the Organization

The following listing discusses the possible fraud schemes considered during the fraud risk assessment sessions. This listing is not all-inclusive and addresses only the fraud schemes considered during this assessment.

Let's look at Wikipedia again as to see how it deals with the term "fraud scheme".

"...The page "Fraud scheme" does not exist. You can ask for it to be created, but consider checking the search results below to see whether the topic is already covered.
For search help, please visit Help:Searching.

Ponzi scheme
A Ponzi scheme is a fraud ulent investment operation that pays returns to its investors from their own money or the money paid by ...

Tax evasion (redirect from Tax fraud schemes)
Under the federal law of the United States of America , tax evasion or tax fraud, is the purposeful illegal attempt of a taxpayer to evade ...

Tobashi scheme
A Tobashi scheme is a financial fraud where a client's losses are hidden by an investment firm by shifting them between the portfolios of ...

Omega Trust
Omega Trust was a fraud ulent US investment scheme in Illinois. Clyde D. Hood is a former electrician from Mattoon, Illinois . ...

Flim-flam
Confidence trick , a fraud scheme. Flim-Flam! Psychics, ESP, Unicorns, and Other Delusions , a book by James Randi. See also : The Flim-Flam Man ...

Mail and wire fraud
In the United States, mail and wire fraud is any fraudulent scheme to intentionally deprive another of property or honest services via mail ...

Fraud
In criminal law , a fraud is an intentional deception made for personal gain or ... Gamboa's banking and investor fraud schemes was described ...

James Paul Lewis, Jr. (redirect from Jim Lewis (convicted of fraud, Ponzi scheme 2006))
The ploy Lewis was running was a classic "Ponzi scheme "; in this ... earlier ones keep getting a return on their investment and the fraud continues. ...

Phillip E. Hill, Sr.
(born 1956) was the ringleader of the largest mortgage fraud scheme ever prosecuted in the State of Georgia . 168 counts of fraud and money ...

Bernard Madoff (section Affinity fraud)
the NASDAQ stock market, and the admitted operator of a Ponzi scheme that is considered to be the largest financial fraud in U.S. history ...

Advance-fee fraud (redirect from "Funds forwarding" scheme)
An advance-fee fraud is a confidence trick in which the target is persuaded to ... the average loss per victim is less than other fraud schemes. ...

Madoff investment scandal (redirect from Madoff fraud)
admitted that the wealth management arm of his business was an elaborate Ponzi scheme . ... estimated the size of the fraud to be $64.8 billion, ...

Foreign exchange fraud
Foreign exchange fraud is any trading scheme used to defraud traders by convincing them that they can expect to gain a high profit by ...

Pyramid scheme (section Connection to franchise fraud)
A pyramid scheme is a non-sustainable business model that involves promising ... franchise fraud schemes was described by the Italian ...

Franchise fraud
Franchise fraud is defined by the United States Federal Bureau of Investigation as a pyramid scheme . Franchise fraud in U.S. federal ...

Securities fraud (section Ponzi schemes)
Securities fraud, also known as stock fraud and investment fraud, is a practice ... stock manipulation schemes, and embezzlement by stockbrokers ...

2010 Medicaid fraud
The 2010 Medicaid fraud was a case of Medicaid fraud allegedly carried out by an ... armenians-indicted-medicare-fraud-scheme | title Savannah ...

Operation Power Outage
The group is accused of racketeering offenses, bank fraud schemes, kidnapping s, and drug trafficking Investigation: date February 2011 ...

Tim Montgomery
Since retiring from athletics he has been tried and convicted for his part in a New York –based check fraud scheme and for dealing heroin ...

Frank Dunn
and Exchange Commission filed civil fraud charges against him, and three former senior executives, in a wide-ranging financial fraud scheme ...

View (previous 20 | next 20) (20 | 50 | 100 | 250 | 500)"[8]...

We will continue with another set of fraud and corruption schemes shortly described below.

Conflict of Interest

- Nepotism

- Insider Trading

- Economic Extortion
- Purchase Schemes—Turnaround Sales
- Sales Schemes—Writing Off Sales

Bribery and Incentives Schemes

- Bid-Rigging Schemes
- Need Recognition Schemes
- Specifications Schemes
- Kickback Schemes
- Illegal Gifts
- Bid Pooling

Cash

- Cash Larceny
- Theft of Cash from the Register (of Cash on Hand)
- Reversing Transactions
- Register Manipulation
- Altering Cash Accounts
- Cash Larceny from the Deposit
  - Deposit Lapping
  - Deposits in Transit
- Skimming
  - Sales Skimming
  - Receivables Skimming
- Forcing Account Balances or Destroying Transaction Records
- Lapping
- Writing Off Account Balances

Inventory and Other Assets

Inventory and Other Assets: There are basically two ways a person can misappropriate a company asset: the asset can be misused or it can be stolen.

- Misuse of Inventory and Other Assets

- Larceny - Purchasing and Receiving Schemes
- Larceny - Asset Requisitions and Transfers

Fraudulent Disbursements

- Billing Schemes
- Invoicing Via Shell Companies/Forming a Shell Company
- Invoicing Via Non-accomplice Vendors/Pay-and-Return Schemes
- Personal Purchases with Company Funds
- Payroll Schemes
- Ghost Employees
- Falsified Hours and Salary
- Expense Reimbursement Schemes
- Mischaracterized Expense Reimbursements
- Fictitious Expense Reimbursements
- Overstated Expense Reimbursements
- Altered Receipts
- Over purchasing
- Multiple Reimbursements
- Check Tampering (for USA)
- Forged Maker Schemes
- Forged Endorsement Schemes
- Altered Payee Schemes
- Register Disbursement Schemes
- False Refunds
- False Voids
- More

Computer and Internet Fraud

- Identity Theft
- Theft of Internal Information
- Spyware

- Spam and viruses
- Many others

Function 4. Recognition of a fraud scenario and its variations, concerning different levels, processes and activities of the organization

Fraud Scenario usually presents the story of how a fraud has been occurred, is occurring or maybe will occur.

Dinev's 3D FRAM Fraud Scenario describes 13 (8W+5H) fatal for the potential fraudster descriptive questions shown on the Fig. 3-2 below.

You should be aware that the situations and the actors in every Fraud Scenario and its Variations will be specific for any organization but the key elements will be the same.

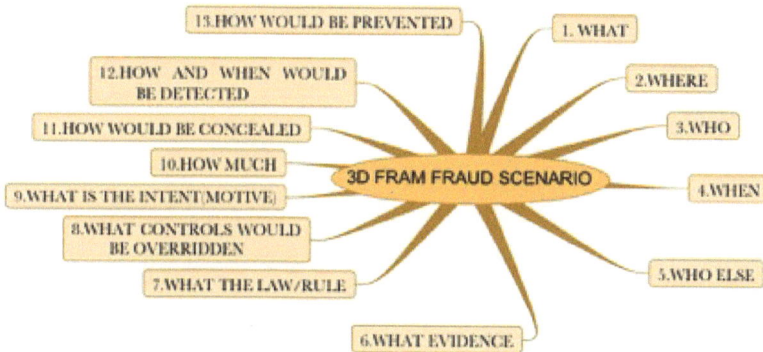

Fig. 3-2 3D FRAM Fraud Scenario Elements

The Fraud Scenario shown above and applied with our 3D FRAM requires the answers to the following 13 fatal for the potential fraudster questions:

1. WHAT is the target - MONEY, TANGIBLE AND/OR INTANGIBLE ASSETS
2. WHERE is possible - WITHIN, FROM OUTSIDE
3. WHO could be the actor - WHO HAS OPPORTUNITY
4. WHEN would be happen - WHEN POSSIBLE
5. WHO ELSE will take part - COLLUSION
6. WHAT EVIDENCE would be available - NO, RUMOURS or PAPER TRAIL

7. WHAT THE LAW/RULE says - MISCONDUCT, ERROR, MISTAKE, IRREGULARITIES, FRAUD

8. WHAT CONTROLS WOULD BE OVERRIDDEN - IF ANY

9. WHAT IS THE INTENT(MOTIVE) - SELF GAIN

10. HOW MUCH would be the loss or the impact - MUCH - ONCE OR LESS - MANY TIMES

11. HOW WOULD BE CONCEALED - COLLUSION, CONNECTIONS, DESTRUCTION

12. HOW AND WHEN WOULD BE DETECTED - TIME LAG, TIPS, CLAIMS, ANTI-FRAUD CONTROLS

13. HOW WOULD BE TO PREVENTED - IN FACT, THERE WILL BE A RESIDUAL RISK

The Fraud Scenario Variations could be another point for a fraud risk assessment and valuation.

It would be necessary the following potential issues to be discussed:

- What kind of scheme would be applied? Maybe internal, external or both and what kind of process, functions or relationship would be the target?

- When would be the possible scheme applied? The expert team should be aware of the opportunities and limitations described in our 3D FRAM and in the recently published "COSO 2012 Internal Control - Integrated Framework"!

- What kind of tools and techniques would be used for the concealment of the deception?

  - Falsifying documents?

  - Financial or operational misstatements?

  - Avoiding or overriding the controlled levels of statutory requirements (procurement, for example)?

  - Blocking the assess to the information?

  - Significant geographical distance between the locations where the documents are prepared?

  - Statements and/or the lousy controls, and

  - Direct or indirect pressure on "the naughty boy"?

- What kind of complexity and the intricacy would be applied and used by the fraud perpetrators?

- Who will be the main actor and/or his "friends"? The owner, the management, the retired employee, the vendors, the clients?

- What kind of the approach would be applied or the way of perpetrating fraud? Alone, with co-partners, with whom else?

- How the intent would be recognized? The difference between error and fraud consists of the intent! Don't forget that the intent is very difficult to be proven and are irregularities or anomalies are explained as errors, first!

- Motives or pressures for committing fraud are numerous and diverse. One executive may believe that the organization's business strategy will ultimately be successful, but interim negative results need to be concealed to give the strategy time. Another one needs just a few more coins per share of income to qualify for a bonus or to meet analysts' estimates. The third executive purposefully understates income to save for a rainy day.

- What kind of fraud patterns, indicators or red flag could be present and how to recognized them properly?

- How the gains would be converted? Direct or indirect, personally or trough relatives or friends, spending for real estate properties or for visiting exotic destinations?

Let's continue with the Q&A sequence of our Fraud Scenario!

- When comes the effect of the benefit?
  - Immediately
  - After a while
  - Directly
  - Indirectly
- It depends on the time lag of possible detection and on
  - Business Cycle
  - Processes
  - Changes
  - Fraud Risk Assessments
  - Perception of Detection
  - Resistance to Fraud

Fraud Detection as element of the "Dinev's Resistance to Fraud Cube"

This phase as a part of the "Dinev's Resistance to Fraud Cube" would provide a visual tool for assessing the different fraud scenarios of the client database for possible fraud risk occurrence and its assessment. For example, if one activity or process has more opportunities and high risk (procurement process, for example), you may want to increase level of the significant fraud occurrence and hence, significant fraud risk for the organization as a whole. For low-risk activities or processes, you may want to lower the level of the likelihood of significant fraud occurrence and, hence, to diminish the fraud risk for the organization as a whole.

An in-depth knowledge of the past, current status and of course, the prospects of the organization is essential to stay alert about the potential of fraud occurrence and its detection. Some of the benefits include improved perception of detection and fraud resistance development. Profile analysis here is an excellent way to get to know the organization as your customer and its prospects. It involves measuring common characteristics within a fraud risk pool of interest.

To understand the fraud and corruption risks to which the client's organization is exposed, the expert team will need to ask what could be achieved by a dishonest, motivated person, or fraudster, whether internal or external. The most effective way to achieve this, used by many anti-fraud experts, is for employees to look at control procedures and job functions from the fraudster's viewpoint and ask whether they can be bypassed by using a particular method of fraud. In other words they need to stop believing that fraud and corruption are not possible and 'think like thieves'. We use the term 'profiling' to describe the process.

Let's describe several situations or fraud scenarios which could be subjects to fraud risk assessment.

Employee as Vendors

Some very basic and fundamental checks can be performed on company data sources to check addresses or phone numbers from an employee master file against the vendor master file to expose any potential commonalities. For example, the fax number listed for a company turns out to be the same as the number listed for the emergency contact information of an employee. Although simple, it does occasionally expose some questionable relationships within the operations of a business, especially some of the larger entities.

In other cases, there could be less obvious connections that require the incorporation of additional sources of data. Many times corporations are run or influenced by a cadre of people including owners/founders, senior management, and board directors. Often, these people also have similar roles in other corporations. Therefore, knowing the chain of command often helps in understanding how decisions can be influenced. Of course, each of these businesses can be further expanded thereby extending the network of influence even more.

This information is more directly based on corporate ownerships and which companies own other companies. Each company will have a president or a CEO that will act as the official figurehead and there will be a multitude of senior executive vice presidents and others not explicitly listed. Some individuals can prove to be quite active and represent multiple companies or subsidiaries at the same time. These just represent other avenues where improper procurement practices could be encountered due to the indirect nature of these kinds of relationships.

Vendors as Vendors

Companies or organizations can operate in an official capacity and subsume, control, purchase, own, and influence other companies/organizations. There are also more cozy and comfortable relationships that are forged where a company (e.g., vendor) is indirectly associated with other vendors, potentially doing similar work. There is concern about these types of situations because a vendor might act as a front company, submitting unreasonably high quotes for a job only to make another vendor look more favorable, yet both companies are owned or controlled by the same entity.

Expanding on this concept, the use of common phones and addresses is one way to help identify inconsistencies in the underlying data and potential areas of fraud against the corporation.

Most likely, this situation exists because the procurement staff did not take the time to see if an existing entity was already present in the data, or their search was unable to return an exact match. Not knowing the duplications that are present in the data can complicate accounting matters because there is never a true accountability of how much money has been spent with the vendor overall. One or more of the vendors could also be a front for special pet projects or kickbacks. Regardless, it represents circumstances that should be inquired.

To further exemplify how inconsistencies impact the overall reliability and integrity of procurement systems, very large networks can be produced from just the different variations present in the data. They do not always reflect any type of fraud, but often poor controls in the accounting and procurement systems that, if allowed to persist, make it harder to differentiate legitimate activity from fraud.

Clearly, some better internal controls need to be employed by the management organization because this degree of repetition could easily lead to duplicate invoicing and other improper posts or ledger errors.

Corporate Expenses

This next round of examples is based on some fundamental processes common to all businesses large and small, from around the globe - namely, expense reimbursements. They are one of the necessary tribulations associated with doing business, especially when travel is involved. There are many ways in which to "embellish" an expense report, which is just another form of stealing from a company through padding costs, fabricating expenses, and bait-and switch expenditures.

Often it can help supplement the salary of a disgruntled employee and will tend to repeat itself over and over. It is also a nice loophole for earning money as a form of nontaxable income.

In one scenario, large furniture manufacturing company was concerned that there were employees embezzling money through various loopholes in their expense-reporting systems. The security office had excellent physical measures to keep their equipment from being stolen from their facilities and warehouses, but they had little control of or insight into how the employees were expensing their travel costs.

The company's main interest was in determining whether there were any patterns of theft that could be detected without too much room for ambiguity with respect to the nature of the activity.

In this particular application the fraud patterns were derived from two electronic data sources. The first was an online expense-reporting system developed for internal use, which contained employee reports of business expenses, out-of-pocket charges, and travel reimbursements. The second data source contained actual charges incurred on the company owned credit cards issued to company employees.

In continuing with defining the fraud pattern, the next logical step was to extract all travel expense reports with an associated airline ticket purchase. Most of the expense reports flagged looked fairly typical and included airfare, meals, lodging, and local transportation, such as cab fare or rental cars. At this point it was easy to spot those employees that traveled frequently, those who had high-euro reports, and those who were more compliant with submitting their reports and properly breaking down each expense.

Human Resources

The cliche"good help is hard to find" applies throughout all levels of business. Periodically reviewing the indirect relationships among employees can help to spot trouble areas that may lead to future problems, especially when an employee is terminated. The indirect relationships can be established through e-mail networks, interoffice phone calls, and personal residences.

Phishing/Click Fraud

Another example comes from cyberspace, where fraud and deception are commonplace in a number of online resources. Everyone is familiar with the spam e-mails they receive for every type of male enhancement pill, insider stock pick, and winning lottery scheme. A lot of spam also comes in the form of phishing where a legitimate-looking e-mail from a bank, a retailer, or some other industry tries to acquire personal information under false pretenses stating that one's account will be suspended or closed. Webopedia defines phishing as: "A way of attempting to acquire information such as usernames, passwords, and credit card details by masquerading as a trustworthy entity in an electronic communication[9]".

Tax Evasion

Finally, tax evasion is a type of fraud against the government and its taxpayers where individuals and corporation try to structure their earnings and losses in a way as to maximize their savings. Unfortunately, many resort to blatant misrepresentations, undervalued reporting, and other fabricated values and figures to justify their tax returns.

Additional Examples

There are too many different fraud scenarios to cover in this section; however, understanding the parameters, boundaries, and relationships goes a long way in uncovering patterns and trends.

Generally, the types of fraud patterns found in one domain can typically be abstracted and used in other domains because the structure of the patterns is often similar in terms of connections, frequencies, and sequences of activities. The following quick examples simply show the concept of employing visualizations to better understand novel patterns.

Demographics such as average age, gender (percent male), marital status (percent married, percent single, etc.), and average length of residence are typically included in a fraud risk scenario analysis. Other measures may be more business specific, such as age of customer relationship or average fraud risk level. Others may cover a fixed time period and measure average money sales, average number of sales, or average net profits. Profiles are most useful when used within segments of the fraud universe and fraud risk pool of interest.

Let's continue with the following real fraud scenarios!

"An email arrives at head office alleging that certain directors have been buying personal items on the company's account and that some of the marketing expenses are not genuine. Furthermore, people who have spoken up are being quietly dismissed. It's not the first email of this kind and rumors to this effect have been circulating for a while. However, financial results in the region are strong and local management resents interference. The tone of the emails is increasingly angry and some of the claims about fraud and corruption are hard to believe.

You are one of seven recipients of this email. You are not directly responsible for the division concerned and it is easier to close your eyes to unsubstantiated claims by assuming that they cannot be true.

What you are unaware of is that if enough resources were actually dedicated to uncovering the whole truth then you would find that many of the allegations are in fact true and just the tip of an iceberg. In reality profits are declining, losses are being systematically hidden in the books, some managers have covert ownership in business partners via offshore companies, property frauds are taking place and bribes are being paid in violation of the code of conduct."

Yes, maybe such situation is impossible for your organization but the variations could only confirm the lack of resistance to fraud.

And now several excerpts from Chapter 61 of "The Fraud Casebook: Lessons from the Bad Side of Business", Wiley&Sons, 2006:

"One morning I was just sitting down for my first cup of coffee, and our office manager brought me an envelope that had been sent from Paris. To my surprise, I found copies of e-mail correspondence between the top management of Water Luxury and InvestCap 1 and InvestCap 2. The sender of this envelope was anonymous. After reading some of the e-mails, I was shocked. We had been concerned that Mich Jacobs and his cohorts from the investment companies had intentionally diverted funds. These e- mails provided exactly what we needed.

I nearly spilled my coffee as I began reading the first e-mail. It was sent by Mich to one of the principals in InvestCap 1:

Patrick,

I am aware that you received a copy of the draft letter handed to us by Mr. Mechev [the deputy mayor]. The last few days I have had a number of meetings with the Concession Screening Unit (CSU) and Christiane Mancheva [the advisor to the mayor and a member of the board of directors of Water Luxury] to ensure that there is absolute clarity that the payments made by Water Luxury to InvestCap 1 and InvestCap 2 are according to the Contract and if the Mayor does write a letter to Board that the numbers we give him are at least factually correct and at best any reference to the 16.2m and 5.82m [investment amounts not used to provide services] is removed.

In speaking with Christiane this morning, she believes the only thing that could cause embarrassment is the fact that there is no "contract" between InvestCap 1 and InvestCap 2 and Water Luxury to cover the reimbursement of these costs. I am not aware of a contract but I believe it would be simple to put one in place with the appropriate date and perhaps we should take this action.

The Aquamon continues to ask questions, but these will be on the quantum, and proof of benefits which while a nuisance, cannot constitute a threat to the Concession. For example they would like copies of all InvestCap1/InvestCap 2 timesheets for development costs and also would like proof of the deliverables from this work. In my meeting with Christiane and Mechev my aim is to provide them with enough confidence in the legality that they will place pressure on Aquamon to reduce these ridiculous requests.

Regarding the capital program, clearly we were slower off the mark than the municipality would like. This, coupled with the higher level of expenditures on transition than anticipated, has created a difficult comparison between material and non-material assets.

In addition, we recharged a significant figure of operating expenses to capital expenditures which in the Municipality's eyes is not real work. Of course, this will be corrected over time. This subject needs two clear activities:

firstly, demonstrable delivery. It is far too risky and could provide an opportunity for termination if the Municipality strongly contests the contents. Secondly, we need a "charm offensive," particularly on the capital program, explaining step-by-step the progress and benefits. With the arrival of Jens and now Jean Paul, I am sure we have the team in place.

Regards, Mich

After investigating the facts presented in this e-mail, we were able to confirm these points:

- Water Luxury management had sent money received as a credit from MIRBD to its mother companies in the United Kingdom.

- There was no legal contract as a basis for this transfer.

- A fake contract would be prepared and simply put it in place with the appropriate date.

- The management of Water Luxury had some high-level accomplices—the deputy mayor and his advisor were members of the board of directors of Water Luxury.

- Pressure would be placed on the concession screening unit to stop its "textbook requests" for information.

- The company was engaging in accounting gymnastics by changing the allocation of operating expenses to capital expenditures in order to manipulate the amount spent on material assets.

After reading the first e-mail, I was eager to know what other information our anonymous benefactor provided. Another important e-mail, from Mich again, follows.

Patrick,

Further to our meeting today, I briefly note the following actions: (i) Gudsen [one of the principals of InvestCap 1 and 2] will produce a note which outlines a commercial structure to undertake capital works and which allows the withdrawal of fees for InvestCap 1 and InvestCap 2; (ii) Gudsen will review the transfers to maximize capital expenditures; (iii) Gudsen will arrange to adjust the "non revenue water" (NRW) graph to ensure that it meets the Level of Service Schedules given to the city as part of the capital program.

Mich

Based on this e-mail, we learned:

- Fees paid to the investment companies would be disguised as payments for capital works.

- The transfers were indeed used to maximize reported capital expenditures.

- The achievement of level of services would be falsely presented.

The third e-mail to one of Mich's executives regarding inflating prices follows.

Subject: Invoice for Models

David,

Please arrange for an invoice to be submitted to Water Luxury from InvestCap 1 "for the provision of hydraulic software and licenses." Total invoice of $113,000 should be dated 28 September.

The actual cost to InvestCap 1 of these licenses will be approximately $53,000 and the net difference of $60,000 is to be shared equally between InvestCap 1 and 2 in the same manner as the billing software.

I believe that the rates at which we are billing for this software and licenses is in line with the prevailing prices and we could be criticized if we try for more, but probably only by engineering companies who know the market, and only then if they had access to the numbers.

We could invoice more if we were comfortable, but I would suggest that we only do this in the event that we need to make up our 75% investment for the year.

Mich

Again, Mich had advised one of the executives to inflate the prices, and he set forth how "the investors" would share the margin and cover the clues. The fact that that was a repetitive action ("in the same manner as the billing software") shows his real intent to defraud the company.

Still reeling from these revelations, I read the next e-mail:

Subject: Modeling Project Structure

Gudens,

Please see attached note. This is a summary of what I believe to be successful discussions last week in regard to modeling in Sofia and I think it meets all our objectives in respect of project delivery. Gudens, please advise if you have any comments before I progress with the software purchase and the procurement of project managers from Ivan Stroj. The procurement will be backdated to be included in the first year.

Mich

Attachment:

Ivan Stroj Ltd. provides project managers through InvestCap 1 at close to market rates. These are then passed through to Water Luxury under the TSA (Technical Service Agreement) as InvestCap 1 staff. InvestCap will have a confidential contract with Ivan Stroj to cover this.

During an initial three-month evaluation and development period, a contract will be developed to provide all necessary modeling support that is not capable of being provided by Water Luxury staff. A public procurement process must be followed, subsequently for the tendering of this contract. But this must be presented in a way that allows the Fobos Joint Venture to win.

A success fee will be payable to Fobos (only Fobos—as lead of the JV) who will pass this through to InvestCap 1 and 2. It is proposed that the money should be equal to the penalties for three months delay in the delivery of the Strategic Models. This is approximately $600K to be paid over three stages of $200K each, at the end of months three, nine, and eighteen. This level of success fee is seen as realistic, given the high level of penalty that can be levied on Water Luxury.

It seemed that there was no end to the chicanery of Mich Jacobs and his friends—inflated bills, fake contracts and consulting services, phantom ventures, big margins, offshore affiliates, possibly even tax fraud and money laundering. Conducting some further searches, I found that Ivan Stroj was a company formed in the United Kingdom. Its Web site noted that the business had recently secured a record number of framework contracts, creating a deluge of career opportunities. Dozens of posts were being advertised, ranging from divisional directors and principal engineers to technicians and graduates, during what was called its most exciting period of growth in the past 20 years.

Obviously, the business it was receiving from Mich Jacobs was paying off—particularly for Mich and the other participants in the InvestCap companies. Although we still had many details to confirm, this information was extremely damning, and we thought it best to notify the mayor and the city leaders about our discoveries.

When we informed the mayor about all evidence, he immediately called Mich Jacobs. Not surprisingly, Mich denied everything and insisted that none of it was true. He proposed that the anonymous sender was simply a disgruntled former employee who just fabricated these stories to seek revenge. Unfortunately for the citizens of Sofia, the story was true. But two events transpired that would prevent swift justice.

First, we were notified that our investigation would end. Aquamon's contract with the city for screening and monitoring was being cancelled. The main reason was that there was now a new state water regulator whose responsibilities would include the same oversight services. Second, a new mayor was elected who did not believe that the investigation of Water

Luxury was a high priority—or a priority at all. He declined to meet with us and although he said he would correct the problems we identified in our report, he never took any action.

However, the municipal council reviewed the evidence and stated that it was ready to consider all options available to revise the concession contract for the operation of Sofia's water and wastewater services with Water Luxury. Bowing to pressure, the mayor presented a list of 15 conditions to the company that it would have to meet in order to preserve the concession. Also, in response to public interest, prosecution authorities said again they were investigating the alleged violations.

Some members of the Sofia city council asked for immediate termination of the contract with Water Luxury. However, other council members opposed such an extreme measure, mainly fearing the penalties for early termination.

Several of the council's advisors claimed that the termination of the contract could cost the city in excess of $30 million. Additionally, they said a ruling would be required from an international court of arbitration in order to end the ordeal, which could take years. The advisors believed that the water concession should continue, and, if possible, the city should share in the dividends of the corruption since it was a shareholder!

Prosecution is reportedly ongoing, but no charges have yet been filed. The city was able to renegotiate the terms of the contract with Water Luxury (under new management), and the citizens of Sofia continue to have water. Mich Jacobs was a master magician - he truly turned water into gold…"

P.S. After enacting The UK BRIBERY ACT 2010 the foreign UK company-investor - concessionaire sold its shares in the enterprises in Bulgaria, Estonia and Poland - my hypothesis was that the only reason was - to comply with the Act!

Function 5. Collecting and obtaining external and internal information about the existing controls, applied for detection and prevention fraud in the organization, if any.

To the function "Collecting and obtaining external and internal information about the existing controls, applied for detection and prevention fraud in the organization, if any" we will also append the information about the possible tools and techniques for concealment fraud. Such information could be generated during the interviews with the client - the owner or the managers - and during the brainstorming sessions with the expert team members.

For applying this function the expert team could use data mining, the interviews, Internet search engines, questionnaires, specialized software and all other techniques described in detail in Part 4.

There are two main approaches used for the assessment of the likelihood of fraud occurrence concerning the availability of the anti-fraud controls.

The first one is that the likelihood of fraud occurrence could be determined applying an analysis of the collected data and the second one uses the traditional way of identifying the existing or non existing controls.

The identification of the existing or non existing controls in our case is based on the idea that the properly established and working controls would minimize the likelihood of fraud occurrence. The progress of the process of the identification includes 1) the linking of the internal controls with the fraud risks and 2) with the assessment of the adequacy of the controls, established to deter fraud occurrence.

We would like to remind you here that one of the goals of the fraud risk assessment using our 3D FRAM is to determine the likelihood of the fraud scenario occurrence in the specific business system.

The assessment is subjective and is based on the adequacy of the internal controls, linked with the fraud scenarios ant it variations.

Therefore, the key element of the fraud risk assessment is the identification of the internal anti-fraud controls, which would be able to minimize the fraud scenario occurrence.

As this identification to be performed, however, what first should be done is the controls to be defined, to be categorized and criteria to be developed as the likelihood of fraud occurrence to be measured and calculated based on the existence or non existence of the internal controls established for fraud deterrence.

After identifying and linking the internal controls with the fraud scenarios the process of assessment of the likelihood of fraud occurrence should begin. This process includes the calculation of the final score about the significance of the fraud risk in the organization.

The data sampling (using the discovery sampling) should probably show whether a probable fraud scenario doesn't exist in the searched population and time period or the transactions fit to the profile of the fraud scenario where the established internal controls show that fraud risk should not exist.

From the point of the strategy chosen for fraud risk assessment, the selection of the right for the organization approach is very important stage in this process.

The common characteristics for the both approaches is the identification of the fraud scenarios linked with the existing or non existing controls and the understanding of how these scenarios could occur in the business systems.

Potential Inherent Risk Conditions

The specific conditions listed below may indicate the presence of inherent risks, some of which may also be fraud risks. Some of these may affect many processes, statements and activities. The examples shown below may assist the expert team in considering each of the inherent risk factors and the fraud risk factors relating to industry conditions, operating conditions, financial stability, corruption, fraud and susceptibility of assets to misappropriation, although it is not all inclusive. The expert should link and asses any other relevant factors and conditions based on the existing or non existing anti-fraud controls.

- Competent Personnel with Sound Ethics
- Organizational Structure and Organizational Locations
- Assignment of Authority and Responsibility and Possible Collusion
- Human Resource Policies and Practices regarding Anti-Fraud Resistance
- Management's Control Methods over Policy Formulation and Execution
- Management's Control Methods over Compliance with Laws and Regulations
- Participation of Those Charged with Governance for creating "Anti-Fraud Tone On The Top" (including oversight groups, such as Audit Committee)
- Setting Reasonable Objectives
- Identifying and Analyzing Fraud Risk
- Managing Change and Minimizing The Fraud Opportunities
- Internal Communication and Internal Values
- External Communication To Related Parties
- Control Activities Concerning Fraud
- Ongoing Monitoring and Fraud Risk Assessment
- Separate Evaluations under Anti-Fraud Legislation, if available
- The Effectiveness of Other Experts - External and Internal Auditors and Consultants

After collecting the necessary data the expert team begins its analysis regarding the fraud risk occurrence.

3.2.2. Fraud Risk Analysis

Function 6. Identification of the opportunities for occurrence of fraud and abuse and for their concealment

As noted, fraud is any intentional act or omission designed to deceive others, resulting in the victim suffering a loss and/or the perpetrator achieving a gain. Regardless of culture, ethnicity, religion, or other factors, certain individuals will be motivated to commit fraud.

A 2007 Oversight Systems study[10] discovered that the primary reasons why fraud occurs are "pressures to do 'whatever it takes' to meet goals" (81 percent of respondents) and "to seek personal gain" (72 percent). Additionally, many respondents indicated that "they do not consider their actions fraudulent" (40 percent) as a reason for wrongful behavior.

For example, potential fraud risks to consider in the ACFE's[11] three general categories include:

1) Intentional manipulation of financial statements, which can lead to:

a) Inappropriately reported revenues.

b) Inappropriately reported expenses.

c) Inappropriately reflected balance sheet amounts, including reserves.

d) Inappropriately improved and/or masked disclosures.

e) Concealing misappropriation of assets.

f) Concealing unauthorized receipts and expenditures.

g) Concealing unauthorized acquisition, disposition, and use of assets.

2) Misappropriation of:

a) Tangible assets by:

i) Employees.

ii) Customers.

iii) Vendors.

iv) Former employees and others outside the organization.

b) Intangible assets.

c) Proprietary business opportunities.

3) Corruption including:

a) Bribery and gratuities to:

i) Companies.

ii) Private individuals.

iii) Public officials.

b) Receipt of bribes, kickbacks, and gratuities.

c) Aiding and abetting fraud by other parties (e.g., customers, vendors)."

The recognition of the opportunities for fraud occurrence and its concealment relies on the collected, obtained and developed data, the comparison of the current situation with the possible and expected fraud scenarios in any specific situation, the time lag for fraud detection and the analysis of the impact - the losses in quantitative and qualitative measures.

The definitions of the applied system for the assessment consider the opportunities for fraud occurrence, implanted in the fraud scenario. The following examples will illustrate the used definitions for the assessed system:

1. The design of the internal controls would minimize the fraud scenario occurrence plus minimizing the delaying effect of internal controls application.

2. The design of the controls would make it possible the fraud scenario occurrence to be minimized.

3. The design of the controls wouldn't make it possible the occurrence of the fraud scenario.

Function 7. Analysis of the data available for patterns of fraud, corruption, abuse, errors, intent, irregularities

This function encompasses all knowledge and skills necessary for fraud risk assessment engagement regarding fraud and corruption taxonomy, the national legislation (EU legislation wold be an advantage!) and, of course, all data collected, obtained and developed.

Analysis for patterns of fraud, corruption, abuse, errors and irregularities could be performed as follows:

According the Sources

- Internal - in the name of organization for personal or for related parties gains but against the organization
- External - in the name and for gains to the organization but against an individual or legal entity external to the organization

According Legal Status

- Individual
- Corporate
- Combination of both

According Ownership and Management Level

- Owners
- Directors
- Managers
- Employees

- Non Employees

According Activity Significance

- Financial and Managerial Accounting
- Procurement
- Financing and funding
- Investments
- Insurance and Reimbursements
- Social Security and Medicare
- Purchasing and Delivering
- Computer and Internet
- E-commerce
- Taxation
- Non-for-profit
- Donations and Charities

More

3.2.3. Fraud Risk Assessment Phase

Function 8: Ranging the fraud risks according their source, ownership level and significance using two measures - quantitative and qualitative

The ranging the fraud risks could be made using the analysis performed above and range for this function from 1 to 10 point could be assigned according the expert team's judgement.

For example, ranging the fraud risks (from 1 to 10) could be performed as follows:

According the Sources - 1 point

- Internal - in the name of organization for personal or for related parties gains but against the organization
- External - in the name and for gains to the organization but against an individual or legal entity external to the organization

According Legal Status - 1 point

- Individual

- Corporate
- Combination of both

According Ownership and Management Level - 5 points

- Owners - 2
- Directors - 1
- Managers - 1
- Employees - 1/2
- Non Employees - 1/2

According Activity Significance - 3 points

- Financial and Managerial Accounting
- Procurement
- Financing and funding
- Investments
- Insurance and Reimbursements
- Social Security and Medicare
- Purchasing and Delivering
- Computer and Internet
- E-commerce
- Taxation
- Non-for-profit
- Donations and Charities
- More - regarding the specifics

Don't forget that the ranging shown above concerns the current situation and the current fraud risk assessment engagement. After any small change in the breakdown above the rates should be changed!

The calculation of the final score for the likelihood of fraud should allow a consistence and integrity in the fraud risk assessment process. The technique should be coordinated and understandable by the client. For achieving this goal you may comply with the following rules:

- Keep the ranging system uncomplicated

• Use two rates for ranging the fraud risk

• The less points - the less fraud risk. This is valid for both approaches used in 3D FRAM - form 100 to 0 and from 0 to 100

• Present definitions for every ranging level

• The fraud risk assessment should use fraud scenarios on every ranging level

• The final score presenting the likelihood or risk of fraud should be an aggregate value based on the rates for all 10 functions of the 3D FRAM

Function 9. Determination of the level of fraud risk in two rages - significant or nonsignificant.

3D FRAM offers you own to choice how to determine the fraud risk significance for the organization but we advise you to follow the sequence described below.

The methodology is as follows:

1. The total score for determination of the fraud risk as SIGNIFICANT is equal to 100 points.

2. All 10 functions of 3D FRAM have equal weights.

3. Every weight has 10 points.

4. Every function is a source for information used for applying from 0 to 10 points.

5. Total score of the all functions is 100.

6. Significant is the fraud risk with score more than 50.

7. Initial inherent fraud risk is 0 or 100 depending on the used technique described in Part 4.

8. Residual risk is equal to inherent fraud risk plus significant risk minus the fraud risk response. It is impossible to be ZERO.

9. The opinion is subjective and the arguments and evidence of the expert team provided to the client is the best defense to any objections.

10. For an initial Fraud Risk Assessment engagement the starting point will be 100 and the final could be 0 points as a total score. For a next 3D FRAM engagement the starting point will be 0 and the final score will be 100 points.

It is very important the preliminary presented awareness about the fraud risk assessment methodology to be consistent with the conclusions and recommendations made to the client.

Table Below is as follows: 3-1 Example for a 10 Grades Table for Fraud Risk Assessment According 3D FRAM

N	FUNCTION	Fraud Risk Significance 10/0	
I.	FRAUD EXPOSURE, AWARENESS AND RECOGNITION PHASE	Yes - 10	No - 0
1	Providing awareness to the client about the nature, scope, fraud exposure and specifics of the fraud risk assessment process - management is not aware about fraud and fraud schemes	10	
2	Collecting, obtaining and developing of external and internal information to get understanding of the legal status and business of the organization - inherent risk is significant	10	
3	Identification of the possible exposure of fraud types, corruption and fraud schemes at different levels, processes and activities of the organization - many possible types of fraud and fraud schemes are identified	10	
4	Recognition of a fraud scenario and its variations, concerning different levels, processes and activities of the organization - many different fraud scenarios and variations are available	10	
5	Collecting and obtaining external and internal information about the existing controls, applied for detection and prevention fraud in the organization, if any - no recognized anti-fraud controls	10	
II.	FRAUD RISK ANALYSIS		

6	Identification of the opportunities for occurrence of fraud and abuse and for their concealment - there are many and different opportunities for fraud	10	
7	Analysis of the data available for patterns of fraud, corruption, abuse, errors, intent, irregularities - tips, complaints, pending legal claims, penalties etc.	10	
III.	**FRAUD RISK ASSESSMENT PHASE**		
8	Ranging the fraud risks according their source, ownership level and significance using two measures - quantitative and qualitative - no 0 tolerance and political interference	10	
9	Determination of the fraud risk in two rages - significant or nonsignificant - difficult to determine	10	
IV.	**FRAUD RISK RESPONSE**		
10	Development of recommendations for an adequate response and timely measures according the significance of the assessed fraud risk as to develop and/or to enhance the resistance to fraud - no adequate response and significant residual risk	10	
V.	**TOTAL RISK SIGNIFICANCE:**	100	

The detailed prescription of all data necessary for a development of the grade scale shown above will be specific and unique for every one organization! The phase "Fraud Risk Response" is described below.

3.2.4. FRAUD RISK RESPONSE

Function 10. Development of recommendations for an adequate response and timely measures according the significance of the assessed fraud risk as to develop and/or to enhance the resistance to fraud.

This function proposes an adequate response and timely measures according the significance of the fraud risk as to "Find The Right People at The Right Place and on The Right Time!" as not to be too late for any actions then!

A fraud risk response model is usually the first type of targeting model that a company/organization seeks to develop. If no targeting has been done in the past, afar risk response model can provide a huge boost to the efficiency of a anti-fraud campaign by increasing responses and/or reducing legal expenses. The goal is to predict who will be responsive to an offer for a ethical behavior product or service. It can be based on past behavior of a similar population or some logical substitute.

A response can be received in several ways, depending on the offer channel. A "hotline" offer can direct the responder to reply anonymously by phone, or Internet. When compiling the results, it is important to monitor the response channel and manage duplicates. It is not unusual for a responder to mail a response and then respond by phone or Internet a few days later. There are even situations in which a company may receive more than one mail response from the same person.

This is especially common if a ant-fraud program receives multiple or follow-up offers for the same service that are spaced several weeks apart. It is important to establish some rules for dealing with multiple responses in fraud risk response model development.

It is possible to establish the following 5 sub-functions as like:

- Targeting,
- Profiling,
- Segmentation,
- Profiling analysis and
- Response

These sub-functions will be discussed in more detail in our next updates of 3D FRAM.

Although the majority of organizations have realized that prevention of fraud and corruption should be an important element of a organizational strategy, there are gaps in their knowledge about fraudsters and the way that they operate. The key areas where improvements can be made are:

- establishing a clear, visible and credible tone at the top aimed at eliminating fraud and corruption;
- investing time in understanding where fraud and corruption takes place by conducting profiling workshops right across the organization and then taking action to eliminate

- the gap between what employees know as reality and what executives believe to be the case;
- encouraging all employees to participate actively in the fight against fraud and corruption, including training all staff to be aware of the red flags which might indicate fraudster and corruption;
- employing techniques which are successful at continuously monitoring and identifying the red flags of fraud and corruption;
- systematically measuring the organization's resistance to fraud and corruption rather than testing the completeness of controls.

Let's dive in the ocean of the 3D FRAM methodology now!

Part IV: 3D FRAM - Methodological Dimension

In this part:

- The Nature of The Methodological Dimension
- The Methods and Techniques for Collecting Data
- The Data Analysis Methodology

4.1. THE NATURE OF "THE METHODOLOGICAL DIMENSION"

This part will learn you "How To Do" or apply different methods and techniques for conducting all the functions necessary for the 3D FRAM. The methods and techniques like data mining, discovery sampling, Internet search engines, specialized software, what-if-analysis, cost benefit and sensitivity analysis will help you to receive and analyze quantitate and qualitative data as to reach the final conclusion.

"The Methodological Dimension" includes the necessary professional judgment and experience, the scope and the design of methods and techniques, used for the fraud risk assessment process.

Don't forget that the goal of the described methodology here is not to become a substitute of the professional judgement and experience but to enhance the quality of the iterative activities and outcomes. We would remind you again that the corruption and fraud risks differ in their nature (fraud is crime!) in comparison with the traditional control risk.

From another point, the intent to deceit is the critical element of the fraud risk and the adequate response should be prepared considering this intent. And again, the intent is the difference between the error and the fraud.

3D FRAM in its Methodological Dimension uses the methods described as follows:

- Method 1: Providing awareness of the engagement
    - Techniques 1.1: Interviews
    - Technique 1.2: Presentations
- Method 2: Collecting, obtaining, searching and reviewing of information
    - Technique 2.1: Data Mining
    - Technique 2.2: Discovery Sampling
    - Technique 2.3: Internet search engines
    - Technique 2.4: Questionnaires

- Method 3: Documentation Review
    - Technique 3.1: Documentation Inspection
    - Technique 3.2: Check the events for authenticity and real accomplishment

- Method 4: Walking, talking, watching, listening
    - Technique 4.1: Be On The Place
    - Technique 4.2: Body Language
    - Technique 4.3: Tips and Claims

- Method 5: Data Analysis
    - Technique 5.1: Content Analysis
    - Technique 5.2: What-if-Analysis
    - Technique 5.3: Hypothesis Testing

- Technique 5.4: Trend and Ratio Analysis

- Technique 5.5: Cost-benefit Analysis

- Technique 5.6: Sensitivity Analysis

- Method 6: Ranging Fraud Risks

  - Technique 6.1: From 0 to 100

  - Technique 6.2: From 100 to 0

4.2. THE METHODS AND TECHNIQUES FOR COLLECTING DATA
4.2.1. Providing Awareness of the Engagement

Technique 4.2.1.1: Interviews

3D FRAM uses the interview is a personal, controlled conversational meeting in which experts could obtain needed information from the clients' owners, management, employees or from who have it.

Interviews are a very important part of a fraud and corruption risks assessment process, because by putting on a expert or think-like-a-thief hat, management and employees can be guided to avoid concentrating on existing controls which they believe to be strong and instead to think about how they could be bypassed.

The advantages of the interviews could be as follows:

- Interviews could be very productive information-gathering methods for experts engaged in the fraud risk assessment, second only to tedious review of documents and financial records.

- Interviews can produce information from nonverbal behavior that no other information-gathering technique can produce.

- From interviews could be obtained necessary background and off-record information unavailable from documents and public records.

- Interviews can provide important interpretations of other data from knowledgeable people.

- Meeting knowledgable and involved people gives the experts an understanding and sense of the activity they are assessing that they cannot get otherwise.

The parties interviewed by the experts during the fraud risk assessment could be:

Owners. Owners can provide information about the entire organizations, including the past or current issues, objectives and future activities.

Managers. Managers can provide detailed information about missions, objectives, policies, procedures, internal controls and general workings in their areas.

Employees. Employees can provide valuable information about day-today operations in specific functions and offices from a unique perspective. Often, they are reliable sources of information about what's right, wrong or needs improvement in their work areas. Any differences between what is heard from various management levels and what is heard from workers will reveal the fraud patterns.

Contractors. Principals, managers and employees of contractors to the company or organization can provide detailed information about the services they provide under their contracts, as well as knowledge of their areas of expertise. Such people are very valuable source of information especially in a case of risk assessment of capital projects.

Vendors. Vendors can provide information about their products and services, their official business relationships with the client, and their personal relationships with your client's employees, which could reveal possible patterns of conflict of interest.

Lawyers and Consultants. The clients's internal and external lawyers and consultants can provide useful information about pending claims, management and technical aspects in general and/or regarding the specific area you are assessing.

Specialists. Independent specialists can provide useful information, answer questions and assist your analyses of the general assessed area, for example, academic fraud risk assessment. Examples include professors, doctors, psychologists, lawyers, environmentalists, biologists, agriculturists and researchers.

Choosing who to interview is an important part of the exercise. Not every employee needs to partake – just those who have hands-on knowledge of the operation. Usually these are team leaders, section heads, supervisors and line managers. The success or failure of the profiling exercise lies in transferring awareness to these employees who then identify the loopholes.

Loopholes in controls exist for various reasons, especially detective and anti-fraud controls, if any: for example, because they are historically present in a process, because new systems have been installed, as a result of breakdowns in processing, or because no one has ever looked at the controls through the eyes of a fraudster.

If employees have worked in a function for some time, they may develop blind-spots which prevent them from seeing how dishonest persons or criminals can bypass the controls and systems.

It is vital to provide employees with the necessary stimulation to be able to see around the controls and identify the methods of fraud and corruption. For example, in-house anti-fraud specialists (who do not believe that controls alone prevent fraud and corruption) are usually able to identify the most common methods which can affect a particular operation.

Alternatively, external anti-fraud specialists or certified fraud examiners can be of assistance in providing that necessary stimulation and insight.

The important point is to make the management and employees aware of the schemes and methodology used by possible fraudsters. Once employees understand the method, they can by default readily evaluate whether or not the existing controls will prevent its use. There is therefore no need to produce detailed maps of the controls and processes which operational risk and fraud risk assessment teams may have already produced.

Quite often, the management and employees would say that they are unable to see a way around the controls because they and their colleagues are all honest and would not attempt a fraud. In this instance, it is easier to ask them to imagine that they are on holiday and that a person has taken their job who is completely dishonest, and then ask what could that person do.

Experience has shown once honest employees imagine that a fictitious dishonest person is in their seat or in the seat of their colleague, they can readily identify methods of fraud.

It should be stressed to employees that the intention of the exercise is not to look at their own honesty or that of their colleagues. The intention is to evaluate the potential for fraud and corruption in the job function assuming they were not there.

A useful method to assist employees to identify exactly what a fraudster sitting in their seat might be interested in is to draw a box and ask them to describe what crosses their desk.

They should consider the different assets relating to their own job function which they can access, for example:

- Incoming and outgoing payments, cheques, cash
- Salable information – personal, operational, security
- Physical assets
- Company resources, such as computer and communications systems
- Proprietary information: brand, patents, intellectual property
- Inventory
- Property, land,

some of which provide ready cash, while others can be converted into a benefit.

Employees should also bear in mind that a number of different opponents may target the organization, ranging from professional criminals to dishonest suppliers, customers, contractors, as well as dishonest employees.

Interviews could be used for obtaining a valuable information about the issues relating to fraud and corruption risks, namely:

- Performance/Productivity Problems

- Interpersonal Problems

- Insubordination

- Excessive Absenteeism and Sick Leave Use

- Drugs and Alcohol

- Theft and Dishonesty

- Violence

- Morality Issues

Questions that can reveal fraud risk and fraud occurrences could concern:

- Fraud Risk. Certain employee attitudes and aspects of their personal lives can indicate a risk of fraud.

- Fraud Occurrences. Contradictory, questionable and inconsistent statements and stories can indicate that fraud might have occurred.

The specific nature of each fraud case will warrant different types and depths of probing questions. Whether to ask probing questions, which questions to ask and how deep to probe must be decided on each case. There is no "cookie cutter" for these questions.

Note that we emphasize "fraud cases." Asking questions to reveal fraud risk or occurrences would be appropriate in fraud risk assessments of activities where fraud is possible, likely or suspected.

Examples for types of questions are as follows:

- How do you feel about your organization, superiors, peers, job, customers? Employees with negative attitudes about the organization, their supervisors, their peers and themselves are more prone to committing fraud than are employees with good attitudes.

- When filing your expense reports, do you submit actual receipts or the per diem allowance?

- Employees who are willing to bend rules or push the envelope toward their benefit might be more prone to committing fraud than are employees who follow the rules.

- How do you feel when you see numerous other people in your office ignoring office policies?

- Employees who justify violations because they see others doing it are more prone to fraud than are employees with scruples to keep themselves honest.

- Do you feel there's enough opportunity in this organization for you to realize your potential and your goals?

- Ambitious employees who feel they have no opportunities are more prone to fraud than are employees with lower ambitions and employees who still see opportunity.

- Do you feel it's all right for people to borrow from the organization as long as they return it?

- Employees who justify questionable actions are more prone to committing fraud than are employees who reject questionable actions.

- Do you feel you are paid fairly? Employees who sincerely feel underpaid are prone to compensating through fraud.

Group Interviews. You can sometimes maximize your results while minimizing your time and effort by interviewing groups of people simultaneously. Use them when you expect to receive similar information from everyone in the group, you expect no contentious information, it doesn't matter if people feed answers to other people, and togetherness makes people more comfortable about discussing an issue.

Advanced-Question Interviews. You can receive good results while minimizing your time and effort by submitting questions to some interviewees in advance. Use this method when you expect no contentious information, it doesn't matter if people research and revise their answers, it doesn't matter if people discuss their answers with other people, you're in the early planning stages and their background information can help you plan other interviews and formulate other interview questions, and/or you intend to interview them personally or by telephone to be sure you understand their answers.

Telephone Interviews. Some interviews can be conducted over the telephone: short interviews, noncontroversial interviews in which no contentious information is expected, repetitive interviews in which several people will be asked similar questions for laying foundations or comparing answers, familiar subjects whom you've interviewed before and/or know well, and/or distant interviewees.

Telephone interviewing can be inefficient and ineffective in some situations: The information you need might be sensitive or contentious. You might need to see nonverbal signals such as facial expressions and body movements. Your subject might feel intimidated by answering questions over the phone. Your subject doesn't know and trust you. Your subject might be distracted by activities you cannot control at their end. Your interview is going to last a long time.

Interviewing by telephone requires planning, too, as well as a few special techniques: Plan it just as you would a personal interview to maximize productivity and efficiency. Introduce yourself and explain your purpose right away. If you don't, you might confuse then antagonize your interviewee. Ask if the time is convenient. If it isn't, your interview might produce flawed results. Speak clearly, calmly and slowly so they can hear your questions accurately. Listen very attentively so you can hear their answers accurately. Listen for voice inflections and pauses. They're to telephone interviews what nonverbal signals are to in-person interviews.

Concentrate on the interview. If you let activities in your office distract you, you'll waste the interview. Repeat answers to be sure you heard them correctly. If you don't, you might write down the wrong answers. Keep the interview moving. If you allow silences of only a few seconds, your subject might get distracted. Provide verbal cues to indicate that you understand the answers.

Using different methods provides different advantages and disadvantages applying in different situations.

For example, the first step for asking questions is to formulate the broad, overall questions to be answered by the assessment or evaluation.

Why is the assessment being done? What do we hope to be able to say or prove? Are we primarily describing what has taken place in a process? Do we want to compare what has happened with some established or implied standard, a normative-type question? Or do we want to determine if a process has made a difference, a cause-and-impact type question?

Examples of such questions are

- Descriptive: "How do employees of the ABZ organization treat the possible fraud patterns of embezzlement in their organization?"

- Compliance: "How well does the anti-fraud training meet its goals for placing employees in their jobs?"

- Cause-and-impact: "Why do some employees are more susceptible to fraud and abuse than others?"

The type of question asked will dictate the fraud risk assessment strategy. Also, certain strategies are more appropriate to answering certain questions. However, structured interviews, being simply a method of data collection, can be used with several evaluation strategies and, thus, in a variety of fraud risk assessment engagements.

After the broad overall questions are developed, they must could be translated into measurable elements in the form of hypotheses or questions. For the example mentioned above, to evaluate how employees treat possible fraud patterns would require developing such measures as the sources through which participants learned of available fraud patterns, the number of employers contacted, and the number of fraud risk assessment interviews arranged. Next, the target population must be identified. The target population is the source level (individuals, groups, or organizations) at which the information is to be gathered. Thus, in the study of how anti-training program employees treat fraud patterns after leaving the program, the target population is the individual participants of the program who were trained.

Next, develop a pool of questions that attempt to measure the variables under consideration. The questions may include various ways of measuring the same variable. For example, for age, you might ask, "How old were you on your last birthday?" or "On what day, month, and year were you born?" Both questions help you determine the individual's age, but the second elicits much more information. Decide which to use. From the pool of questions, then, the most useful or appropriate are chosen.

Using your interviews as data/evidence. Information obtained properly from interviews serves usually as important evidence for fraud risk assessment reports. Evidence is data on which factual statements can be based, which in turn support conclusions. It is a requisite source of facts in fraud risk assessment Regarding fraud risk assessment, evidence is a collection of relevant and sufficient facts offered in verification of an fraud risk assessment conclusion.

Data/Evidence from interviews. Evidence obtained from interviews differs from all other evidence because of its distinctive advantages and disadvantages.

Advantages. Interviews have distinct advantages over other forms of evidence that make interviewing a crucial fraud risk assessment method. The information has special qualities that cannot be obtained any other way. The advantages could be as follows:

- Information about each interviewee's skills and knowledge can be valuable evidence you will not find elsewhere.
- Interviews can reveal whether missions, policies and procedures are reaching all levels in the organization.
- First-hand knowledge of problems can surface in any interview but not be available anywhere else.
- Knowledge about the client that is not and might never be documented can surface in interviews.
- Personal analyses from managers and employees can be useful in developing your findings.
- Eyewitness accounts of problems, incidents, accidents and other situations can be just the evidence you need to solidify your findings. It might never be available anywhere else.

- Leads to other information that the expert might never have found without this assistance from interviewees can help develop findings.

- Stories that describe the situation under discussion but do not typify it can be useful sometimes for making points clear to report readers.

- Office grapevines are frequently reliable sources of background information or leads to other sources. Not much information flowing on the office grapevine appears in any documentation.

- People's emotions, sentiments, positions and viewpoints are sometimes useful in analyzing fraud risk assessment evidence. They rarely appear in formal documentation. As examples: Poor employee morale is a rarely documented emotional position of employees toward management and/or the organization. Deliberate noncompliance is rarely documented, because memos documenting it are either not written or are destroyed.

- Comparisons of evidence obtained from interviews can be very valuable in analyzing the body of fraud risk assessment evidence and leading to finding elements. As examples:

  - Compare statements made during an interview with other statements made during the same interview for inconsistencies. Some inconsistencies might result from nervousness or confusion, and others might result from lack of candor.

  - Compare statements made in some interviews to statements made in other interviews for inconsistencies from the same person or among various people. Such inconsistencies require close examination and followup.

  - Compare statements made in interviews with other physical or documentary evidence for inconsistencies. If you are able to corroborate the testimony, that's great, but if the testimony does not corroborate with other evidence, a problem has been revealed.

- Confidential and Off-books Information. Information given under agreements of confidentiality can help you understand or lead you to other evidence.

From this short list, we can see how evidence obtainable from interviews is deep, varied and helpful in numerous ways. Inconsistencies from comparisons of evidence plus confidential and off-record information would probably warrant additional fraud risk assessment work that had not been planned when the fraud risk assessment began.

Disadvantages of interviews. The advantages of testimony notwithstanding, not all evidence obtained from interviews is useful to experts. Hazards abound. As examples:

- Most fraud risk assessment interviews are conducted on basic trust. Without oaths, there's little recourse if any information is untruthful. This is why corroboration is so important.

- Some evidence obtained from people in interviews is not reliable for a lot of reasons. Different people can naturally have different perceptions, interpretations and recollections of the same incident. The more time between the incident and the interview, the more the recollection and interpretation will be tainted or faded. Some data is hearsay – the person heard it from someone else and doesn't know for certain. Some data is conjecture – the person doesn't know for certain but concludes on preliminary evidence and convinces himself that his conclusions are valid. Some people give answers to questions they are not truly capable of answering, usually because they don't want to feel or appear inadequate.

- Some people deliberately misrepresent and/or withhold information, telling only what the experts ask or what they want the experts to know. Some people lie outright.

- People's attitudes and biases can naturally interfere with their recollections, interpretations and accounts. It's inadvertent most of the time.

- Secrecy agreements limit the usefulness of some information as evidence. Information obtained confidentially cannot be substantiated by revealing its source. Information obtained off the record cannot be used in the report or the working papers. Some of that information cannot be corroborated, either.

Value of Evidence. The evidence obtained from interviews has weight, or value, depending on its nature and sources. Given the unique advantages and disadvantages of so called testimonial evidence, the prudent expert determines that value carefully. The values of evidence could be described below as follows:

- Competent evidence is appropriate to the circumstance, suitable for the purpose and the best obtainable through the use of professional fraud risk assessment techniques. Evidence obtained from planned, prepared and well conducted interviews is usually competent.

- Relevant evidence helps you answer the questions posed by the fraud risk assessment objective and is logically related to the issue. Interviewing people who are in positions to know and asking them the right questions will ensure that your interview evidence will be relevant.

- Material evidence is significant enough to affect decisions or outcomes. The mere existence of misstatements or contradictory statements might not warrant reporting if they do not affect decisions or outcomes.

Significance is very important to be looking for throughout the interviews. It will concern the following aspects:

- Perspective is (1) the relationship of aspects of a subject to one another and to the whole, and (2) subjective evaluation of relative significance. To be meaningful, your testimonial evidence must be collected, analyzed and reported in relation to the whole issue you are assessed.

- Adequate evidence is of high enough quality to be used for analysis and proof. For example, legible time cards are adequate for verifying hours worked, and illegible time cards are adequate for verifying sloppy time-keeping practices. Similarly, testimony from supervisors about how they train their staff and from workers about how they perform procedures would be generally adequate.

- Sufficient evidence is enough to lead a prudent person to the same conclusion that you reached. Determination of how much evidence is sufficient requires judgment and experience. Interviewing enough people to depict situations from various viewpoints will usually provide sufficient testimonial evidence.

- Corroboration means the evidence is strengthened by links to other reliable evidence that verifies it. Usually, three corroborating items are sufficient, but sometimes more are needed. Almost all testimonial evidence must be corroborated.

Analyzing the interview results. Analysis is "separating an intellectual whole into its parts for individual study," and "the results of that study." Analyze your interview promptly, while the spirit of the interview is still fresh in your mind.

Look for value. Most of the information the expert team obtains from your interviews should have some value. Some will have more value than others, and each type of information will have a different value. Look for those values in the information you obtained.

Analyze step by step. The expert team should follow a methodical, step-by-step approach to analyzing the information obtained from its interviews. Using a logical approach based on the nature of that information and the relationships among the answers will help to analyze all of it and not omit anything.

Documenting the Interviews. Document every interview as soon as possible after finishing it. Three documentation formats would be available to the team: transcripts, recaps and summaries. The team might find one, two or all three useful, depending on the nature of information obtained from your interview.

Interview Summaries. Interview summaries synopsize the main relevant information obtained from interviews. They are appropriate for short interviews that produce few details and are unlikely to be contested. Additionally, summaries should be written for every interview transcript and recap. These summaries in the working papers enable other people to understand the working paper.

Technique 4.2.1.2: Presentations

3D Fraud Risk Assessment Model (3D FRAM) uses the presentations as a tool for providing awareness to the client/owner/management and to the employees in the organization where an fraud risk assessment engagement is provided.

Normally, a presentation follows the phases described below:

- Determine the objectives of the presentation
- Focus the attention on the key fraud issues
- Plan to provide awareness about fraud and fraud risks to your audience
- Take care about your clothes and first impressions
- "Ice breaking" is a Must
- Prepare carefully the slides and handouts
- Present the importance of the topic with confidence and impact
- Take care about the body language – yours and your audience
- Maintaining eye contact - the affect on the audience
- Controlling your voice effectively
- Timing your delivery
- Using visual aids
- Ask for questions and comments
- Don't forget and don't repeat the mistakes made during similar presentation

4.2.1.2.1.Presentations Before Owners/Stakeholders/Management

While everything in the preceding chapters is relevant in presenting to management, there are some additional things that you'll want to keep in mind. This chapter focuses on tips for presenting to anyone from your client - owner or board of directors. If they're the highest in rank, the following tips apply:

- Tailor your presentation to their perspective
- Get to the point
- Incorporate an appropriate level of complexity
- Accommodate their communication preferences
- Be cautious about using humor
- Rehearse.

Tailor the presentation to their perspective

Presentations to the client - owners and/or management are typically for the purpose of informing and persuading. The key to successfully informing or persuading is to consider the audience's perspective. In the case of your client - the management, what do they need to know or do to be successful - and to be perceived as successful by their own superiors. What do you need to know to put your presentation in their terms?

In preparing to present to management, consider their priorities, pressures, fears, and frustrations. What drives their key decisions? Fighting fraud? Reducing costs? Improving on-time delivery? Increasing customer satisfaction? Overcoming a negative public image? Doing more with less? Learn what's important to those you're presenting to and tailor your presentation accordingly.

Get to the point

Don't pontificate. Synonyms for pontification in my online thesaurus include sound off, preach, go on, and hold forth - all things to avoid doing in presenting to your superiors. As busy people with numerous competing priorities, they are in a position to stop you half-way through if they don't find your material relevant and compelling. Therefore, stick to what's important and omit the rest.

Keep in mind the inverted pyramid approach (or inverted triangle, as it's often drawn). This refers to presenting the most important information first and then successively less important material.

This approach, which derives from the newspaper industry, is based on the realization that most people don't read a newspaper article beyond the first few paragraphs. With the most important information at the top, readers can quickly glean the essential information. In addition, if space originally intended for the article is needed for an ad or a breaking story, editors can cut from the end without being concerned about slashing critical information.

This same idea applies to presenting to the client. Something may come up that requires them to make an early exit. Therefore, begin with your conclusion and then provide supporting information, going from most important to least important. That way, even if circumstances prevent you from giving the entire presentation, they'll at least have heard your most important information.

Incorporate an appropriate level of complexity

Having urged you in Part 5 to minimize the use of text-filled slides, 3D FRAM now offers a possible exception based on a personal experience. I was once invited to speak at an executive retreat that my client, a CPA organization, was holding for its customers, senior managers of technology divisions. The partner who invited me, assigned a graphic artist to design slides for my presentation. In each of the resulting slides was a few words to make the key point, plus a whimsical cartoon that supported that point. The partner reviewed my presentation and slides and signed off on both. I knew my slides would be a big hit. I was wrong.

It quickly became evident from the executives comments and facial expressions that they found my slides too simplistic. The next presenter's slides, which were filled with complex charts and tiny type, apparently met their expectations of what constituted executive-oriented slides. The audience loved his presentation.

Accommodate their communication preferences

This suggestion may not be practical if you're presenting to a large audience, but if you're presenting to just one or two individuals or a small group, consider how they like to receive information. Do they favor colorful charts and graphs? Visual images? Text? Statistics?

Do they prefer to view slides or read printed information? Do they prefer high-level or in-depth information? And relative to the simplicity/complexity issue, would it be smarter to keep your slides simple or make them look complex?

When I was an financial director, our new executive director didn't want formal presentations. She was a let's-get-on-with-it guy. If we couldn't give her the facts swiftly and concisely, she wasn't interested. Look at slides? Not a chance. Her communication preferences were altogether different from her bullet-point-driven predecessor. We quickly learned that we had to change our ways to accommodate her.

Think about what you know about the communication preferences of those you'll be presenting to, and seek input from colleagues. Tailoring your presentation to their preferences may make them more receptive to your information than they might otherwise be.

Be cautious about using humor

Using humor is important in presenting to upper management Why?

Because they may take themselves seriously - or at least want to be seen as taking themselves seriously. As a result, they may not find your humor amusing, even if they'd find it uproariously funny if they heard it from one of their peers. If they already know you and they appreciate your light-hearted approach to serious issues, then go for it. Otherwise, use caution.

I'm certainly not implying that senior managers are humorless nor would I insist that you never use humor in presenting to them. Just think twice before you do so. Or maybe three or four times. Especially, when you are going to talk about corruption and fraud!

Anticipate possible questions and objections

If you can't answer a question while presenting to your coworkers, it's not the end of the world. If you can't answer a question while presenting to your clients, the end of the world may be a bit closer than you'd like. Therefore, contemplate the questions they might ask and make very sure you can respond.

If you're making a proposal, or seeking backing for an engagement, prepare to respond to objections. To do this, take a position opposed to the case you're making and identify – and write down – all the objections you can. This isn't easy to do; after all, you're arguing against your own interests.

But by identifying possible objections, you can formulate ways to counter them. In the process, you may be able to strengthen your case by weeding out flaws and weaknesses.

Several audit managers have asked me whether it's better to anticipate questions and answer them before anyone asks them or hold back in order to respond competently if someone asks. In a presentation to management, it's usually better to be forthcoming. If you withhold key information in anticipation of a question, your listeners may see you as unprepared. Why, the executive might wonder, did you not provide this information without my having to ask?

Of course, if it's a point that might damage your persuasive case, and it's a point your audience is unlikely to ask about, maybe (just maybe) it's worth holding back.

Rehearse

Rehearsing is crucial for presentations to a company's top officials. People who give presentations to this level often every point, practicing the entire presentation, and giving special attention to any part that seems weak.

A great strength of many technical professionals is they have a vast body of knowledge that they're often eager to share. But this strength can turn into a problem if you're giving a presentation that requires that you adhere closely to an agreed agenda. A CEO had recently given a presentation to a board of directors to seek funding; he told me how critical it was that he and his team should stick to their script and not make impromptu remarks that could undermine their message.

To recap

In preparing to present to the client - an owner and/or his management, consider their issues and concerns, their fears and frustrations, their priorities and pressures, and their communication preferences, and tailor your presentation accordingly In particular:

- Frame your presentation in terms of their perspective

- Present the most important information first

- Make sure your material is appropriately complex

- Accommodate their communication preferences

- Be cautious about using humor, especially examples about corruption and fraud

- Prepare to respond to possible questions and objections.

- Practice and practice some more.

These issues are important in presenting to all levels of management, but the higher up they are, the more important these issues become.

In conclusion

Management can be a tough audience, especially if your goal is to persuade. To the extent feasible, build credibility in advance so that when you present, you will receive a fair hearing. Never underestimate the power of your reputation to give you an advantage when you present to management.

4.2.1.2.2. Presentations Before Employees/Vendors/Specialists

- Consider your clients' perspectives

- Guard against potentially ambiguous terminology

- Show that you understand their business

- Watch their attitude

- Allow ample time for questions

- Be careful how you sell fraud risk assessment engagement

- Remember that appearances count

- To recap

- In conclusion

4.2.2. Collecting, Obtaining, Searching and Reviewing of Information

Technique 4.2.2.1. Data Mining

According Wikipedia[12]: "Data mining (the analysis step of the knowledge discovery in databases process), a relatively young and interdisciplinary field of computer science is the process of discovering new patterns from large data sets involving methods at the intersection of artificial intelligence, machine learning, statistics and database systems.

The goal of data mining is to extract knowledge from a data set in a human-understandable structure and involves database and data management, data preprocessing, model and inference considerations, interestingness metrics, complexity considerations, post-processing of found structure, visualization and online updating."

For the purposes of the 3D FRAM we will use data mining as a process of discovering interesting knowledge trough different patterns about likelihood of fraud from large amounts of data stored either in databases, data warehouses, or other information repositories. Additionally, data mining is an integrated process of data analysis that consists of a series of activities that go from the definition of the objectives to be analyzed, to the analysis of the data up to the interpretation and evaluation of the results.

Data mining can be useful greatly in the fraud risk assessment process by helping to answer several important questions about the data collected:

- What fraud patterns are there in our database?
- What is the likelihood that a fraud will occur?
- Which fraud patterns are significant?
- What is a high level summary of the data that gives us some idea of the significant fraud risk which is contained in my database?

The use of terms like "red flags"and "indicators" is common for the fraud theory. In 3D FRAM we introduce the use of the term "pattern".

Again, according Wikipedia (http://en.wikipedia.org/wiki/Pattern): "A *pattern*, from the French *patron*, is a type of theme of recurring events or objects, sometimes referred to as elements of a set of objects."

Patterns can be any combination of values that contain meaning within the context or domain for which they are being reviewed. There are many different ways to expose patterns, including clusters, sequences, or relationships.

Look at Fig. 4-1 below for a visual understanding of these concepts.

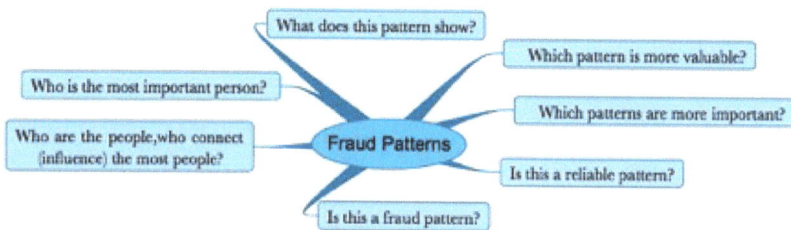

Fig. 4-1 Fraud Patterns

In the real world, there are no right answers and there are no wrong answers. Patterns are based on individual interpretation of the data, the environment, the circumstances, and the quality of the data collected.

One must also take into account that not all patterns hold true 100 percent of the time, that there are always exceptions to the patterns, that there are always exceptions to the exceptions, and that the patterns are always evolving.

Patterns, such as fraud, exist in data because the controls established by the organization, business, or entity have allowed the situation to exist in the first place—albeit unintentionally. In many cases fraud, malpractice, and malfeasance succeed because people do not know how to interpret their datasets or recognize the telltale symptoms. Most theft and fraud is usually achieved through a series of frequent claims or transactions with relatively modest amounts of money being stolen on any one occasion, rather than in a single, large, obvious heist.

Over an extended time period, an organization may pay out millions of currency in small amounts. This sort of fraud is subtle and not directly detectable through usual methods of oversight. Of course, upon detecting a pattern, the goal is to determine what processes need to change to remove and increase the future resistance to fraud. Practically speaking, detecting patterns is useless unless the corporation or agency affected is in a position to change their processes (collection, enforcement, or fraud risk assessment) - otherwise, it is a waste of money, time, and resources to even initiate.

During the phase of collecting, obtaining go and searching for data it would be useful to find the answers of the following questions:

- Which patterns are more important?
- Is this a reliable pattern?
- Is this a fraud pattern?
- Which pattern is more valuable? - for example, total money lost to a fraud or a scheme

- What does this pattern show? For example, a key employee connected with 2 phone numbers etc.
- Who is the most important person?
- Who are the people, who connect (influence) the most people? For example, if removing one of them what kind of impact will be on the network - negative or positive?

As a final example, an unlikely member of the group, John, could be considered the most important even though he is on the perimeter of the network.

In addition to working with some great and wonderful people, perhaps the most fun and exciting part of any new fraud risk assessment engagement is learning about the environment, the processes, and the overall operations of a program, system, or agency. The challenge is in conquering the unknown. To see data for the first time can be exhilarating and stimulating, while at the same time it can also be somewhat nerve racking and make one somewhat apprehensive.

This is especially true in "fraud scenario" or "find the bad guy" scenarios where there is a lot riding on targeting "entities" of interest and uncovering the hidden patterns. This becomes exceedingly evident, where, for example:

- A fraud perpetrated against an organization can cost hardworking people a lot of money

- A foreign investor pays bribes to the politicians and don't make any capital expenditures as negotiated

- A transshipment of drugs is smuggled across a border without interception and threatens the integrity, well-being, and futures of the youth in the society

- A criminal escapes detection by law enforcement agencies and perpetrates additional crimes that ruin people's property and lives.

As was reiterated many times, there are no right or wrong answers, only interpretations and subjective opinions.

Inevitably, core business processes will need to be updated, upgraded, and adjusted to respond to a possible significant fraud risk revealed. The revealed patterns themselves need to be vetted, and all relevant, repeatable, and actionable patterns need to be addressed and new procedures put in place to deal with the findings about existing fraud risk. Thus, patterns related to fraud would require existing business processes to be adjusted to minimize their occurrences, to reduce losses resulting from these schemes, where as patterns exposing an increased resistance to fraud in the near future would be maximized. It is all a matter of proactive approach and timely and adequate response.

The various phases of the process of pattern analysis could be as follows:

- Definition of the objectives for analysis

- Selection, organization and pre-treatment of the data
- Exploratory analysis of the data and their transformation
- Evaluation and comparison of the methods used and choice of the final model for fraud risk analysis
- Interpretation of the chosen model and its use in the fraud risk assessment process.

Having seen the benefits we can get from data mining, it is crucial to implement the process correctly in order to exploit it to its full potential. The inclusion of the data mining process in the fraud risk assessment of the organization must be done gradually, setting out realistic aims and looking at the results along the way. The final aim is for data mining to be fully integrated with the other activities that are used to support fraud risk assessment process.

The quality of data in terms of consistency, correctness, and precision impacts the accuracy and reliability of analytical and monitoring systems. During the fraud risk assessment process, simple mistakes, such as spelling errors, phonetic interpretations, or abbreviations, account for a large amount of the inconsistent data recorded and a significant likelihood for fraud occurrence.

Don't forget the old adage "garbage in, garbage out" continues to be true.

Therefore, whenever possible experts should evaluate and change the collection process to minimize errors or inconsistencies, thus better facilitating the analytics that will be performed. The quality of the data always plays a critical role within the analytical and fraud risk assessment specialists.

The quality of data has a tremendous impact on the quality of the analytics that can be performed. Value errors, missing data, and bad structures directly, and usually in a negative fashion, affect the outcomes and results of a system. Seemingly simple searches can be fraught with challenges due to misspelled words, transposed characters, or improperly formatted content. The level of trust placed in using the results from such systems is marginal at best.

Errors and inconsistencies in the data are most often seen as the result of typos, misspellings, or abbreviations in the data. Generally, without strong validation controls (e.g., lookup tables, entry masks, etc.), and especially when data can be entered in a free-form format, there will be problems with the quality of the data. Additionally, in adversarial collections (e.g., money laundering, terrorism, fraud) there is often intentionally misrepresented data.

The only real issue to factor in is the time frame for which the information has been reported because the relationships (e.g., ownership, renter, leaser, etc.) may change over time. Furthermore, additional checks regarding the real-world classification of the address (e.g., vacant lot, bus terminal, office building, residential, etc.) or even if the address actually exists would prove vital for many types of analyses to help expose questionable activities, patterns, and misrepresentations.

Fortunately, there are ways to help deal with these situations by transforming, cleaning up, and restructuring the data to better accommodate the analyses. Additionally, the use of entity resolution techniques within the law enforcement and intelligence communities will begin to transition from the larger, well-funded projects to become a more commonplace offering across all systems. These advancements also lay the foundation for expanding the use of anonymous resolution capabilities to enable sharing among systems with different security requirements as well as with external agencies, including foreign allies. However, a lot of the disparity encountered in the data can be addressed during its collection.

There have been a multitude of new technologies introduced into the anti-fraud marketplace over the past several years, including link analysis and other systems for detecting non obvious relationships and associations. Perhaps even more important are the refined analytical methodologies that help to interpret the complex networks and patterns presented by these technologies. Better understanding of the data will inevitably lead to better pattern detection, and ultimately, lower fraud incidence.

Once a pattern has been exposed, it is up to the affected company to act on that knowledge by changing business processes to flag related or similar occurrences of the pattern. Remember that there are always exceptions to the rule, and there are exceptions to the exceptions.

One of the first areas dealing with a large collection of digital data is probably text mining. It aims at analyzing large collections of unstructured documents with the purpose of extracting interesting, relevant and nontrivial knowledge.

As an example we provide you with a description of the activities of the software "Data Mining"[13] which could be useful applying the data mining technique.

Help Menu of a "Data Mining" Software
"Data Mining" was developed to find the number of hits (string occurrences) within a large text. To use "Data Mining", use the File>Open menu to load a plain text file or paste the plain text to be searched into the window, enter the strings (case-sensitive) into the fields (28 fields provided) and click on the "Start Mining" button.

Hits will be shown to the left of each string. The contents of the 28 search fields are saved when you quit and reloaded when you relaunch. To use the Ad Hoc search capability, type the search string (case-sensitive) into the Ad Hoc String field and click on the "Ad Hoc" button.

The number of hits will appear above the "Ad Hoc" button. The Ad Hoc String is not saved between sessions. There is also a Find capability. Type the search string (case-insensitive) into the Find field and click on the "Find" button.

The window will scroll to that row (just above the red line in the middle of the window) and the search string will be highlighted. You can click on the "Find Next" button to step through all string occurrences. The total number of text characters is displayed. Click on the "Reset" button to clear the text window, Hits and the Ad Hoc and Find search strings. Click on the "Clear Hits" button to clear just the Hits.

"Data Mining" is optimized for speed. A search of one million characters for 28 strings takes approximately one second. A Help window is available. This utility is freeware.

Note: If you paste text into the window (instead of loading a text file), click on the window and click on the "Return" key five times and then paste the text. This will set the red line offset.

Hits	String	Hits	String
776	*_*	0	
774	speedreading.	0	
306	speedreadingii.	0	
902	games	0	
58	mealplanning	0	
93	misc	0	
63	dees	0	
61	crossword	0	
48	icecream	0	
327	mathpractice	0	
50	picks	0	
1712	speedreadingiii.	0	
187	ebook	0	
39	datamining	0	

Start Mining   Fine Scroll Up
Reset   Fine Scroll Down
Clear Hits   Scroll Row: 2317
Total Characters: 1574356
Ad Hoc String   902
games   Ad Hoc
Find String   23
mathpractice   Find   Find Next   Find Row: 2317   Char #: 62899

Displayed above, raw data of web site activity for a short period of time is mined for 14 strings. Plain text has been pasted into the text window and unique strings have been entered into the 14 fields. In this case, the text window has approximately 1.6 M characters. In the above case, there were 327 hits for the "mathpractice" string.

The Ad Hoc string search for "games" matches the number of Hits for "games in the fourth string. The window is scrolled to row 2317 where the 23rd string of "mathpractice" is found using the Find capability. Note the Find String in the row above the red line in the window is highlighted. This string started at character 62899. On the Mac platform, clicking the arrows (or moving the handle) on the scrollbar results in jumps of more than one row. The jump size depends on number of rows. The "Fine Scroll Up" and "Find Scroll Down" buttons scroll the window one row at a time; the scroll row number is displayed when these buttons or the "Find" and "Find Next" buttons are used.

Below is an example of using Data Mining with non-English text having accented characters.

Hits	String		Hits	String
6	moitié		30	Tu
43	l'ai		100	tu
1	échappés		2	éclos
1	'Océan		60	après
13	Où		0	
10	propriétaire		0	
2	À monsieur		0	
152	Léon		0	
15	parlé		0	
1	l'appartient		0	
21	prêt		0	
13	envoyé		0	
3	aisément		0	
1	mît		0	

On était là depuis un bon quart d'heure, et le train avait repris sa course en sifflant, et les omnibus des divers hôtels s'étaient lancés l'un après l'autre au grand trot dans l'avenue qui conduit à la ville; et le soleil de juin ne se lassait pas d'éclairer cet heureux groupe de braves gens. Mais Mme Renault s'écria tout à

Start Mining   Fine Scroll Up
Reset   Fine Scroll Down
Clear Hits   Scroll Row: 228
Total Characters: 329240
Ad Hoc String

Ad Hoc

Find String   2
après   Find   Find Next   Find Row: 228   Char #: 6453

There is also a personal challenge associated with performing these types of analyses, especially when it comes to assess the fraud risk detecting criminals trying to outsmart "the system" by taking advantage of the loopholes, flaws, or vulnerabilities inherent in any process. A small percentage of dishonest people adversely affect the millions of people who lead decent and honest lifestyles. For some, they have been lucky, avoided detection, and gotten away with their scams, frauds, and embezzlements for personal gain. Everyone has a rationale and justification for their actions and many feel they are entitled to the money or benefits they steal.

At the end of each day, someone's life changes—for better or worse— depending on the outcomes of the analyses performed by reviewing the data sources. Ultimately, the goal is to improve the resistance to fraud in the organization by providing better, faster, and more effective analytics against the data and enabling the fraud risk experts to be more timely and efficient with their limited resources. Small improvements in fraud risk assessment process can result in significant levels of returns.

There are many examples of these types of fraud schemes across the world. What works well in one country is often refined and adjusted in other countries.

Technique 4.2.2.2. Discovery Sampling

Below are the answers of the following questions:

Why discovery sampling is used in 3D FRAM?

The shortest answer is: "The random types of sampling don't fit the requirements of the fraud risk assessment engagement!"

And now - with more details!

Discovery sampling is a form of attribute sampling. Attribute sampling is usually used as a statistical means of estimating the proportion of a population containing a pattern, or attribute, of interest. Pure attribute sampling could be used by the experts reviewing internal anti-fraud controls and evaluating transactions processing for deviations from specified control policies and procedures. The attribute or fraud pattern of interest is compliance with or deviation from the specified control policy or procedure. The discovery sampling is also called purposeful sampling.

What discovery sampling in 3D FRAM is?

- It is a tool designed to address fraud risk factors and probe for potential fraud

- It is used as an external check of internal records

- It is an economical, effective form of controls availability verification

In discovery-level testing, the expert contacts a small sample of managers or employees and asks three straightforward questions: "Did you order the product? Did you pay for it? Did you receive it?"

It is that simple and unobtrusive. Most answers are completed in about a minute. On average, more than 90 percent of the managers or employees you contact readily answer these basic questions.

What discovery sampling in 3D FRAM is not:

- It is not projectable – meaning the expert does not statistically project problem findings at the discovery level onto a product's total average paid circulation

- It is not intrusive to the managers or employees selected; The discovery sampling does not inquire about payment amount or personal financial information

- It is not appreciably time-consuming or costly

- It is not inevitable that discovery testing leads to products circulation deductions

Discovery sampling is a type of purposeful samplings and when you look through the examples below, remember that purposeful sampling is different from random (statistical/ probability) sampling. As such, purposeful sampling is rife with trade-offs and ambiguities, even though people who seek to manipulate data often do purposeful sampling but report results as though based on random sampling.

The most notable trade-off is that the more narrowly you define your population, sample, or respondents, the less likely you are to produce information that really represents any population at all. This contradiction points up the fact that you must often have a high tolerance for ambiguity when using purposeful sampling.

Note, too, that there are no statistical rules for this type of sampling. The rules for random sampling do not really apply. In purposeful sampling, sample size depends on what you want to know, what is at stake, and what can be done within existing resource constraints. Samples must be judged on the purpose of each engagement, and samples should be pulled for that purpose. In this sense, purposeful sampling can be quite valuable, especially as a device for identifying or initially exploring potential fraud patterns or fraudulent characteristics of interest. Just be aware that you should not confuse such exploration with representation of a population or confirmation of a finding.

How to use discovery sampling in 3D FRAM?

Discovery sampling is a tool used in the 3D FRAM. In the 3D FRAM the experts measure a random sample of items from the documentation with policies, rules, codes, controls to provide evidence that the whole rules and controls comply with a given set of criteria. Experts expect the items in a sample to be free of fraud patterns because they believe that the entire database has very few (if any) defects. As part of their engagement, experts are usually required to provide a confidence statement about the such as: "We are 95% confident that less than 1% of the items in the documentation are fraud risk exposed."

The standard statistical tool for making this kind of statement uses the classical method of confidence intervals. A confidence interval brackets the estimated number of defects in the documentation based on the number of defectives in the sample (usually zero in a discovery sampling). The size of the sample is chosen so the tolerance level (maximum number of defectives) appears at the upper end of the confidence interval. If the interval would span the actual number of defects in (say) 95% of future fraud risk assessment engagements, then it's called a "95% confidence interval."

Discovery sampling usually specify tight tolerances such as 1% or even 0.1%. Tight tolerances come with a steep price: large sample sizes. For example an expert would need to sample nearly a quarter of a large documentation to achieve 95% confidence for a 1% tolerance. The reason classical confidence intervals require large samples stems from an implicit assumption which becomes evident once a Bayesian framework is adopted. The assumption becomes very pessimistic for tight tolerance fraud risk assessment.

As mentioned, discovery sampling is a type of attribute sampling, based on an expected error rate of zero. It is used when the expert wants to know whether a population contains *any* pattern or error indicative of fraud. For instance, an account should not include any payments made out to a vendor name that is known to be fictitious unless there is that type of fraud in the account. If there is no such fraud in the account, there should be no payments to fictitious vendors.

Thus, finding even one such error has critical implications with respect to the existence of fraud. If the expert were to assess some of the payments in an account for fraud patterns and were to find a payment made out to a fictitious vendor, the expert would know that fraud pattern existed in the account but would not know the extent of fraud in the account.

Conversely, if the expert obtained some information about the payments in the account and did not find any payments made out to the fictitious vendor, he or she could not conclude that no fraud patterns of fictitious payments existed in the entire account. Discovery sampling allows the expert during the fraud risk assessment engagement to answer questions such as the following:

- If the expert examines a randomly selected sample and finds no patterns or errors indicative of fraud, how confident can he be that the population contains no more than a specified rate of such error and what the rate of the fraud risk is?

- If the expert finds one or more patterns an/or errors indicative of fraud in the sample examined, how confident can he or she be that the population has at least a specified rate of such error and what the rate of fraud risk is?

- How large a sample of data must the expert examine to have a desired level of confidence as to a specified rate of error and risk indicative of fraud in the population?

The expert is interested in the confidence of finding at least one fraud pattern or error (such as a payment to a fictitious vendor) because even one such fraud pattern or error could indicate fraud. If the expert finds even one such fraud pattern or error, there is a fraud risk in the account and all (or at least many more) payments in the account must be assesses to find the fraudulent ones. (That's why, sometimes discovery sampling is called stop-and-go sampling. If one patterns or error is found in the sample, the sampling is stopped and other assessment procedures are applied to the population.) If the expert finds no such fraud pattern or error, the confidence that the population does not contain fraud greater than a specified extent can be quantified.

Technique 4.2.2.3: Internet search engines

Most of us know our information is on the Web because we share it every day.

What you may not know is that your information is collected, stored, and sold between hundreds of companies around the world. So much information makes it easy for identify thieves to find you.

Anyone with a computer can search for information about you because your personal data is already online. The expert team could make the same searches, of course!

What people can see using Internet search engines? The answer is:

- Religion
- Net Worth
- Address History
- Ethnicity
- Home Value
- Phone Numbers
- Politics
- Legal History
- Email Addresses
- Marriages
- Date of Birth
- Friends + Photos

Google is the undisputed king of 'spartan searching'. While it doesn't offer all the shopping center features of Yahoo!, Google is fast, relevant, and the largest single catalogue of Web pages available today. Make sure you try the Google 'images', 'maps' and 'news' features... they are outstanding services for locating photos, geographic directions, and news headlines.

Google makes it possible to reach not just publicly available Internet resources, but also some that should never have been revealed

If your search yields millions of search results, your search query is probably too broad. Rather than wading through pages and pages of search results, use these search refinement tips[14]:

- Multiple words: Avoid making one-word queries.
- Case insensitivity: There's no need to capitalize.
- Superfluous words: Drop overly common words.
- Exact phrases: Put quotes around phrases.
- Word order: Arrange your words in the order you think they would appear in the documents you're looking for.
- Singular versus plural: Use plural if you think the word will appear in that form in the documents you're looking for.
- Wilcard: * can substitute for a whole word in a multiword search.
- Number range: .. between numbers will match on numbers within that range.

- Punctuation: A hyphenated search word will also yield pages with the un-hyphenated version. Not so with apostrophes.

- Accents: Don't incorporate accents into search words if you don't think they'll appear in the documents you're looking for.

- Boolean logic: Use OR and - to fine-tune your search.

- Stemming: Google may also match on variations of your search word unless you tell it otherwise by preceding the word with + .

- Synonyms: ~ in front of a word will also match on other words that Google considers to be synonymous or related.

On Table 4-1 below are presented Google search Operators which could be used during hte collection phase of the fraud risk assessment engagement.

Table 4-1 Google Search Operators[15]

Operator Description	Format Example	Description
filetype:	marketing plan filetype:doc	Restrict search results by file type extension
site:	google site: sec.gov	Search within a site or domain
inurl:	inurl:marketing plan	Search for a word or phrase within the URL
allinurl:	allinurl: marketing plan	Search for multiple words within the URL
intext:	intext:marketing	Search for a word in the main body text
allintext:	allintext: marketing plan	Search for multiple words within the body text of indexed pages
intitle:	intitle:"marketing plan"	Search for a word or phrase within the page title
allintitle:	allintitle: marketing plan	Search for multiple words within the page title
inanchor:	inanchor:"marketing plan"	Search for a word or phrase within anchor text
allinanchor:	allinanchor: marketing plan	Search for multiple words within anchor text

Another source of useful information about the Google Query Operators is shown on Table 4-2 below.

Table 4-2 Google Query Operators

Operator	Description	Sample query
site	restricts results to sites within the specified domain	site:google.com foxwill find all sites containing the word fox, located within the *.google.com domain
intitle	restricts results to documents whose title contains the specified phrase	intitle:fox firewill find all sites with the word fox in the title and fire in the text
allintitle	restricts results to documents whose title contains all the specified phrases	allintitle:fox firewill find all sites with the words fox and fire in the title, so it's equivalent to intitle:fox intitle:fire
inurl	restricts results to sites whose URL contains the specified phrase	inurl:fox firewill find all sites containing the word fire in the text and fox in the URL
allinurl	restricts results to sites whose URL contains all the specified phrases	allinurl:fox firewill find all sites with the words fox and fire in the URL, so it's equivalent to inurl:fox inurl:fire
filetype, ext	restricts results to documents of the specified type	filetype:pdf firewill return PDFs containing the word fire, while filetype:xls fox will return Excel spreadsheets with the word fox
Numrange	restricts results to documents containing a number from the specified range	numrange:1-100 fire will return sites containing a number from 1 to 100 and the word fire. The same result can be achieved with 1..100 fire
link	Restricts results to sites containing links to the specified location	link:www.google.comwill return documents containing one or more links to www.google.com
inanchor	restricts results to sites containing links with the specified phrase in their descriptions	inanchor:firewill return documents with links whose description contains the word fire (that's the actual link text, not the URL indicated by the link)

allintext	restricts results to documents con- taining the specified phrase in the text, but not in the title, link descrip- tions or URLs	allintext:"fire fox"will return documents which con- tain the phrase fire fox in their text only
+	specifies that a phrase should occur frequently in results	+firewill order results by the number of occurrences of the word fire
-	specifies that a phrase must not oc- cur in results	-firewill return documents that don't contain the word fire
""	delimiters for entire search phrases (not single words)	"fire fox"will return documents containing the phrase fire fox
.	wildcard for a single character	fire.foxwill return documents containing the phrases fire fox, fireAfox, fire1fox, fire-fox etc.
*	wildcard for a single word	fire * foxwill return documents containing the phrases fire the fox, fire in fox, fire or fox etc.
|	logical OR	"fire fox" | firefoxwill return documents containing the phrase fire fox or the word firefox

Both in European countries and the U.S., legal regulations are in place to protect our privacy. Unfortunately, it is frequently the case that all sorts of confidential documents containing personal information are placed in publicly accessible locations or transmitted over the Web without proper protection. To get our complete information, an intruder need only gain access to an e-mail repository containing the CV we sent out while looking for work. Address, phone number, date of birth, education, skills, work experience – it's all there.

For the purposes of fraud risk assessment engagements inn the educational organization, thousands of such documents can be found on the Internet – just query Google for intitle: "curriculum vitae" "phone * * *" "address *" "e-mail". Finding contact information in the form of names, phone number and email addresses is equally easy. This is because most Internet users create electronic address books of some description. There are many cases of "Diploma Mills" and other types of academic fraud revealed recently in Europa.

While these may be of little interest to your typical intruder, they can be dangerous tools in the hands of a skilled sociotechnician, especially if the contacts are restricted to one company. A simple query such as filetype:xls inurl:"email.xls" can be surprisingly effective, finding Excel spreadsheet called email.xls.

All the above also applies to instant messaging applications and their contact lists – if an intruder obtains such a list, he may be able to pose as our IM friends. Interestingly enough, a fair amount of personal data can also be obtained from official documents, such as police reports, legal documents or even medical history cards.

From another point of view, the Web also contains documents that have been marked as confidential and therefore contain sensitive information. These may include project plans, technical documentation, surveys, reports, presentations and a whole host of other company-internal materials. They are easily located as they frequently contain the word confidential, the phrase "Not for distribution" or similar clauses. Table 4-3 presents several sample queries that reveal documents potentially containing personal information and confidential data.

As with passwords, all the organizations can do to avoid revealing private information is to be cautious and retain maximum control over published data. Companies and organizations should (and many are obliged to) specify and enforce rules, procedures and standard practices for handling documents within the organization, complete with clearly defined responsibilities and penalties for infringements.

The experts conducting a fraud risk assessment engagement should be aware that many administrator downplay the importance of securing such devices as network printers or webcams. However, an insecure printer can provide an intruder with a foothold that can later be used as a basis for attacking other systems in the same network or even other networks. Webcams are, of course, much less dangerous, so hacking them can only be seen as entertainment, although it's not hard to imagine situations where data from a webcam could be useful (industrial espionage, robberies etc.). Table 4-3 contains sample queries revealing printers and webcams, while Table 4-4 shows a printer configuration page found on the Web.

Table 4-3. Searching for personal data and confidential documents

Query	Result
filetype:xls inurl:"email.xls"	email.xls files, potentially containing contact information
"phone * * *" "address *" "e-mail" intitle: "curriculum vitae"	CVs
"not for distribution" confidential	documents containing the confidential clause
buddylist.blt	AIM contacts list
intitle:index.of mystuff.xml	Trillian IM contacts list
filetype:ctt "msn"	MSN contacts list
filetype:QDF QDF	database files for the Quicken financial application

`intitle:index.of finances.xls`	finances.xls files, potentially containing information on bank ac- counts, financial summaries and credit card numbers
`intitle:"Index Of" -inurl:maillog maillog size`	maillog files, potentially containing e-mail
`"Network Vulnerability Assessment Report" "Host Vulnerability Summary Report" filetype:pdf` `"Assessment Report"` `"This file was generated by Nessus"`	reports for network security scans, penetration tests etc.

Table 4-4 Queries for locating network devices

Query	Device
`"Copyright (c) Tektronix, Inc." "printer status"`	PhaserLink printers
`inurl:"printer/main.html" intext:"settings"`	Brother HL printers
`intitle:"Dell Laser Printer" ews`	Dell printers with EWS technology
`intext:centreware inurl:status`	Xerox Phaser 4500/6250/8200/8400 printers
`inurl:hp/device/this.LCDispatcher`	HP printers
`intitle:liveapplet inurl:LvAppl`	Canon Webview webcams
`intitle:"EvoCam" inurl:"webcam.html"`	Evocam webcams
`inurl:"ViewerFrame?Mode="`	Panasonic Network Camera webcams
`(intext:"MOBOTIX M1" | intext:"MOBOTIX M10") intext:"Open` `Menu" Shift-Reload`	Mobotix webcams
`inurl:indexFrame.shtml Axis`	Axis webcams
`SNC-RZ30 HOME`	Sony SNC-RZ30 webcams
`intitle:"my webcamXP server!" inurl:":8080"`	webcams accessible via WebcamXP Server
`allintitle:Brains, Corp. camera`	webcams accessible via mmEye
`intitle:"active webcam page"`	USB webcams

The opportunities for using other free search engines for the purposes of an fraud risk assessment engagement are described below[16].

"The Ask/AJ/Ask Jeeves search engine is a longtime name in the World Wide Web. The super-clean interface rivals the other major search engines, and the search options are as good as Google or Bing or DuckDuckGo. The results groupings are what really make Ask.com stand out. The presentation is arguably cleaner and easier to read than Google or Yahoo! or Bing, and the results groups seem to be more relevant. Decide for yourself if you agree... give Ask.com a whirl, and compare it to the other search engines you like.

At first, DuckDuckGo.com looks like Google. But there are many subtleties that make this spartan search engine different. DuckDuckGo has some slick features, like 'zero-click' information (all your answers are found on the first results page). DuckDuckgo offers disambiguation prompts (helps to clarify what question you are really asking). And the ad spam is much less than Google. Give DuckDuckGo.com a try... you might really like this clean and simple search engine.

Bing is Microsoft's attempt at unseating Google. Bing used to be MSN search until it was updated in summer of 2009. Touted as a 'decision engine', Bing tries to support your researching by offering suggestions in the leftmost column, while also giving you various search options across the top of the screen. Things like 'wiki' suggestions, 'visual search', and 'related searches' might be very useful to you. Bing is not dethroning Google in the near future, no. But Bing is definitely worth trying.

The Internet Archive is a favorite destination for longtime Web lovers. The Archive has been taking snapshots of the entire World Wide Web for years now, allowing you and me to travel back in time to see what a web page looked like in 1999, or what the news was like around Hurricane Katrina in 2005. You won't visit the Archive daily, like you would Google or Yahoo or Bing, but when you do have need to travel back in time, use this search site.

Yippy is a Deep Web engine that searches other search engines for you. Unlike the regular Web, which is indexed by robot spider programs, Deep Web pages are usually harder to locate by conventional search. That's where Yippy becomes very useful. If you are searching for obscure hobby interest blogs, obscure government information, tough-to-find obscure news, academic research and otherwise-obscure content, then Yippy is your tool.

Yahoo! is several things: it is a search engine, a news aggregator, a shopping center, an emailbox, a travel directory, a horoscope and games center, and more. This 'web portal' breadth of choice makes this a very helpful site for Internet beginners. Searching the Web should also be about discovery and exploration, and Yahoo! delivers that in wholesale quantities.

Mahalo is the one 'human-powered' search site in this list, employing a committee of editors to manually sift and vet thousands of pieces of content. This means that you'll get fewer Mahalo hit results than you will get at Bing or Google. But it also means that most Mahalo results have a higher quality of content and relevance (as best as human editors can judge). Mahalo also offers regular web searching in addition to asking questions. Depending on which of the two search boxes you use at Mahalo, you will either get direct content topic hits or suggested answers to your question.

Years ago, *Dogpile* was the fast and efficient choice before Google. Things changed, Dogpile faded into obscurity, and Google became king. But today, Dogpile is coming back, with a growing index and a clean and quick presentation that is testimony to its halcyon days. If you want to try a search tool with pleasant presentation and helpful cross link results, definitely try Dogpile.

Webopedia is one of the most useful websites on the World Wide Web. Webopedia is an encyclopedic resource dedicated to searching techno terminology and computer definitions.

Teach yourself what 'domain name system' is, or teach yourself what 'DDRAM' means on your computer. Webopedia is absolutely a perfect resource for non-technical people to make more sense of the computers around them."

And several words about the use of existing national search engines!

Baidu is a Chinese web services company which offers many services, including a Chinese language search engine for websites, audio files, and images. Baidu offers 57 search and community services including **Baidu Baike**, an online collaboratively-built encyclopedia, and a searchable keyword-based discussion forum. During Q4 of 2010, it is estimated that there were 4.02 billion search queries in China of which Baidu had a market share of 56.6%. In December 2007, Baidu became the first Chinese company to be included in the NASDAQ-100 index. Baidu provides an index of over 740 million web pages, 80 million images, and 10 million multimedia files.

Another example for a national search engine could be the very useful Bulgarian search engine "Diri.bg", used searching and finding documents, maps, news, flights, music, images etc. on the territory of Bulgaria!

Technique 4.2.2.4. Questionnaires

Questionnaires are popular because they can be a relatively inexpensive way of getting people to provide information. But because they rely on people to provide answers, a benefit-risk consideration is associated with their use. People with the ability to observe, select, acquire, process, evaluate, interpret, store, retrieve, and report can be a valuable and versatile source of information under the proper circumstances. And if we do not ask the right people the right questions in the right way, we will not get high-quality answers.

Writing questionnaires is the science and art of asking the "right" questions of the "right" people in the "right" way. It is a science in that it uses many scientific principles developed from various fields of applied psychology, sociology, and evaluation research. It is an art because it requires clear and interesting writing and the ability to trade off or accommodate many competing requirements. For example, a precisely worded, well-qualified, unambiguous question may be stilted and hard to read and understand. The experts who conduct a fraud risk assessment engagement have to learn how to write questions in a clear, concise, interesting, and easy-to-read format with a minimum loss in qualifying precision.

The main goal of the questionnaires is to ask people for behavior, figures, statistics, amounts, and other facts. The expert asks them to describe conditions and procedures that affect the work, organizations, and systems with which they are involved, and he/she asks for their judgments and views about processes, performance, adequacy, irregularities, fraud patterns. The expert have to ask people to share their views about past and current events as to make forecasts, to tell him/her about their attitudes and opinions, and to describe their behavior and the behavior of others.

After deciding to use a questionnaire, experts must:

- Plan the questionnaire,
- Develop measures,
- Design the sample,
- Develop and test the questionnaire,
- Produce the questionnaire,
- Collect the data and follow up with nonrespondents,
- Perform checks to ensure the quality of responses, and
- Reduce and analyze the data.

Except for the data collection, these processes are very similar regardless of whether the questionnaire is to be designed for the e-mail or a telephone or face-to-face interview.

Prepared together with Dr. Joseph T. Wells (The Founder & Chairman of ACFE) on the tables are presented the questionnaires used for a fraud risk assessment process concocted in one of Bulgarian universities on the tables 4-5 as examples are presented below.

Table 4-5

FRAUD RISK ASSESSMENT QUESTIONAIRE – SAMPLE

Statement I. Within your college or university, have you or anyone you know cheated on an examination by:				
N o	DESCRIPTION OF QUESTIONS	ANSWERS		
		YES	N O	N/A
1.	Using unauthorized materials such as textbooks, notes, electronic devices or other unauthorized sources?			
2.	Copying from the test of another student?			
3.	Allowing another student to copy from you?			
4.	Leaving during the exam to obtain unauthorized help?			
5.	Allowing another student to take your exam?			
6.	Taking the exam for another student?			
7.	Taking the exam papers outside the examination room?			
8.	Stealing an advance copy of the exam?			
9.	Making copies of the exam for use by other students?			
10.	Using personal contacts to obtain an advance copy of the exam?			
11.	Offering or giving a bribe to the instructor to obtain a good grade?			
12.	Threatening the instructor to obtain a good grade?			
13.	Asking one instructor to influence your grade with another instructor?			
	SIGNIFICANT FRAUD RISK GRADE:			

N o	DESCRIPTION OF QUESTIONS	ANSWERS		
	Statement II. Within your college or university, have you or anyone you know cheated on an essay or thesis by:	YES	NO	N/A
1.	Submitting the work of another author as your own?			
2.	Allowing your work to be submitted by another student as his or her own?			
3.	Hiring another person to prepare your assignment?			
4.	Preparing an assignment for another student?			
5.	Falsely claiming information from the Internet as your own?			
6.	Submitting one work for two or more classes?			
7.	Adding fake bibliographic references to make the work appear more substantial?			
8.	Presenting material or ideas of another author as your own without proper credit?			
9.	Obtaining assistance from others for an assignment that requires you to complete it on your own?			
	SIGNIFICANT FRAUD RISK GRADE:			

N o	DESCRIPTION OF QUESTIONS	ANSWERS		
	Statement III. Within your college or university, have you or anyone you know committed other dishonest acts by:	YES	NO	N/A
1.	Using contacts within the institution to change your grade?			
2.	Preparing false documents, such as a doctor's report, to delay an assignment or exam?			
3.	Paying for a fake diploma?			
4.	Obtaining preferential treatment in dorm assignments or housing by the use of bribes, gratuities, or false information?			
	SIGNIFICANT FRAUD RISK GRADE:			

Because it is difficult to write good questionnaires, they are one of the most misused of data collection techniques. Part of the problem is that good practices cannot be well documented by a few easy-to-remember principles. For every rule on questionnaire design and implementation, there is a host of exceptions.

Another problem is that the development and use of questionnaires looks easy but is not. How to determine the right questions to include in the data collection instrument? First, you must carefully analyze the overall questions the fraud risk assessment engagement was designed to answer. The line of questioning on the instrument, along with other aspects of the evaluation design, must lead to answers to the project questions.

Second, the questions in the instrument must be asked in a way such that different people with very different experiences will provide similar answers under similar circumstances.

How do the expert find the "right people" when those he/she needs are experts with firsthand knowledge in' finance and investment trading business? The expert can just contact a few people who are conveniently located or appear to be approachable but this will a wrong approach. The experts have to find out if they can and will obtain the information they need. Then they have to select samples of respondents that are compatible with overall fraud risk assessment.

To ask good questions is very hard to do, especially regarding fraud. They must be asked in a way that encourages people to respond—and to respond accurately. Asking questions about fraud risk occurrence in the organization triggers a very complex and not very well understood introspective and cognitive process.

Respondents (for example, the students at one of the Bulgarian Universities, shown on the tables above) have to understand what is being asked, retrieve relevant information from memory, analyze this information, make judgments about which information best answers the question, perhaps combine this information, and select an answer.

People are different; they read, perceive, think, interpret, value, remember, and respond differently. Unless we are knowledgeable about, and can anticipate, their cognitive processes and adjust our inquiry to account for these differences, the experts may get as many different answers to the same question as there are people.

Method 3. Documentation Review

Technique 3.1. Document Inspection

Inspection is a reliable source of fraud risk assessment data and is used in multipurpose testing of documents, policies, rules etc. Because evidence of performance is documented, this type of test can be performed at any time. The evidence previously obtained from (1) the inspection of documents in walk-throughs (in which inspection is performed to a lesser extent than in sampling control tests) and (2) observation or inquiry tests may provide sufficient evidence of control effectiveness. However, the the experts should consider discover sampling items for inspection if additional fraud risk assessment evidence is needed.

Since documentary evidence generally does not provide evidence concerning how effectively the controls were applied, the experts should supplement inspection tests with observation and/or inquiry of persons applying the controls. For example, the expert should supplement inspection of initials on documents with observation and/or inquiry of the individual(s) who initialed the documents to understand the procedures they followed before initialing the documents. The expert may also reperform the controls being tested to determine if it was properly applied and if there is a risk of fraud.

For example, the documentation inspection could be applied to all phases of a basic procurement process, shown below:

- How are defined and documented the goals and objectives for the procurement process.
- How are determined the nature, scope, and location of the procurement process in the organization structure.
- How the policies, procedures, and controls needed for the procurement process are identified, documented, and implemented.
- What kind of schedule for procurement activities exists.
- How documented are the received requisitions and and developed specifications.
- How many bids are solicited from vendors.
- How the bids are evaluated and awarded.
- What kind of documentation exists as to confirm the receiving, inspecting and storing the items
- How is monitoring and evaluating the procurement process.

The expert conducts inspection tests by examining documents and records for evidence (such as the existence of initials or signatures) that a control activity was applied to those documents and records. System documentation, such as operations manuals, flowcharts, and job descriptions, may provide evidence of control design but do not provide evidence that controls are actually operating and being applied consistently. To use system documentation as part of the evidence of effective control activities, the expert should obtain additional evidence on how the controls were applied.

Technique 3.2. Check the events for authenticity and real accomplishment

This technique is widely used by all auditing or inspecting professionals in all areas of business and nonbusiness activities and will be discussed in details in our future updates of Dinev's SMARTGuide.

Method 4. Walking, talking, watching, listening

Technique 4.1. Be On The Place

This techniques is very important because gives the expert the opportunity personally to:

- See,
- Talk to different people,
- Listen carefully what somebody wants to say him/her "tete-a-tete",
- Take pictures and

- Use its own "nose" and,

- Perception of detection during the fraud risk assessment engagement.

Technique 4.2: Body Language

Gestures and other Nonverbal Patterns. Nonverbal patterns are those that do not use words. Instead, they use visual signals such as facial expressions, gestures and postures. They are usually subconscious and sometimes deliberate. Either way, they can be more revealing than oral responses and can lead you to important information that you would not otherwise have found.

It is important that the interviewer be aware of characteristic nonlinguistic cues such as change in voice, facial expressions, or gestures, since as much as half of the communication that takes place during the interview is conveyed by these modes of expression. Failure to understand these cues may result in miscommunication.

The expert's appearance, verbal mannerisms, body language, and voice will determine the rapport, starting with the contact that sets up the interview. Since this is usually done by telephone, your voice and verbal mannerisms are extremely important (as they are later in the interview setting). Of course, voice and verbal mannerisms are key factors in the success of the interview.

Make your verbal and voice cues calm and unflustered. Speak so the interviewee need not strain to hear and understand. Changes in voice inflection, sighs, or other noises give clues to your feelings or moods, as do your facial expressions and body language. Control these so that the interviewee does not pick up impatience, disapproval, or other negative feelings. Ideally, you should not experience such feelings during the interview, since you are supposed to be an impartial, unbiased, and tolerant observer. Likewise, you should control expressions of positive feelings or agreement with what the interviewee is saying.

Your appearance is still another variable that influences rapport and, therefore, the tone of the interview. Dress to fit both the interview and the interviewee. If the interview is with a state welfare official in his office in the capitol, it is appropriate, perhaps mandatory, to wear office-type clothing (suit and tie for men, and suit or dress for women). This is what you would expect the interviewee would be wearing. Try to live up to the expected standards of the interviewee in this case. Not doing so might get the interview off to a bad start.

If, however, the interview is to take place at a construction site or with young people at a summer youth-recreation site, wear more casual clothing. This makes sense in that it gives interviewees the feeling that you understand the nature of their circumstances. Also, you are not set off as being totally different from the interviewee.

Observing your interviewee's nonverbal signals enhances your interviews, because it gives you a greater understanding of their verbal message. Here are nonverbal signals you should observe in interviews.

Facial Expressions are different and numerous of nonverbal patterns. They include eye and eyebrow movements and smiles, frowns and grimaces.

Hand and arm gestures used for communication are difficult to count. Waving, shooing, welcoming, beckoning, and inviting, are only a few. In particular, look for open or closed arms and hands for sincerity or obstruction.

A person's posture sends nonverbal signals about attitude and feelings. Sitting or standing in straight or slouched positions are worth observing.

The nature of a person's environment could draw the expert's attention too. Office accessories can indicate attitudes and luxury preferences. Office furniture, arrangements and accessories indicate something about the office holder. Quality of office furniture can indicate status or perceived status. Open, comfy office arrangements indicate sociability, while close arrangements indicate control or self-protection.

Timeliness sends clear messages. Being generally prompt indicates regard for other people on the job or project, supervisors, staff and clients; an ability to plan, organize, manage and control one's workload; and an ability to prioritize work according to what is needed when and by whom.

While being timely is not always possible, being frequently late could show disregard for the job, project, people on the project, supervisors, staff, clients and you; inability to plan, organize, manage and control; and inability to prioritize work. These indications can have some relation to the way the activity is managed.

Technique 4.3: Tips and Claims

Mostly of the detected cases indicating fraud have been initiated accidentally or by tips and claims. From my own experience I could say that using such technique is very useful and important tool for further fraud response in the organization. If possible, the expert should require a personal meeting with the person providing tips and claims. During the meeting is very important for the expert to use the approaches described below.

- Listen Carefully

- Accept the Personality of the Person

- Participate in the Conversation

- Concentrate on the person's general message and details

- Draw the main point from his/her message

- Make yourself interested in what you listen

- Get away from distractions such as noises, interruptions and other people

- Talk less, listen more

- Take notes and concentrate on the message

- Avoid all behaviors that inhibit listening

- Focusing on specific statements diverts the attention from the whole message

- Interrupting cuts off the speaker's message
- Taking too many notes will make difficult the concentration to the main topic
- Listening attentively is impossible when preoccupied with evaluating, judging and arguing with people who are trying to give you information
- Changing the subject is among the worst enemies of listening
- Don't lose your self-control

Of course, the list with such expert advices could be expanded after gaining more experience with such fraud risk assessment engagements.

4.2.3. Data Analysis Methodology

Method 4.3.1: Data Analysis
- Technique 4.3.1.1: Content Analysis
- Technique 4.3.1.2: Trend and Ratio Analysis
- Technique 4.3.1.3: What-if-Analysis
- Technique 4.3.1.4: Hypothesis Testing
- Technique 4.3.1.5: Cost-benefit Analysis
- Technique 4.3.1.6: Sensitivity Analysis

Every organization, bureau, agency, and corporation has fundamental analytical needs that traditionally require a significant amount of data integration and resources to best understand the data. Whether trying to identify risk of money laundering, insider trading, insurance fraud or other forms of the activities of "white collar" criminals, the analytical processes and system architectures are very similar to each other.

In fact, the types of patterns exposed in one domain can frequently be used in another, and it is often not necessary to reinvest and re-create these capabilities across different industries when a common approach can be used.

Analysis is usually associated with separating an intellectual whole into its parts for individual study and with the results of that study. Analytical methods are the tools to obtaining the evidence needed to support the fraud risk assessment findings. Analytical evidence is among the four types of evidence together with physical, documentary, and testimonial evidence. Analytical methods used in the 3D FRAM could include:

- Separating the whole in its parts
- Identifying trends
- Making comparisons,

- Making judgements,

- Making calculations,

- Hypothesis testing and, finally making

- Synopsis.

Analytical evidence can often complete or corroborate documentary evidence used for proving the final conclusions about the rate of fraud risk in the organization.

Let's look at the different analytical methods used in the 3D FRAM.

Technique 4.3.1.1. Content Analysis

Content analysis is a methodology used in our 3D FRAM for determining the content of written, recorded, or published communications via a systematic, objective, and quantitative procedure. Thus, it is a set of procedures for collecting and organizing information in a standard format that allows analysts to draw inferences about the characteristics and meaning of recorded material.

Content analysis can be used to make numerical comparisons among and within documents. It is especially useful for tabulating the results of open-ended survey questions and multiple interviews.

It can also be used to analyze entity documentation to determine compliance with laws, rules, policies, and procedures; to clarify trends in agency activity; to assess alignment between such activity and stated goals, objectives, and strategies; or to examine differences between groups within the entity on of issues of interest.

The content analysis could include the following steps:

- Determination whether content analysis is appropriate. Selection of content analysis as a method will depend on fraud risk assessment engagement's objectives and issues, availability of accurate recorded material, and the kinds of comparisons sought.

- Identification of the fraud universe. That is, determine what material should be included in the analysis. Consider what content material exists, the types of fraud and fraud patterns will identify, the types and locations of samples you will obtain, and what time frame(s) is of interest. Such material can be in any media yielding information on which reanalysis can be performed. Note that discovery sampling may be needed if the fraud universe is too extensive to be reviewed in its entirety.

- Usually most commonly, written documentation is explored. Appropriate written media include plans, policies, procedures, reports, work samples, correspondence, memoranda, staff or client records, responses to interviews or questionnaires, agendas, minutes, resumes, job descriptions, etc. Possible other media include Internet Websites, audio and video recordings, television and radio programs, movies, and photographs.

- Examples of the content to be analyzed are obtained. One distinction between content analysis and other analyses is that the development of the analysis instrument is highly dependent on the content to be analyze concerning fraud risk occurrence in our example. Thus, be sure that the examples you obtain are consistent with the content.

- Review content examples to determine if the information available meets the objectives of the fraud risk analysis. Identify and explore alternate sources, as needed. You may also need to redefine or expand the universe of content.

- Select the coding units, i.e. the unit(s) of analysis which best capture data (words, phrases, ideas, etc.) in the body of work being analyzed.

The advantages of using the content analysis in the 3D FRAM could be:

- Quantification of largely qualitative information

- Cope with large volumes of source material

- Help experts learn more about fraud risk assessment issues

- Validation of evidence from other sources

- Application to virtually any fraud risk assessment engagement

The disadvantages of using the content analysis in the 3D FRAM could be:

- Knowledge and skill for applying the content analysis needed

- Costly and time-consuming

- Possible reliability and validity problems

- Challenged as subjective

Technique 4.3.1.2 Trend and Ratio Analysis

For the purposes of the 3D FRAM we will use trend analysis for seeking out and examining systematic historical fraud patterns in financial statements or other quantitative data. Such analysis of data over time can vary from primarily descriptive techniques to more complex cause-and-effect methods. This technique will be used for cause-and-effect analysis and focuses on the descriptive methods of trend analysis and two closely related analytical techniques - fluctuation analysis and common-size statements analysis.

The underlying assumptions using trend analysis in the 3D FRAM could be as follows:

- There was a fraudulent trend of changes in the past

- There is no a fraudulent trend of changes currently

- There won't be any fraudulent trend of changes in the future
- If there was a fraudulent trend of changes in the past there will be such trend in the future

Keeping in mind the assumptions above the experts should very carefully choose one fiscal period as a base period and then express subsequent quantities as a percentage of the data associated with this base period. In the case of an income statement, changes in all items could be assessed in relation to the base period. Significant changes can then be assessed further. Note that trend analysis can be performed to determine changes in the number of physical units as well as money amounts. The subcategories of the trend analysis are fluctuation analysis and common-size statement analysis.

Fluctuation analysis is closely related to trend analysis and consists of comparing the absolute and percentage differences of current period balances to those of prior periods. Variances may then be further explored for their causes, effects, and reasonableness.

Common-size statements analysis expresses balance sheet components as a percentage of total assets and income statement components as a percentage of total revenue. This approach facilitates identifying deviations in the components of statements by focusing on relative differences through time.

The advantages of the trend analysis could be defined as follows:

- Reveal potentially fruitful areas of fraud risk assessment investigation
- Detect significant variations over time
- Be easily understood and communicated
- Be readily accepted due to its widespread use

The disadvantages of the trend analysis could be defined as follows:

- Little insight into the causes and impacts of variations
- No possible to indicate what the entity's normal or benchmark position is
- Undermined by frequent changes in financial reporting formats
- Influenced by the choice of the base fiscal period

There is an example for common financial statement trends shown on Table 4-6 below.

Table 4-6 Example for Common Financial Statement Trends

In fact, an accounting "system" will interact with every stage of the business cycle. Here's a table of the typical business cycle along with the related accounting entries at each point with their related trends.

Steps of Business Cycle	Accounting Entries
1. Purchase raw materials	Debit (increase) inventory; Credit (decrease) cash (if paid on spot); Debit (increase) accounts payable (if not paid in cash)
2. Begin manufacturing or assembly process	Transfer inventory to intermediate stage called Work in Process (WIP)
3. Pay suppliers and employees	Credit (decrease) accounts payable; Credit (decrease) cash (or payroll account)
4. Complete the manufacturing or assembly process	Reduce WIP inventory; Increase finished goods inventory
5. Sell the product	Reduce finished goods inventory; Debit (increase) accounts receivable; Debit (increase) sales revenue
6. Collect payment for credit sales	Credit (decrease) accounts receivable; Debit (increase) cash

Usually for the most companies and organizations, there are trends in the increases and decreases of financial statement amounts. Unexpected increases or decreases may be a symptom of fraud. However, while analytical techniques are useful, they are not absolute patterns/indicators of fraud.

The following interactions between accounts often exist:

Sales and

Accounts Receivable

Cost of Sales

Selling Expenses

Outbound Freight

Commissions

Inventory and

Accounts Payable

Warehousing Costs

Wages and Salaries Expense and

Payroll Taxes

Health Insurance

Interest Expense and

Long-term Debt

Accounts Receivable and

Bad Debt Expense

Legal Expense (for collection of bad debts)

Cash and Investments and

Investment Income (such as interest and dividends)

The experts conducting a fraud risk assessment engagement may also wish to review relationships of financial statement amounts to items or totals that are not necessarily part of the financial statements. The following are examples of these items which could reveal fraud patterns:

- *Utilities expenses.* Trends in revenues should be relatively consistent with electricity and water usage.

- *Inventory.* If a particular component is important to a whole product, it might be possible to analyze trends in inventory, production, and sales based on the use of that component.

- *Labor Hours or Number of Employees.* As to reveal the risk of "ghost" employees the number of employees can be compared to a variety of financial statement amounts, including labor costs, production costs, or revenue.

- *Sales of Companion Products.* A particular product usually has a companion product often sold with it, such as optional equipment, installation kits, or service contracts. In those cases, as to reveal possible fraud patterns, it may be useful for the expert to study trends in sales of both core products and companion products.

- *Number of Sales Transactions.* It may be useful to study trends in sales transactions as well as total revenue.

To be effective, look for bases that (a) would be expected to have a reasonable relationship to the accounts being questioned and (b) could not easily be manipulated by the perpetrators.

Another useful technique is to analyze trends in the components of certain accounts or transaction types. Common examples include:

- Credit Sales versus Cash Sales

- Accounts Payable Components

Whatever the specific mathematical techniques used, the expert should obtain a clear understanding of the transactions and conditions affecting each financial statement amount. It is often useful to look at several trends and relationships to identify inconsistencies or unusual patterns.

Widely used trend analyses are shown below:

Common-sized Financial Statements (Vertical Analysis). Each line in the financial statements is presented as a percentage of a base number.

Fluctuation or Trend Analysis (Horizontal Analysis). It computes the change in balance sheet and income statement items from one year (or period) to the next and usually expresses the change in percentage terms.

Performing such an analysis requires that the experts understand the company's business and industry in order to know what relationships would be expected to exist, what relationships would be considered unusual or unlikely, and what plausible explanations might exist for observed relationships.

Ratios analysis

Ratio analysis is an attempt to express the relationship between two or more accounts or variables in a simpler, more comprehensive way. Ratios are usually derived from financial statements as a basis of comparison, evaluation, and prediction.

Given the large number and variety of possible financial ratios, it is important to focus on those amounts that are functionally related. For example, the relationship between bad debt expense and credit sales is more meaningful than the relationship between bad debt expense and total sales.

Many of the performance measures in the governmental agencies, for example (outcomes, outputs, efficiencies), are expressed as ratios -- for example, administrative support cost as a percentage of total expenditures. This module focuses only on analysis of financial ratios.

Ratio analysis is useful when the goal is to reduce financial data to fewer expressions or variables. This goal often arises when the underlying relationships between the elements of the ratio are of interest, when data are not expressed in absolute dollar amounts, and/or when financial condition must be reviewed over time.

The ratio may be compared to the same ratio for a prior period (or several prior periods) and unusual or significant variations assessed. For example, thefts of inventory might be concealed by manipulating those accounts, causing unusual changes in the inventory turnover ratio.

For example, a business that is a front for money laundering might engage in an on-the-books fraud involving the over reporting of revenues (because a portion of the revenues is money obtained from an illicit activity). In such a case, unless the business was one with relatively fixed costs to sales (such as a movie theatre), the result would be costs unusually low in relation to reported sales. If so, comparing the ratio of costs to sales might indicate fraud patterns.

In performing ratio analysis, the expert should be aware of that unusual fluctuations can be caused by legitimate economic factors or by honest accounting errors rather than by fraud. Also, ratio analysis will not reveal unusual relationships or fluctuations caused by fraud unless the amount stolen and concealed in the financial statements is material. Immaterial amounts will not significantly affect the ratios. In addition, ratio analysis may not be revealing if applied to consolidated financial statements; in such a case the financial statements of the branch, division, or subsidiary in which fraud is suspected should be isolated and analysed.

Examples for ratios used in the educational institutions are shown below.

Contribution and demand ratios

Endowment Income/Total Educational and General Expenditures and Mandatory Transfers

Governmental or Local Revenues/Total Educational and General Expenditures and Mandatory Transfers

Tuition and Fees/Total Educational and General Expenditures and Mandatory Transfers

Additional demand ratios are created by dividing each of the following expenditures by total educational and general revenues:

- Academic support
- Institutional support
- Instruction
- Operation and maintenance of plant
- Public service
- Research
- Scholarships and fellowships
- Student services

The advantages of the ratio analysis could be described below. It:

- Communicates the aspects of an entity's overall economic situation more broadly and succinctly than financial statement data alone
- Facilitates understanding how certain variables may influence each other
- Helps determine a variety of financial aspects

The disadvantages of the ratio analysis could be described below. It:

- Is costly to track over time, especially when norms change
- Is difficult to obtain for use in public sector fraud risk assessment
- Leads to misleading conclusions if viewed out of context

- Ignores unique factors which make entities fundamentally incomparable

4.3.1.3. Technique: What-if Analysis

3D FRAM uses this type of analysis applying 2 approaches:

1. Using What-if Analysis applying the standard spreadsheet softwares as like Microsoft Excel and Apple Numbers, and

2. Using the What-if Analysis applying the 3D FRAM Fraud Scenario.

Using the first approach, here's a simple, brief way to describe the Excel what-if tools:

- You use Goal Seek in Excel when you want to work backward from a solution to a problem - when you know the result of a single worksheet formula but not the input value that the formula needs to figure out the result. For instance, Goal Seek would be a good way to get a rough estimate of how much you could afford to pay for a home mortgage if you already know the mortgage's interest rate, the mortgage term, and how much you were willing to pay on the mortgage each month.

- Data tables are helpful when you want to view and compare the results of all of the different variations of a formula on a worksheet. A simple example of this might be one of those multiplication tables or metric conversion tables that you learned in school.

- Scenarios are a great tool for saving, in a worksheet, sets of values that Excel can switch between automatically so that you view different results. For instance, you could create best-case and worst-case scenarios, and then compare these scenarios' results next to each other.

- You use Solver when you want to work backward from a solution to a problem. It's similar to Goal Seek, but you use Solver when you also want to apply restrictions on the problem. Using the previous Goal Seek example, you could use Solver if you wanted to further restrict the total home price to not exceed a certain price.

The second approach will use What-if Analysis applying our 3D FRAM Fraud Scenario asking the questions which follows!

For example:

- What would be happen If certain assets as money, fixtures or software would be embezzled?

- What would be happen If certain vendors or suppliers will commit fraud against the client's organization?

- What would be happen If the owner, certain directors (John, Michael etc.) or managers could perpetrate fraud depending their authority?

- What would be happen If fraud has been occurring, is occurring without any patterns/indicators/red flags and will be occurring in such situation?

- What would be happen If certain employee perpetrates an assets embezzlement in collusion of the owner, the executive director or the supervisor?

- What would be happen If there is no any evidence available - no fraud patterns, indicators, no paper clue, only rumours?

- What would be happen If there is no obvious misconduct or a law/rule noncompliance?

- What would be happen If there are no any specific anti-fraud controls or the controls are overridden?

- What would be happen If the intent (motive) is difficult to be recognized?

- What would be happen If the embezzled sum of money is not much?

- What would be happen If it is difficult to prove that the fraud is going to be concealed this or other way?

- What would be happen If there are signs for an unusual increasing of the personal wealth of the owner the director, the manager, the employee?

- What would be happen If there tips, customer claims and obviously fraud pattern/indicators/red flags?

- What would be happen If there is not any adequate response to the final conclusion that the fraud risk in the organization is significant?

We are absolutely sure that the analysis of the answers would be very helpful for the phase of ranging the fraud risk during the fraud risk assessment engagement.

4.3.1.4. Technique: Hypothesis Testing

Hypothesis testing is used in the 3D FRAM for:

- Drawing inferences about a the events based on sample data from such population using discovery sampling

- Assessing the significance of the difference between the likelihood an event would be happen or not

- Populations on a variable of interest based on sample data from such populations

- Choosing among alternative courses of action

Hypothesis testing is appropriate when the goal is to test an assumption about population parameters based on samples from such populations. Hypothesis testing will be used to assess the probability that a management assertion about a population or condition is correct or not correct.

The underlying assumptions using this technique could be as follows:

- There was a fraudulent trend of changes in the past

- There is no a fraudulent trend of changes currently

- There won't be any fraudulent trend of changes in the future

- If there was a fraudulent trend of changes in the past there will be such one in the future

- Reject the null hypothesis, in which case one concludes that sufficient evidence exists to indicate that the alternative hypothesis is true

- Do not reject the null hypothesis, in which case one concludes that insufficient evidence exists to indicate that the alternative hypothesis is true

Thus, the null hypothesis can be rejected or not rejected. More definitive conclusions can be drawn if the null hypothesis is rejected. The conclusion would be that the null hypothesis is false, at a particular level of confidence, i.e. beyond a reasonable doubt.

If a null hypothesis is not rejected, the same degree of certainty is not obtained. One can assume that null hypothesis is reasonable, but the level of certainty could be specified only if one knows the true population parameter, the mean weekly output in the sample application above. This is rarely possible to obtain since surveying entire populations is expensive and time-consuming.

The zero and alternative hypotheses for each fraud could attain the following forms:

- Fraud, including inflation of prices by the suppliers through deals with associated parties, does not exist.

- Fraud, including inflation of prices by the suppliers through deals with associated parties, does exist. Hence, two types of errors could occur when testing the hypotheses by using indicators.

The hypothesis testing for null H or alternative H hypotheses could be applied for our 3D FRAM Fraud Scenario more in details described in Part 3 and shown below:

FRAUD SCENARIO (8W+5H): 13 FATAL FOR A POTENTIAL FRAUDSTER QUESTIONS!

1. WHAT?

2. WHERE?

3. WHO?

4.WHEN?

5.WHO ELSE?

6.WHAT EVIDENCE?

7.WHAT'S THE LAW/ RULE?

8.WHAT CONTROLS ARE OVERRIDDEN?

9.WHAT IS THE INTENT(MOTIVE)?

10.HOW MUCH?

11.HOW TO CONCEAL?

12.HOW AND WHEN TO DETECT?

13.HOW TO PREVENT?

Applying to all 13 questions hypothesis testing may reveal that the first type of errors occurs when fraud patterns/indicators have not been detected, and the fraud indeed exists. This type of error could occur because of incorrect classification of the hypotheses, of the type of fraud that could exist, of the types of indicators generated by frauds, or of the methods used for search of fraud indicators.

The first type of errors could also occur when the researches reveal appropriate patterns/ indicators which however are incorrectly interpreted, are not identified by examiners, or are studied in an inappropriate way.

The second type of errors occurs when a document or action (inaction) are indicated as fraud indicators, but indeed they are not. This type of errors could occur due to all the causes, leading to the first type of errors.

Except in fraud risk assessment process as a stand-alone engagement, hypotheses generating is considered critical for the efficiency and effectiveness of the diagnostic processes and in external and internal fraud risk assessment.

4.3.1.5. Technique: Cost Benefit Analysis

First question asked by the expert assessing the fraud risk regarding different project, especially capital expenditures projects, should be: "What says the cost-benefit analysis for this project?" and second question would be: "Is there any such cost-benefit analysis conducted at all?". The sequence could be reversed, of course!

But how 3D FRAM uses the cost-benefit analysis? Let's describe it!

Cost-benefit analysis is a process used to aid managers in making decision choices between strategies. Through definition and evaluation of costs and perceived benefits associated with particular alternatives, reasonable decisions can be made about whether to proceed with a given strategy. Cost-benefit analysis can also apply to the fraud risk assessment process as a way to determine which fraud risk assessment technique would be most appropriate.

Cost-benefit analysis is similar to cost effectiveness analysis, though some distinctions exist. While cost-benefit is primarily concerned with economic efficiency, cost effectiveness focuses on technological efficiency. Cost-benefit would more likely inform long-term public sector decisions, such as whether to commit capital to a new project. Cost effectiveness has a more narrow short term focus, such as in determining an existing program's resource priorities.

Distinctions between the two are less pronounced now that cost-benefit analysis is less used in global situations where potential benefits and costs are not easily expressed in dollars. Such circumstances are quite common in the public sector.

Cost-benefit analysis is most commonly used to determine which of a series of alternative actions will be most economically efficient. As noted earlier, many real-world situations have benefits and costs which may be difficult to quantify.

For example, the legislature may be considering several strategies for lowering the crime rate. One strategy might target more dollars toward substance abuse prevention, another might seek longer prison sentences for criminals, while a third might advocate boot camps for youthful offenders.

In reality, more than one strategy might be appropriate. What criteria, then, should one use for this decision? If all strategies were expected to reduce crime by equal amounts, it would seem that the decision hinges on the financial cost to implement the strategy. Yet, this is an unlikely assumption. It is more probable that actual decision criteria would be more complex. Even so, cost-benefit analysis in this example could be used to inform the policy decision.

Fraud risk assessment applications also exist for cost-benefit analysis. For example, when determining the nature and extent of ant-fraud controls, the experts must weigh the cost of detective or anti-fraud controls against the benefits of having the controls in place. This is necessary since resources available for implementing anti-fraud controls are limited.

Similarly, cost-benefit analysis can help justify recommendations for adding or eliminating specific internal controls. The experts can also use the process to asses and evaluate the cost effectiveness of prior management decisions. Finally, cost-benefit analysis can facilitate quantifying findings.

Cost-benefit analysis can:

- Allocate resources to anti-fraud strategic objectives
- Take the economic efficiency of anti-fraud strategies into account
- Specify assumptions, costs, and benefits of anti-fraud strategies more fully

- Focus on the outcomes and effects of anti-fraud strategies
- Help gather data on and quantify objectives and outcomes
- Show where intangibles, fraud patterns and uncertainties exist
- Posit and compare alternate approaches to the same policy objective
- Highlight long-term effects of policy decisions on population segments
- Summarise a great deal of information
- Encourage factoring intangibles and politics into strategic anti-fraud decisions

Cost-benefit analysis can:

- Be constrained by problems in quantifying key variables
- Become confusing on complex projects
- Be challenged as subjective, particularly with respect to fraud patterns
- Lend itself to political or bureaucratic manipulation
- Appear to be more precise and comprehensive than it really is
- Be seen as a prescription for decision-making rather than as one tool among many

According Wikipedia[17], more detailed description of cost-benefit analysis is presented below:

"...Cost–benefit analysis is often used by governments and others, e.g. businesses, to evaluate the desirability of a given policy. It is an analysis of the expected balance of benefits and costs, including an account of foregone alternatives and the *status quo*, helping predict whether the benefits of a policy outweigh its costs, and by how much. Altering the status quo by choosing the lowest cost-benefit ratio can improve Pareto efficiency, in which no alternative policy can improve one group's situation without damaging another. Generally, accurate cost-benefit analysis identifies choices that increase welfare from a utilitarian perspective. Otherwise, cost-benefit analysis offers no guarantees of increased economic efficiency or increases of social welfare; generally positive microeconomic theory is moot when it comes to evaluating the impact on social welfare of a policy.

The following is a list of steps that comprise a generic cost-benefit analysis.[2]

1. List alternative projects/programs.
2. List stakeholders.
3. Select measurement(s) and measure all cost and benefits elements.
4. Predict outcome of cost and benefits over relevant time period.
5. Convert all costs and benefits into a common currency.

6. Apply discount rate.

7. Calculate net present value of project options.

8. Perform sensitivity analysis.

9. Adopt recommended choice.

CBA attempts to measure the positive or negative consequences of a project, which may include:

1. Effects on users or participants
2. Effects on non-users or non-participants
3. Externality effects
4. Option value or other social benefits

A similar breakdown is employed in environmental analysis of total economic value. Both costs and benefits can be diverse. Financial costs tend to be most thoroughly represented in cost-benefit analyses due to relatively abundant market data. The net benefits of a project may incorporate cost savings or public willingness to pay compensation (implying the public has no legal right to the benefits of the policy) or willingness to accept compensation (implying the public has a right to the benefits of the policy) for the welfare change resulting from the policy. The guiding principle of evaluating benefits is to list all (categories of) parties affected by an intervention and add the (positive or negative) value, usually monetary, that they ascribe to its effect on their welfare.

The actual compensation an individual would require to have their welfare unchanged by a policy is inexact at best. Surveys (stated preference techniques) or market behavior (revealed preference techniques) are often used to estimate the compensation associated with a policy, however survey respondents often have strong incentives to misreport their true preferences and market behavior does not provide any information about important non-market welfare impacts.

One controversy is valuing a human life, e.g. when assessing road safety measures or life-saving medicines. However, this can sometimes be avoided by using the related technique of cost-utility analysis, in which benefits are expressed in non-monetary units such as quality-adjusted life years. For example, road safety can be measured in terms of *cost per life saved*, without formally placing a financial value on the life. However, such non-monetary metrics have limited usefulness for evaluating policies with substantially different outcomes. Additionally, many other benefits may accrue from the policy, and metrics such as 'cost per life saved' may lead to a substantially different ranking of alternatives than traditional cost-benefit analysis.

CBA usually tries to put all relevant costs and benefits on a common temporal footing using time value of money calculations. This is often done by converting the future expected streams of costs and benefits into a present value amount using a discount rate. Empirical studies and a technical framework suggest that in reality, people do discount the future like this.

The choice of discount rate is subjective. A smaller rate values future generations equally with the current generation. Larger rates (e.g. a market rate of return) reflects humans' attraction to time inconsistency—valuing money that they receive today more than money they get in the future. The choice makes a large difference in assessing interventions with long-term effects, such as those affecting climate change. One issue is the equity premium puzzle, in which long-term returns on equities may be rather higher than they should be. If so then arguably market rates of return should not be used to determine a discount rate, as doing so would have the effect of undervaluing the distant future (e.g. climate change).

Risk associated with project outcomes is usually handled using probability theory. This can be factored into the discount rate (to have uncertainty increasing over time), but is usually considered separately. Particular consideration is often given to risk aversion—the irrational preference for avoiding loss over achieving gain. Expected return calculations does not account for the detrimental effect of uncertainty.

Uncertainty in CBA parameters (as opposed to risk of project failure etc.) can be evaluated using a sensitivity analysis, which shows how results respond to parameter changes. Alternatively a more formal risk analysis can be undertaken using Monte Carlo simulations.

CBA was later expanded to address both intangible and tangible benefits of public policies relating to mental illness, substance abuse, college education and chemical waste policies. In the US, the National Environmental Policy Act of 1969 first required the application of CBA for regulatory programs, and since then, other governments have enacted similar rules. Government guidebooks for the application of CBA to public policies include the Canadian guide for regulatory analysis, Australian guide for regulation and finance, US guide for health care programs, and US guide for emergency management programs.

CBA application for transport investment started in the UK, with the M1 motorway project in 1960. It was later applied on many projects including London Underground's Victoria Line. Later, the New Approach to Appraisal (NATA) was introduced by the then Department for Transport, Environment and the Regions. This presented cost–benefit results and detailed environmental impact assessments in a balanced way. NATA was first applied to national road schemes in the 1998 Roads Review but subsequently rolled out to all transport modes. As of 2011 it was a cornerstone of transport appraisal in the UK and is maintained and developed by the Department for Transport.

The EU's 'Developing Harmonised European Approaches for Transport Costing and Project Assessment' (HEATCO) project, part of its Sixth Framework Programme, reviewed transport appraisal guidance across EU member states and found that significant differences exist between countries. HEATCO's aim is to develop guidelines to harmonise transport appraisal practice across the EU.

In the US, both federal and state transport departments commonly apply CBA, using a variety of available software tools including HERS, BCA.Net, StatBenCost, Cal-BC, and TREDIS. Guides are available from the Federal Highway Administration, Federal Aviation Administration, Minnesota Department of Transportation, California Department of Transportation (Caltrans),[28] and the Transportation Research Board Transportation Economics Committee.

The value of a cost–benefit analysis depends on the accuracy of the individual cost and benefit estimates. Comparative studies indicate that such estimates are often flawed, preventing improvements in Pareto and Kaldor-Hicks efficiency[citation needed]. Causes of these inaccuracies include[:

- Over-reliance on data from past projects (often differing markedly in function or size and the skill levels of the team members)
- Use of subjective impressions by assessment team members
- Inappropriate use of heuristics to derive money cost of the intangible elements
- Confirmation bias among project supporters (looking for reasons to proceed)

Reference class forecasting was developed to increase accuracy in estimates of costs and benefits.

Interest groups may attempt to include or exclude significant costs from an analysis to influence the outcome.

In the case of the Ford Pinto (where, because of design flaws, the Pinto was liable to burst into flames in a rear-impact collision), the company's decision was not to issue a recall. Ford's cost–benefit analysis had estimated that based on the number of cars in use and the probable accident rate, deaths due to the design flaw would cost it about $49.5 million to settle wrongful death lawsuits versus recall costs of $137.5 million. Ford overlooked (or considered insignificant) the costs of the negative publicity that would result, which forced a recall *and* damaged sales.

In health economics, some analysts think cost–benefit analysis can be an inadequate measure because willingness-to-pay methods of determining the value of human life can be influenced by income level. They support use of variants such as cost–utility analysis and quality-adjusted life year to analyse the effects of health policies.[citation needed]

In environmental and occupational health regulation, it has been argued that if modern cost-benefit analyses had been applied prospectively to decisions such as removing lead from gasoline, building Hoover Dam in the Grand Canyon and regulating workers' exposure to vinyl chloride, they would not have been implemented even though they are considered to be highly successful in retrospect. The Clean Air Act has been cited in retrospective studies as a case where benefits exceeded costs, but the knowledge of the benefits (attributable largely to the benefits of reducing particulate pollution) was not available until many years later…"

Delivering to you more information about the cost-benefit analysis using Wikipedia we hoped to increase your professional interest as to be applied more intensively in the fraud risk assessment engagements of capital expenditure projects!

4.3.1.6. Technique: Sensitivity analysis

Using Wikipedia as a open source for actual information: *"Sensitivity analysis (SA)* is the study of how the uncertainty in the output of a model (numerical or otherwise) can be apportioned to different sources of uncertainty in the model input. A related practice is uncertainty analysis which focuses rather on quantifying uncertainty in model output. Ideally, uncertainty and sensitivity analysis should be run in tandem.

In any budgeting process there are always variables that are uncertain. Future tax rates, interest rates, inflation rates, headcount, operating expenses and other variables may not be known with great precision. Sensitivity analysis answers the question, "if these variables deviate from expectations, what will the effect be (on the business, model, system, or whatever is being analysed)?"[18]

In more general terms uncertainty and sensitivity analysis investigate the robustness of a study when the study includes some form of statistical modelling. Sensitivity analysis can be useful to fraud risk modellers for a range of purposes, including:

- Support decision making or the development of recommendations for stakeholders;
- Enhancing communication from fraud risk modellers to stakeholders (e.g. by making anti-fraud recommendations for resistance to fraud more credible, understandable, compelling or persuasive);
- Increased understanding or quantification of the system (e.g. understanding relationships between input and output variables); and
- Fraud Risk Model development for the organization (e.g. searching for errors in the model).

Let us give an example: in any budgeting process there are always variables that are uncertain. Future tax rates, interest rates, inflation rates, headcount, operating expenses and other variables may not be known with great precision. Sensitivity analysis for 3D FRAM purposes answers the question, "if these anti-fraud controls deviate from expectations, what will the effect be (on the business, losses, reputation, or whatever is being analyzed)?"

In a decision problem, the expert may want to identify cost drivers as well as other quantities for which we need to acquire better knowledge in order to make an informed decision. On the other hand, some quantities have no influence on the predictions, so that we can save resources at no loss in accuracy by relaxing some of the conditions. Sensitivity analysis can help in a variety of other circumstances which can be handled by the settings illustrated below:

- To identify critical assumptions or compare alternative model structures
- Guide future data collections
- Detect important criteria
- Optimize the tolerance of manufactured parts in terms of the uncertainty in the parameters
- Optimize resources allocation
- Model simplification or model lumping, etc.

However there are also some problems associated with sensitivity analysis in the business context:

- Variables are often interdependent, which makes examining them each individually unrealistic, e.g.: changing one factor such as sales volume, will most likely affect other factors such as the selling price.
- Often the assumptions upon which the analysis is based are made by using past experience/ data which may not hold in the future.
- Assigning a maximum and minimum (or optimistic and pessimistic) value is open to subjective interpretation. For instance one persons 'optimistic' forecast of fraud occurrence may be more conservative than that of another person performing a different part of the analysis. This sort of subjectivity can adversely affect the accuracy and overall objectivity of the analysis.

When reporting a sensitivity analysis, the experts should explain fully their specification search so that the client can judge for themselves how the results may have been affected.

Technique 4.3.1.7 Using specialized software

The application of softwares for analysis such as like ACL, IDEA etc. could be learned from other different sources but in our 3D FRAM will shortly describe the application of the free for use software called "Picalo". Hot to apply Picalo is described below!

"Conan C. Albrecht, Picalo Workbook, 2009, www.picalo.org, pp. 53-65

... Phantom Contractors

Goal: To learn how to use Picalo commands to find a type of fraud.

Now that you know the basics of Picalo tables, import and export, and database connections, let's explore the primary purpose of Picalo: analysis!

In this exercise, you'll complete tasks related to finding phantom contractors.

Use your creativity to solve these problems; there are usually multiple approaches to get to the answers.

This exercise uses the Procurement dataset, which includes the following data:

Bid - Contains the bids on different contracts from the contractors in the Contractor table.

BidDetail - Contains the bid detail for each of the bids in the Bid table. Each contract has a number of items that need to be bid on.

For example, a bridge project would include line items for concrete, labor, etc. This table contains the bid amounts on each line item listed in the ProjectItem table.

Blacklist - Contains a number of contractors that have been blacklisted because of fraud or other problematic behavior.

Contractor - Contains the records for the contractors who have bid on our projects.

Employee - Contains the employee records for our company's employees.

Invoice - Contains invoices for work done on projects by the winning bidder. After a contractor has won a bid, it starts work on the project. The invoices in this table are the bills for that work.

Project - Contains 64 projects that the company has sent out for bids from different contractors. This can be seen as the master table of the entire database.

ProjectItem - Contains the line items for projects. Each contract has a number of items that need to be bid on. For example, a bridge project would include line items for concrete, labor, etc. These line items are contained in this table.

PurchaseCard - Contains purchase card information for our employees. Each employee is issued a credit card to make purchases with. This table is not really related to the project/bidding tables.

PurchaseTransaction - Contains the actual transactions employees have made on their p-cards.

ValidNAICS - Contains the valid places employees can use the p-cards at. Each NAICS code represents a type of business, and our employees can only spend money at certain types of businesses. Note that these NAICS codes are generated (they do not relate to real NAICS codes).

Please ensure you have copied this dataset to your disk before starting. Windows users can copy it to their My Documents folder.

4.1 Set the Project Directory

All of your work in Picalo is contained in a project, which corresponds to a directory (a.k.a. folder) on your computer. The left-side list will show all tables, database connections, queries, and scripts in this directory.

Picalo will create a file called Picalo.history in the directory to keep track of everything you do in the project. You can find this log in the History tab at the bottom of the screen. Picalo keeps the history log forever (unless you clear it), so even your activities in past sessions are available.

1. Open Picalo and set the project directory to Procurement. How many initial tables are in this project?

Answer Key: Set the Project Directory

1. Open Picalo and set the project directory to Procurement. How many initial tables are in this project?

There are 11 tables in this project (they are the same ones we used in the database last exercise).

4.2 Address matching

When employees set themselves up as phantom contractors, they often list their home address so payment checks come to them. Others list P.O. Boxes, which real companies don't normally use. Contractors can also set up ghost companies to decrease competition, such as when all three bidders on a project are actually subs of the same parent company.

Address checking can be difficult because 50 N Maple is essentially the same as 50 North Maple Street. Doing an exact match (which is what database queries do) won't match these addresses. Some analysts modify the addresses in clever ways by removing all instances of North, South, East, West, Way, Circle, Street, Avenue, etc. Others remove all letters and compare only the street numbers.

Another way is to use fuzzy matching. Picalo supports both the Soundex algorithm and normal-style comparisons for fuzzy matching. Both can be effective methods of finding duplicates.

1. Using the Data menu, join the employee and contractor tables to find if any have the same address and zip code (hint: use a fuzzy match join). What did you find?

2. Join the contractor table with itself to see if any have the same address and zip code. Are any the same?

Answer Key: Address matching

1. Using the Data menu, join the employee and contractor tables to find if any have the same address and zip code (hint: use a fuzzy match join). What did you find?

There are three matches that are worrisome: 4399 North Possum Road and 5012 North Possum Road, 446 South First Way and 446 South First, and 7555 East Main Street and 7555 E Main Street. The fuzzy match algorithm can find these matches, but it takes a little experimentation with the match percent. At 30 percent, you'll likely find too many matches (it's too fuzzy for this analysis). At 90 percent, you'll likely find none. 60 percent turns out to be a good happy medium that finds the right records. Many analyses are like this: they require a little experimentation to get the thresholds right.

(a) Open the Employee and Contractor tables by double-clicking them.

(b) Select Data | Join | By Fuzzy Match... to get the `Join By Fuzzy Match' dialog.

(c) Set Contractor as the first table and Employee as the second table.

(d) Select Address as the first match criteria in both tables.

(e) Select ZipCode as the second match criteria in both tables.

(f) Set 60 percent as the fuzzy match percent. Give a results table name and click OK.

2. Join the contractor table with itself to see if any have the same address and zip code. Are any the same?

There are no matching contractors. This exercise simply showed that tables can be joined to themselves to find matching records.

4.3 Name matching

1. Create a new static calculated column in the employee table that represents the initials of each employee (hint: use FirstName[0] for the first character of first name). Join this new column with the contractor names using a Picalo expression that checks to see if any name has these initials (hint: the expression \Field1 in Field2 sees if the text in field 1 exists anywhere in field 2). What do the results mean? What further investigation should be done?

Answer Key: Name matching

1. Create a new static calculated column in the employee table that represents the initials of each employee (hint: use FirstName[0] for the first character of first name). Join this new column with the contractor names using a Picalo expression that checks to see if any name has these initials (hint: the expression \Field1 in Field2 sees if the text in field 1 exists anywhere in field 2). What do the results mean? What further investigation should be done? A bug in Picalo prevents this one right now. We're working on it.

4.4 Interesting addresses

1. Check for contractor addresses that are using PO Boxes. Normally, businesses have real addresses and not post office boxes. What did you find?

2. Check for zip codes that do not match the correct format for zip codes. What is the likely cause of any problems here? What should the follow up be?

Answer Key: Interesting addresses

1. Check for contractor addresses that are using PO Boxes. Normally, businesses have real addresses and not post office boxes. What did you find?

There are two contractors: EVL and RZK Partnerships. These may not be real contractors. These results can be found through Data | Select, Edit | Find, or by filtering the table. To use the filter method, click the magic wand icon to set a simple filter on the word `Box'. Set it to match partial values and to ignore the case. A more robust solution is to use the detectlet (Tools | Detectlets) that is engineered to find post office boxes. It searches for dozens of different ways to write P. O. Box.

2. Check for zip codes that do not match the correct format for zip codes.

What is the likely cause of any problems here? What should the follow up be? There is one contractor with an invalid zip code: RPC Incorporated. To find this contractor, click the magic wand icon to set a filter on the table. The pattern is `#####-####' . Exclude the matching records. Click OK and you'll see the invalid company.

4.5 Interesting names

1. Are there any interesting names of contractors (hint: what would happen if a check were cut to a company named \Cash)? The perpetrator might have been tricky here, so be clever in your searching. Is there only one, or are there two companies of interest here? Have any payments been made to this company?

Answer Key: Interesting names

1. Are there any interesting names of contractors (hint: what would happen if a check were cut to a company named \Cash)? The perpetrator might have been tricky here, so be clever in your searching. Is there only one, or are there two companies of interest here? Have any payments been made to this company?

There are two companies: Cash and The Cash Company. The first company, Cash, would have checks printed to cash, meaning anyone could cash them. The second one is likely a real company and not a problem. These results can be found through Data | Select, Edit | Find, or by filtering the table.....”

3D FRAM presents another specialized software called “EXChecker” already used for identification of 498 errors in a EU ISPA Project Model regarding Water&Wastewater Services in Sofia, Bulgaria! Shortly the applications of EXChecker could be used not only by experts but and by the fraud risk evaluators too and it can be described below!

EXChecker

- Quickly analyze and diagnose errors and fraud in client spreadsheets
- Experts and risk managers are sharpening their focus on end-user applications – especially spreadsheets – as being a source of corporate risk throughout the entire organization.
- Moving beyond financial spreadsheets, analytical and operational spreadsheets are increasingly considered as potential sources of financial impact that need their own controls.
- Designed for experts, risk managers, forensic accountants and spreadsheet developers, EXChecker makes available detailed spreadsheet analysis and documentation capabilities in a standalone package that can be used to forensically examine the structure, formulas, macros, data flow, and data linkages of risky spreadsheets to identify errors or potential sources of fraud.

EXChecker gives experts and fraud risk evaluators the most comprehensive and the deepest set of analytical and documentation functionality available, maximizing client benefits such as:

- Lowers the risk introduced through spreadsheet errors to business operations and compliance initiatives.
- Identifies hidden problems in complex, mission-critical spreadsheets difficult to detect in traditional spreadsheet development and review processes.
- Helps detect fraudulent attempts at misrepresenting or concealing data.
- Creates detailed documentation trail of fraud risk assessment analysis and problem mitigation.
- Increases efficiency of spreadsheet remediation through summary-level analysis and automated spreadsheet control validation.
- Streamlines spreadsheet development and validation process through quick detection and fixing of problems during construction of spreadsheet model.
- Unmatched Forensic Analysis Capabilities Visual, Intuitive Interface for Ease of Use

Spreadsheets allow for free-form user-developed applications, so they are extremely prone to error and fraud and are increasingly the subject of close scrutiny by experts. However, finding and diagnosing problems or assessing the risk of fraud is a challenge - Excel does not provide an adequate set of capabilities itself for this, and there is no documentation facility for such an analysis. EXChecker provides a volume of sophisticated analytical capabilities in an non-plugin, easy-to-use standalone application environment, including:

- Summary-level reporting detailing items such as formula count, sheet count, occupied cells count, named ranges, external references, very hidden sheets and validations
- Interactive visual formula structure and information flow analysis

- Workbook comparison reports detailing the differences between versions
- Hierarchical identification of a cell's precedents and dependents
- Sophisticated, integrated fraud risk assessment documentation environment
- Configurable spreadsheet warnings
- Function Use Analysis tool providing a breakdown of each time a function is used
- Identification and analysis of macros
- User-definable spreadsheet rules that may be applied to multiple spreadsheets to highlight those that break best-practice policies
- Advanced spreadsheet search capabilities using wildcard searches to locate cell values, text patterns, macro code, formula values, notes or worksheet names
- Detailed forensic analysis of advanced functions, such as NESTED IF levels, LOOKUP content analysis, Negative and Positive formula definitions, unlocked cells, etc.

It locates potential concealment strategies and hard-to-find data misrepresentations, such as invisible cells, image masking, hidden rows/columns, unused input cells, formulas with blank or text cells, numerics stored as text, etc.

Method 4.3.6 Ranging Fraud Risks

Technique 4.3.6.1: From 0 to 100
This technique provides for the beginning of the ranging process of fraud risk from 0 to 100 where each step includes 10 rates following the description of all 10 phases presented in the Functional Dimension Methodology described in Part 3.

Technique 4.3.6.2: From 100 to 0
This technique provides for the beginning of the ranging process of fraud risk from 100 to 0 where each step includes 10 rates following the description of all 10 phases presented in the Functional Dimension Methodology described in Part 3.The detailed application of these techniques will be presented in the next 3D Fraud Risk Assessment Model's updates which will continuously follow this issue!

Part V: 3D FRAM - Timing Dimension

In this part:

- Planning the Fraud Risk Assessment Engagement
- Performing the Fraud Risk Assessment Engagement
- Fraud Risk Assessment Conclusions and Recommendations

Time is money! As any business engagement 3D FRAM is limited in time and depends on the other two dimensions the 3D FRAM - Functional and Methodical Dimensions. Proper planning and organizing the conduct of the 3D FRAM is the prerequisite for a successful finalizing of the engagement. Consider many and different obstacles during this engagement because we are talking about Fraud and Fraud Risk Assessment!

All the 3 dimensions could be presented in a form of cube where all sides are proportional. This means that the scope and the length of the Timing Dimension will strongly depend on the other two dimensions - Functional and Methodological.

The Timing Dimension will include the time budget and the length of the phases of the whole fraud risk assessment or, shortly - will encompass all the efforts and costs needed for a such engagement. As an example, 3FRAM will use the length of 4 weeks for the fraud risk assessment engagement which is the minimum length of time for such performance.

The process of conducting the fraud risk assessment engagement is presented in a chronological order and starts with its careful preparation described below.

5.1. PLANNING THE FRAUD RISK ASSESSMENT

3D FRAM requires the preparation of the fraud risk assessment engagement to include creating a professional team, planning the necessary resources, the visits and meetings and the design for collecting and evaluating the data. Very important point here is that the experts should consider the potential attempts for a influence or the pressure of the client to them as regarding the choice of the methodology. The question here is whether the client will expect a significant fraud risk to be revealed after performing such a fraud risk assessment engagement.

The possible influence would be aimed at the manipulating the methodology, the data and/or the conclusions made by the experts. For example, you should state that there is not a significant fraud risk in the managed by John Doe organization. Reversely, the client would make attempts to influence the experts as their final conclusions to show a significant fraud risk in the managed by John or Jim organization.

Being aware of such situation and especially for a such engagement the experts should create a professional team where the term "professional" should include and the term "sound ethics" but not only knowledge, skills and experience.

3D FRAM uses the planning as a development of an overall strategy for the expected conduct and scope of the fraud risk assessment engagement. Successful fraud risk assessment engagements will be built upon the foundation of good planning. Responsibility for planning the engagement should be shared by the expert team and its manager.

The important thing to remember is that all stages of the fraud risk assessment involve planning in some form.

Planning begins before the fraud risk assessment engagement is accepted and continues throughout the entire process until, at the end of the current engagement, fraud risk assessment team begins to plan the next engagement.

Again, time is money! Invest it and Save it!

I. FRAUD EXPOSURE, AWARENESS AND RECOGNITION PHASE - 2 ½ weeks

    1. Pre-Engagement Planning. Creating an engagement team.

    2. An engagement conference is held with the prospective client.

    3. Agreement is reached and an engagement letter is originated.

    4. The experts spend time for collecting, obtaining and developing of external and internal information to get understanding of the legal status, integrity, the industry and the business of the organization-prospective client

    5. Identification of the possible exposure of fraud types, corruption and fraud schemes at different levels, processes and activities of the organization.

    6. Recognition of a fraud scenario and its variations, concerning different levels, processes and activities of the organization.

    7. Collecting and obtaining external and internal information about the existing controls, applied for detection and prevention fraud in the organization, if any.

II. FRAUD RISK ANALYSIS - ½ week

8. Identification of the opportunities for occurrence of fraud and abuse and for their concealment.

9. Analysis of the data available for patterns of fraud, corruption, abuse, errors, intent, irregularities

III. FRAUD RISK ASSESSMENT PHASE - ½ week

10. Ranging the fraud risks according their source, ownership level and significance using two measures - quantitative and qualitative

11. Determination of the fraud risk in two rages - significant or nonsignificant

IV. FRAUD RISK RESPONSE - ½ week

12. Development of recommendations for an adequate response and timely measures according the significance of the assessed fraud risk as to develop and/or to enhance the resistance to fraud.

13. Preparation and presentation of the engagement report

Let's follow the description of The Timing Dimension below.

I. FRAUD EXPOSURE, AWARENESS AND RECOGNITION PHASE - 2 ½ weeks (1) - (7)

(1) Pre-Engagement Planning. Creating an engagement team.

You or your company is approached by a prospective client. Under optimal conditions, the prospective client should contact you well in advance so that you or your experts may have time to assess overall fraud risk of the client. Fraud risk includes external and internal risk factors related to the industry in which the client does business, as well as the history and specific facts about the client, such as (non) competitive position within the industry, pressures, opportunities, financial structure, the existence of related parties and more. Fraud risk is also associated with the integrity and reputation of the client.

Pre-engagement planning continues with creating a professional team for the specific engagement where all of the team members should possess the knowledge and skills described in the paragraph "Performance" which will follow below.

(2) An Engagement Conference is held with the Prospective Client.

The experts provide awareness to the prospective client about the fraud risk assessment engagement using presentation about:

- The nature and goals,
- The scope and timing,
- The types of fraud and abuse exposures

- The specific (3D FRAM) methodology applied, and
- The benefits of using the fraud risk assessment process.

(3) Agreement is reached and an Engagement Letter is originated

It is extremely important that the expert team and the client reach preliminary agreement concerning the work to be done and the responsibilities to be assumed by each. Most consultants recognise the importance of formalising this agreement in the form of a written engagement letter. Although not always required, the written engagement letter has been widely used to avoid misunderstandings between the consultants providing the fraud risk assessment engagement and clients regarding the nature, timing, extent and methodology used by the expert team.

The engagement letter is a written contract between the consulting company (the consultant) and the client, which, among other things, may include:

- The nature of the work to be performed (providing awareness of fraud exposure, collecting and obtaining data, surveys, interviews, analysis and synthesis, review, or any combination of those services).

- The period of time over which the engagement is expected to extend.

- Limitations of the engagement with respect to detection of fraud patterns/indicators, errors, irregularities, or illegal acts.

- In the case of exclusively investigation services, a statement that the engagers is not to be construed as a fraud risk assessment engagement.

- Responsibility of the consultants for communicating findings of the engagement.

- Time to be spent on the engagement and fee arrangements.

The consultants who use written engagement letters typically request that clients sign and return a copy of the engagement letter to indicate their acceptance of an agreement with the contents of the letter.

Since the engagement letter forms a written contract between the consultants and the client, adherence to the terms of the letter is part of the consultant's legal responsibility.

Engagement Planning (4), (5), (6), (7)

Once the consultants and the client have reached an agreement, planning of the engagement enters a more detailed stage. Although the length of time required for the engagement may vary with its complexity, it is not uncommon for planning to cover 2 or more weeks (We use 4 weeks as an example for the timing dimension!). In planning a fraud risk assessment engagement, the expert team should develop an appropriate overall strategy.

This strategy requires identification of areas of potential significant risk of corruption, embezzlement, misappropriation of assets, different misstatements and the establishment of preliminary expectations for the inherent risk of fraud and/or errors. (Don't forget that the difference between them is the intent!).

In doing those things, the expert team relies on their own knowledge and skills, observations, anonymous surveys, tips and claims and analytical procedures using selected financial and operational data of the client and finally on discussions with the client. (Don't forget that the client (especially the management) won't be very warmhearted regarding the significant fraud risk if finally identified!

During this stage, the expert must also obtain an understanding of the control structure and the anti-fraud controls (if any!) of the client (the control environment, the accounting system, and critical control procedures or COSO's 5 elements in the big companies and organizations). Several reviews of internal control procedures may also be performed during this period to ascertain whether the system is operating as it was designed and/or there are real significant fraud risks in this internal control system. The procedures are discussed at length below.

II. FRAUD RISK ANALYSIS - ½ week

(8) Identification of the opportunities for occurrence of fraud and abuse and for their concealment

In many cases, the the expert team may reach an early conclusion regarding inadequacy of the control structure and may begin performing surveys through interviews and anonymous questionnaires as to obtain data necessary for further analysis.

(9) Analysis of the data available for patterns of fraud, corruption, abuse, errors, intent, irregularities

After the expert team leaves the client's office, the working papers for the engagement are typically subjected to several reviews by the team manager and by the responsible company manager. During this period, which can take two to three days, recommended adjustments and supplementary disclosures could be discussed with the client. Of course, the client's management is primarily responsible for the whole organizational resistance to fraud but the expert team is responsible for the final results, conclusions and recommendations to the client. Don't forget that "We are talking about Fraud! Are you talking to ME?"

That's why the adequate planning enables the consultants to schedule their work so that it provides adequate time to decide on the nature, timing, and extent of final reviews and surveys necessary for the final field work—when time deadlines for completing the fraud risk assessment engagement are often critical. Properly timed communication of approximate time frames to the client's personnel would enable them to prepare physical facilities to accommodate the engagement and to provide any client-prepared documents, files or database information that the expert team might be able to use in completing the fraud risk assessment engagement on a timely basis.

III. FRAUD RISK ASSESSMENT PHASE - ½ week

10) Ranging the fraud risks according their source, ownership level and significance using two measures - quantitative and qualitative

This final procedure usually begins immediately after analysis of the data available for patterns of fraud, corruption, abuse, errors, intent, irregularities is performed. This will generally last approximately half a weeks after the end of the filed work. The exact amount of time depends on the nature and extent of rating procedures remaining to be performed. It is during this time that a final evaluation is made of the client's significance of fraud risk, to determine the nature, timing, and extent of future recommendations to be proposed.

11) Determination of the fraud risk in two rages - significant or nonsignificant

The expert team may decide at this time that additional reviews or surveys of internal controls, procedures, incentives, intents, opportunities and/or other fraud risk factors to be performed as finally to confirm or reject the final conclusions. This would occur, for example, when circumstances surrounding the client's system of internal controls have changed substantially since the reviews and surveys of processes and/or transactions were performed.

I.V FRAUD RISK RESPONSE - ½ week

12) Development of recommendations for an adequate response and timely measures according the significance of the assessed fraud risk as to develop and/or to enhance the resistance to fraud.

We have already reminded you that the outcome of 3D FRAM is to develop and/or to increase the whole organizational resistance to fraud and not only to reduce the fraud occurrence. Of course, the recommendations will follow the conclusions made by the expert team and they may require urgent response. As a whole we recommend the development and the consolidation of the sample presented by "Dinev's Fraud Resistance Cube" with its all 6 sides - Ethics, Compliance, Fraud Risk Assessment, Fraud Detection, Fraud Investigation and Fraud Prevention!

(13) Preparation and presentation of the final engagement report

Finally, the report has to be delivered to the client. In addition, the expert team manger may have decided that significant fraud patterns or indicators exist in the client's organization. If so, these reportable conditions should be communicated to the client at this time. This may be done through a management letter, in which the consultant may communicate suggestions for initiating a fraud investigation and/or improvements in operating efficiency as well as in anti fraud internal controls.

The presented length of the Timing Dimension is only for educational and training purposes and serves as a time benchmark. Depending on the size of the organization-client and volume of necessary data to be collected and analyzed, the length will differ.

5.2. PERFORMING THE FRAUD RISK ASSESSMENT

3D FRAM's Timing Dimension encompasses the time of all procedures performed during the engagement and some of the most important will be described below.

Performing the engagement includes creating and training the expert team, presentations and communication with the client (owner, management), documentation reviews, field work on different locations, interviews with the employees, vendors, customers, whistleblowers, direct surveys of business processes and transactions, brainstorming discussions with the expert team members and other experts.

Finally, the application of the model with its 3 dimensions has the main goal to present to all stakeholders a professional assessment of the likelihood for the occurrence of different but specific and real for the organization types of fraud, corruption and abuse.

5.2.1. Creating and Training a Team

Fighting "white collar" fraud usually needs an interdisciplinary approach and a good risk assessment requires input from various sources. There are typically two approaches chosen. First one is, the team to be organizationally independent and the second one, the team to be not organizationally independent and to consist of internal for the organization experts.

Ideally, the client should identify and invite an independent fraud risk assessment team from an external company or organization to conduct the fraud risk assessment. Individuals with different knowledge, skills, and perspectives should be involved in such fraud risk assessment engagement. If the internal sources are used then the requirements for the team members could as follows:

•Accounting/Finance/IT/HR personnel, who are familiar with the operations and internal controls.

• Nonfinancial business unit and operations personnel, to leverage their knowledge of day-to-day operations.

• Legal and compliance personnel, if the organization has.

• Internal fraud risk assessment personnel, for companies or agencies with internal experts.

In this case, the management should participate in the assessment, as they are ultimately accountable for the effectiveness of the organization's fraud risk management efforts. The team experts should be aware of the situations where the same management could collude, conceal or perpetrate different types of fraud against the organization.

3D FRAM introduces the situation for creating an external and independent team of experts who should posses the proper knowledge, skills and experience described below.

When new external or internal experts are assigned the task of looking for risk of fraud, many of them could be found without the necessary skills to do a proper assessment. In this section 3D FRAM will provide an overview of what the new assigned expert needs to know about fraud in his or her first fraud risk assessment engagements.

Before starting our description of the knowledge and skills needed be the new assigned experts we will advise them to read first our SMARTGuide from the beginning and to learn more about the following fraud theoretical and practical concepts:

- Incentive/pressure - Need, greed or revenge. Management, other employees, or external parties (for example, for some improper payments) have an incentive or are under pressure, which provides a motive to commit fraud.

- Opportunity - Circumstances exist, such as the absence of controls, ineffective controls, or the ability of management to override controls, that provide an opportunity to commit fraud.

- Attitude/rationalization—Individuals involved are able to rationalize committing fraud. Some individuals possess an attitude, character, or ethical values that allow them to knowingly and intentionally commit a dishonest act.

- Management is in a position that could permit it to perpetrate fraud by directly or indirectly manipulating accounting records; overriding controls, sometimes in unpredictable ways; or committing other fraudulent or improper acts.

- Control anomalies and weaknesses - no documentary (fraud risk assessment) trails or separation and rotation of duties, no internal fraud risk assessment function, no control policies, no code of ethics

- Formulation of intent - the difference between fraud and error

- Acts of theft, fraud, or embezzlement and abuse

- Off-books fraud - bribes, illegal gifts, skimming

- Concealment - alternation, forgery, or destruction of documents

- Fraud Patterns/Red Flags - tips and claims, variances detected, allegations made, behavior pattern change noted

- Internal investigation initiated - evidence gathered, loss of assets confirmed and documented, interrogation of principals

- Prosecution recommended

- Civil recovery sought

- Trial - presentation of evidence at trial

Most types of fraud risks that a new assigned expert would identify, analyze and assess could fall under one of the following types of fraud:

Misrepresentation of material facts. These cases can be prosecuted criminally or civilly. There are numerous criminal statutes that these crimes can be prosecuted under including:

- false statements,
- false claims,
- mail and wire fraud,
- vendor frauds - false invoicing, including overcharges for quantities, hours worked, duplicate charges, substitution of materials, etc.,
- employee frauds - fictitious vendors, expense report frauds
- financial statement frauds - merger candidates, "rogue" subsidiaries or divisions, distributors, customers and vendors

Concealment of material facts. An action for fraud may be based on the concealment of material facts, but only if the defendant had a duty to disclose them in the circumstances. The elements of this type of fraud include:

- That the defendant had knowledge
- Of a material fact
- That the defendant had a duty to disclose
- And failed to do so
- With the intent to mislead or deceive the other party.

Persons who occupy a special relationship of trust, such as the officers and directors of a corporation, an attorney, an accountant, trustee, stockbroker, or other agent may be found to have a duty to fully and completely disclose material facts to the parties who rely upon them.

Bribery. The elements of bribery vary from jurisdiction to jurisdiction, but typically include:

- Giving or receiving
- A thing of value
- To influence
- A business decision

Bribery is a common and costly fraud in the whole world. Although, often it is thought that purchasing agents and other procurement professionals are the targets, executives, information systems managers, operations managers and the like could be the recipients. In major bribery cases, collusion among numerous employees is not unusual.

Economic extortion. The other side of a bribery could be a demand for payment by the decision maker or influencer. Extortion is defined as the obtaining of property from another with the other party's "consent" having been induced by wrongful use of actual threatened force or fear. Fear may include the apprehension of possible economic damage or loss. A demand for a bribe or kickback may constitute an extortion.

Conflict of interest. All countries in the world probably have enacted legislation that prohibits persons, especially in the governmental agencies and municipalities, from engaging in conduct that involves a conflict of interest. Depending on the national legislations a conflict of interest may be prosecuted both civilly and criminally. Elements of a conflict of interest include:

- A person taking an interest in a transaction
- That is actually or potentially adverse to the principal
- Without full and timely disclosure to and approval by the principal.

Like other corruption schemes discussed above, conflicts of interest are fairly common in governmental entities, municipalities, corporations etc. Generally, they involve some type of related party transaction that is not disclosed, such as a relative, a vendor controlled by the decision maker through family relations, stock ownership, etc.

Theft of money or property. The term theft is often used to describe a wide variety of fraudulent conduct. For 3D FRAM purposes we will use it regarding embezzlement, larceny and misappropriation of trade secrets and proprietary information.

Embezzlement is the wrongful appropriation of money or property by a person to whom it has been lawfully entrusted. The common legal elements are generally:

- The defendant took or converted
- Without the knowledge or consent of the owner
- Money or property of another
- That was properly entrusted to the defendant.

Larceny is defined as the wrongful taking of money or property of another with the intent to convert or to deprive the owner of its possession and use. In larceny, unlike embezzlement, the defendant never had lawful possession of the property. The legal elements of larceny typically include:

- Taking or carrying away
- Money or property of another

- Without the consent of the owner

- With the intent to permanently deprive the owner of its use or possession.

Theft or misappropriation of trade marks or secrets and patents may be usually prosecuted under a variety of national and international laws. Trade secrets include not only secret formulas and processes, but other proprietary information such as customer and price lists, sales figures, business plans, or any other confidential information that has a value to the business and would be potentially harmful if disclosed. The elements typically include:

- That a party possessed information of value of to the business

- That was treated confidentially

- That the defendant took or used by breach of an agreement, confidential relationship, or other improper means.

We could express our concern about the copy rights and how our 3D FRAM and Dinev's SMARTGuide will be treated by the professionals in the world preserving them from unauthorized use and distribution! But time will tell!

Attorney/Client Work Product Issues. It is critical for the expert team members to be aware of the parameters of the legal privileges and protections available to the company – particularly when the company is under active investigation by governmental authorities or is likely to be in the near future. A fraud risk assessment engagement must be structured to take advantages of the protections the law offers. Those protections include the attorney – client privilege and attorney work – product doctrine.

Evidence Issues. In assisting or performing a fraud risk assessment, the expert team members will be looking for evidence to prove or disprove the conclusions. Evidence is anything perceptible by the five senses and any form of species of proof, such as testimony of witnesses, records, documents, facts, data, or concrete objects presented legally at trial. Evidence is used to prove a contention and induce a belief in the minds of the client. So evidence can be testimonial, circumstantial, demonstrative, inferential, and even theoretical when given by a qualified anti-fraud expert. Evidence is simply anything that proves or disproves any matter in question.

Generally, to be legally acceptable as evidence, interviews, documents, objects, or facts must be competent, relevant, and material to the issues being litigated and be gathered in a lawful manner. Some of the evidentiary matters considered relevant and, therefore, admissible and defending the conclusions about significant fraud risk, are:

- The motive for the possible fraud

- The ability of the possible defendant to commit the fraud

- The opportunity to commit the fraud

- Threats or expressions of ill will by the accused
- The means of committing the offense (possession of the tools or skills used in committing the fraud)
- Physical evidence at the scene linking the accused to the fraud
- The suspect's conduct and comments at the time of possible arrest
- The attempt to conceal identity
- The attempt to destroy evidence
- Valid confessions, if any

Chain of Custody. When evidence in the form of a document or object is collected or obtained at a specific place, or discovered in the course of an fraud risk assessment engagement, it should be marked, identified, inventoried, and preserved to maintain it in its original condition and to establish a clear chain of custody until it is introduced at the proper authority. If gaps in possession or custody occur, the evidence may be challenged by the client on the theory that the writing or object introduced may not be original or is not in its original condition and, therefore of doubtful authenticity.

5.2.2. Brainstorming Discussions with the Expert Team Members

Members of the engagement team, including the engagement partner, are required to discuss the susceptibility of the client's performance to corruption and fraud. The discussion could include an exchange of ideas (so called, "brainstorming"). The discussion should also emphasize the importance of exercising professional ethics throughout the fraud risk assessment. The discussion may occur prior to, or in conjunction with, other fraud risk assessment planning procedures, but should take place during every engagement.

The questions for the engagement team discussion could be as follows:

- Why does the company/organization have an fraud risk assessment? What possible motives or fraud schemes does this suggest?
- Who are the users of the company's products/services and how do they use them? Which aspects of the products/services are most likely to influence the users?
- Are there any known pressures that would motivate management to fraudulently perform their duties?
- Which processes, activities, accounts or transaction classes are most susceptible to manipulation?
- Are there any known internal control weaknesses, especially overriden controls that would allow fraudulent activities to occur and remain undetected?

- What would you do as to fraudulently misstate the financial statements at this client?
- How would you conceal fraudulent activities especially corruption and off-books fraud at this client?
- How do think, which individuals in the company have the opportunity to embezzled or steal tangible and/or intangible assets?
- Are there any specific known motives or pressures that would motivate employees with opportunity to embezzled assets?
- Which tangible and/or intangible assets of the company are susceptible to misappropriation, either through physical access or unauthorized transactions?
- Are there any known or unknown internal control weaknesses that would allow misappropriation of assets to occur and remain undetected?
- How would you embezzle assets from this company if you have the opportunity?
- Who and how could materially misstate financial statement accounts by embezzling assets?
- What you do as to conceal corrupted practices and/or embezzlement of assets at this client?
- What factors might indicate that the company has a culture or environment that would enable management or employees to rationalize committing corruption and fraud?
- During your surveys have you observed any attitudes, behaviors, or lifestyle changes that may indicate the presence of corruption and fraud?
- Who in the company/organization is authorized or in a position to override controls? Which controls would you override if you were in their position?
- How would you embezzle trade secrets from this company?
- How could financial statement accounts be materially misstated by corrupted or fraudulent activities?
- How would you convert the embezzled assets at this client?

What if Scenarios for the Engagement Expert Team Discussion

- If you were the owner of the company, what would you embezzle, why and how?
- What could be the main reason you have for wanting to deceive the users of the company's tax return and records?
- If you are the owner how would you misstate the financial statements to intentionally influence the users? Or if you are the manager?
- If you were the accountant, how would you embezzle cash (or assets)?
- If you were the receiving worker, how would you steal inventory?

- If you were the accounts payable supervisor, how would you steal cash?
  - If you were the procurement manager, how would you obtain goods or services or bribes for personal use?
  - What kind of methods would you use as to cover up the fraud to keep from getting caught?

As being able to answer to questions presented above the expert team member should perform the procedures described below

Collecting Information to Identify Fraud Risks

The expert team might identify fraud risks as a result of replies to inquiries. To obtain information about fraud risks, the expert should inquire of management about

- any knowledge of fraud or suspected fraud or related allegations;
- management's understanding of fraud risks, including any specific risks the organization has identified and any account balances, assertions, or classes of transactions having likely fraud risks;
- any anti-fraud programs and controls the company/organization has established;
- whether and how the owner/management communicates to employees its views on anti-corruption practices and ethical behavior; and
- whether management has reported to those charged with governance, such as the owner or an audit committee, or others with equivalent authority and responsibility on how the entity's internal control prevents, deters, or detects fraud.

In addition to inquiring of owners/management, inquiring of others may provide a different perspective or provide other important information. Accordingly, the expert team generally could perform the following inquiries and related procedures:

- To obtain information about instances of fraud and to summarize how cases of reported fraud were committed, and then ask management or the owner whether related controls have been strengthened.
- To understand how those charged with governance know about fraud risks, any fraud or suspected fraud, and how they exercise oversight.
- To inquire of internal audit staff about fraud risks, any procedures to detect corruption and fraud during the assessed period, management's response to any such findings, and any fraud or suspected fraud.
- To inquire of other personnel about fraud or suspected fraud. The expert should use judgment to determine whom to ask and the extent of inquiries. For example, the expert may inquire of employees with varying levels of authority, operating personnel not directly

involved in the financial reporting process, employees familiar with complex or unusual transactions or with improper payments, and in-house legal counsel.

If inconsistencies arise from the expert's inquiries of management and others, obtain additional evidence to resolve the inconsistencies.

Identification and Assessment of Fraud Risks

To identify fraud risks, the expert team could perform the following procedures:

- Evaluate the information obtained in the procedures described before, in the context of the three conditions that generally are present when fraud occurs— motive/incentive/pressure, opportunity, and attitude/rationalization. While fraud risk might be greatest when all three of these conditions are evident, observation of one or more of these conditions might indicate a fraud risk.

- Where revenue is (or is expected to be) material, evaluate whether there are fraud risks related to revenue recognition (for example, through premature recognition or fictitious revenue). If the expert teams concludes that improper revenue recognition does not represent a fraud risk, the expert team should document the reasons supporting that conclusion.

- Evaluate the possibility that management could override controls, even if specific fraud risks have not been identified.

For each identified fraud risk, the expert team could determine whether it relates to (1) specific activity, process, financial statement account balances or classes of transactions and related assertions or (2) more pervasively, to the whole activities as a whole. Generally, relating fraud risks to the individual processes, activities, accounts, classes of transactions, and assertions helps in designing fraud risk assessment procedures in ranging these risks.

As part of understanding internal control sufficient to plan the fraud risk assessment, the expert should (1) evaluate whether programs and controls that address identified fraud risks have been suitably designed and implemented and (2) determine whether these programs and controls mitigate these risks, or whether specific control deficiencies increase these risks. See FAM 350 regarding testing the operating effectiveness of controls that are determined to mitigate these risks.

The expert team could assess the identified fraud risks, taking into consideration the results of the procedures described above. In making this assessment, using professional and ethical judgment, the expert team could evaluate significant aspects of each of these risks, including the type of pattern or misstatement, the significance and pervasiveness of the risk, and the likelihood that a significant impact could result.

Response to Assessed Fraud Risks

The expert must respond to the assessed risks of material misstatement due to corruption and/or fraud as the nature and significance of these fraud risks, as well as programs and controls that address identified fraud risks, influence the expert's conclusions and recommendations. The expert should use professional judgment in determining the appropriate response for the circumstances and exercise professional skepticism in gathering and evaluating fraud risk assessment evidence.

The response should (1) affect the overall conduct of the fraud risk assessment, (2) address fraud risks that relate to management override of controls, and (3) for any of these risks that relate to specific financial statement account balances or classes of transactions and related assertions, involve the nature, extent, and timing of fraud risk assessment procedures. If it is not practicable, as part of a financial statement fraud risk assessment, to design fraud risk assessment procedures that sufficiently respond to the fraud risks, the expert may request assistance from the team manager and evaluate the effect of omitting these procedures on the scope of the fraud risk assessment and the fraud risk assessment report.

In some instances, the fraud risk assessment strategy and fraud risk assessment plan could, for reasons other than responding to fraud risk, include procedures and personnel and supervisory assignments that are sufficient to respond to a fraud risk. In those instances, the expert may conclude that no further response is required. For example, with respect to timing, fraud risk assessment procedures could be planned as of the date that the reporting period ends, both as a response to a fraud risk and for other reasons.

The expert should respond to the fraud risks in ways that have an overall effect on the conduct of the fraud risk assessment, as follows:

- Assignment of personnel and supervision—Assign fraud risk assessment team staffing and/ or supervision so that the knowledge, skill, and ability of personnel assigned significant responsibilities are commensurate with the expert's assessment of the fraud risks. For example, the expert may assign a fraud specialist or more experienced staff member or may increase supervision in response to identified fraud risks (also see FAM 270 related to IS controls specialists).

- Review of accounting principles—Review management's selection and collective application of significant accounting principles, particularly those related to subjective measurements and complex transactions.

- Unpredictability of fraud risk assessment procedures—Incorporate an element of unpredictability in the selection of fraud risk assessment procedures from reporting period to reporting period. For example, perform substantive procedures on selected account balances and assertions not otherwise tested due to their materiality and risk, adjust the timing of fraud risk assessment tests, use a different method to select items for testing, or perform procedures at different locations or at locations on an unannounced basis.

Discovery sampling selection usually provides an element of unpredictability as to the specific items tested. Generally, the expert should not inform entity personnel of specific fraud risk assessment procedures prior to performing them, as personnel may take actions to further conceal any fraudulent activity. However, the expert will usually make arrangements to conduct fraud risk assessment work at specific sites in advance, and will instruct entity personnel to locate certain documentation so the expert may test it upon arrival.

The expert should perform procedures to specifically address the risk that management can perpetrate fraud by overriding controls as follows:

- Examination of journal entries and other adjustments—Examine journal entries and other adjustments for evidence of possible material misstatement due to fraud. These include reclassifications, consolidating entries, and other routine and nonroutine journal entries and adjustments. The expert should

  - obtain an understanding of the financial reporting process and the controls over journal entries and other adjustments;

  - identify and select journal entries and other adjustments for testing;

  - determine the nature, extent, and timing of the testing (ordinarily including tests of journal entries and other adjustments at the end of the reporting period); and

  - inquire of individuals involved in the financial reporting process about inappropriate or unusual activity related to the processing of journal entries and other adjustments.

- Review of accounting estimates—Review accounting estimates for biases that could result in material misstatement due to fraud. In preparing financial statements, management is responsible for making judgments or assumptions that affect significant accounting estimates and for monitoring the reasonableness of these estimates on an ongoing basis. The expert should evaluate whether differences between (1) estimates best supported by the evidence and (2) the estimates included in the financial statements, even if the estimates are individually reasonable, indicate possible bias by management, in which case the expert should reconsider the estimates taken as a whole.

The expert also should perform a retrospective review of significant accounting estimates used in the prior year's financial statements, focusing on sensitive or subjective aspects, to determine whether they indicate possible bias by management, and the expert should be alert for aggressive or inconsistently applied estimates. For example, significant changes in allowances for uncollectible accounts that may be tied to performance measures in an effort to improve collections.

- Evaluation of business rationale for significant unusual transactions—Evaluate the business rationale for any significant unusual transactions, considering whether

- the form of these transactions is overly complex;
- management has discussed the nature of and accounting for these transactions with those charged with governance;
- management is placing more emphasis on particular accounting treatments than on the underlying economics of the transactions;
- transactions that involve related parties require review and approval by those charged with governance; and
- the transactions involve previously unidentified related parties (see FAM 902) or related parties that do not have the substance or financial strength to support the transaction without assistance from the entity.

For fraud risks related to specific financial statement account balances or classes of transactions and related assertions, the specific response will depend on the types of risks and the specific balances or classes and assertions, but it generally should involve both substantive procedures and control tests. The response should involve one or more of the following:

- Nature of fraud risk assessment procedures—for example, obtaining related evidence from independent external sources rather than internal sources.
- Extent of fraud risk assessment procedures - for example, increasing sample sizes.
- Timing of fraud risk assessment procedures—for example, performing substantive procedures at or near the end of the reporting period rather than at an interim date.

Key Implementation Considerations

In applying the 3D FRAM to a client, the expert team considers fraud risk assessment objectives, exercise of professional judgment and ethics, references to positions, knowledge of information systems and use of IT specialists, compliance with legislation, use of technical terms, and reference to sections of the 3D FRAM.

5.2.3. Preparing a Fraud Terminology for The Case

As to prepare a fraud terminology for the case the expert team should consider discussing of the susceptibility of the client's financial statements to material misstatement due to fraud. Specifically discuss the following

- How and where the entity's financial statements (for example, which accounts or transaction classes) might be susceptible to material misstatement due to fraud.
- How management could perpetrate and conceal fraudulent financial reporting.
- How the entity's assets could be stolen.

- External and internal factors that might create incentives/pressures, provide opportunities, or enable rationalization of fraud.
- The nature and risk of management override of controls.
- How the fraud risk assessment team might respond to the susceptibility of the client's financial statements to material misstatement due to fraud.

The glossary of terms used by the expert team throughout the whole fraud risk assessment engagement should be prepared in advance and presented to the client during the initial presentations and entrance conference.

3D FRAM's glossary of terms is presented at the beginning of this Dinev's SMARTGuide - in Part 1 but the most important terms used in each engagements are presented below.

Dinev's Compass for Fraud Detection - a methodology for systematic description of the fraud detection process

Perception of Detection - the established atmosphere and organizational environment where the owners, management and employees to be able reveal the patterns of fraud and to response adequately

Fraud Risk - the likelihood that a fraud has been occurring, is occurring or/and will be occurring

Fraud Risk Assessment (3D FRAM) - systematic and iterative process of assessment of the risks relating to the safeguarding of the entity's assets and fraudulent reporting and management consideration of possible acts of corruption

Fraud Risk Management - includes fraud risk identification, analysis, assessment, response

Reasonable Assurance - concept applied mostly as not for focusing on fraud and abuse

Professional skepticism - concept applied mostly for suspecting errors, irregularities, fraud

Fraud Risk Pool - the myriad of risks of corruption, misappropriation of assets and fraudulent reporting which the organization faces daily

Fraud Risk Analysis - assessing the level of the likelihood of fraud occurring and type of response

Inherent Fraud Risk - the likelihood of existence of a fraud before applying a fraud risk assessment process

Risk Assessment - a dynamic and iterative process for identifying and assessing risks to the achievement of objectives

Risk Impact - the effect of the negative event

Fraud Risk Impact - the effect of fraud

Fraud Risk Response - includes fraud detection, fraud investigation, legal prosecution, elimination

Fraud Risk Tolerance - normally should be accepted as "ZERO"

Fraud Risk Velocity - refers to the pace with which the entity is expected to detect occurrence of fraud

Fraud Risk Appetite - if used and applied it would be a nonsense. It would be dangerous affair to being "hungry" or "greedy" for fraud. Fraud is a crime!

Fraud Scenario - the story of how a fraud is carried out

Dinev's Fraud Scenario - 13 (8W+5H) fatal for the potential fraudster descriptive questions

Risk - the possibility that an event will occur and adversely affect the achievement of objectives

Expert's Fraud Risk - the likelihood that the expert will collude or cover a fraud concerning the financial or nonfinancial statements

Fraud Risk Significance - depends on the type of fraud, detection lag, activities, processes, ownership, managerial judgement

Fraud Risk Assessment (COSO 2012) - management's assessment of the risks relating to the safeguarding of the entity's assets and fraudulent reporting and management consideration of possible acts of corruption, both by entity personnel and by external parties directly impacting the entity's ability to achieve its objectives.

Fraud Resistance - the proactive approach, tone on the top, anti-fraud activities, procedures and legal prosecution against fraud in the organization

Fraud Universe - the totality of fraud that could exist or the whole myriad of fraud and abuse which could occur in an organization. As a little humor, for example: The "galaxies" include corruption, misappropriation of assets, fraudulent reporting, money laundering etc. "The planets" could be the countries, "the stars" - the potential fraudsters etc.

Dinev's Fraud Resistance Cube - Ethics, Compliance, Fraud Risk Assessment, Fraud Detection, Fraud Investigation, Legal Prosecution!

5.2.4. Presentations to The Client

The expert team could provide an awareness of fraud, fraud taxonomy, types of fraud schemes, the approaches for increasing the organizational resistance to fraud using multimedia presentations.

Other methods of presenting the information to the client include (1) preparing an outline and presenting it to the client or (2) sending articles and other information followed by personal contact to see if the client has questions about how they could implement, improve, and/or maintain anti-fraud programs and controls within their company.

Client Personnel Involved

The presentation meeting should include key management personnel involved in the control environment and information systems. In smaller entities, attendees might include the owner/ manager and the senior accountant responsible for overseeing the financial reporting process. In larger entities, a representative of senior management (such as the president or chief executive) should attend, as well as top personnel from accounting (such as the chief financial officer or controller) and other functional areas.

In addition, an internal audit representative and members of the audit committee (or the audit committee chair), and in house counsel might also attend. Use professional judgment and ethics in suggesting meeting attendees to the client. The client may suggest attendees as well.

Timing of the Presentation. Clients should be receptive to discussions about control improvements at any time. When delivering the management letter to the client might be a good time to suggest setting up a meeting. This meeting would ordinarily be held at the client's offices to facilitate their ease of attendance. An office environment would be most conducive to a PowerPoint or Apple Keynote presentations, particularly when more than one or two attendees are involved.

3D FRAM EXAMPLE PRESENTATION SLIDES FOR AN ENTRANCE CONFERENCE

Slides 1-2 Overview

The main points of our presentation include:

• The fraud phenomenon and its exposure to your organization.

• Fraud types and fraud schemes.

• Types of fraud risks affecting your organization.

• The methodology for accomplishing the 3D FRAM.

• 3D Fraud Risk Assessment Model.

• A fraud risk assessment example for bribery.

• Achieving effective resistance to fraud.

• Summarizing the presentation with a few concluding remarks.

• Completing the presentation with an open question and answer period.

Slide 3 Reasons You May Be Interested in This Presentation

• As an non governmental company, you do not fall under the provisions of the national legislation and therefore are not required to report on internal control.

- Managements of public or private companies of all sizes are responsible for the company's anti-fraud policy and thus for maintaining anti-fraud controls over all activities. Those controls should be designed to deter, prevent or detect the fraud patterns that could be significant for diminishing the organizational resistance to fraud.

- As a small company, you face unique challenges in maintaining effective internal control due to your small number of accounting personnel.

Slide 4 The fraud phenomenon and its exposure to your organization.

- Nature and characteristics of fraud

- Legal aspects of fraud

- Fraud taxonomy

- How fraud could hurt your organization?

Slides 5-6 Fraud types and fraud schemes

- Cressy's model of fraud

- ACFE Fraud Tree

- Corruption, misappropriation of assets and financial and nonfinancial misstatement

- Cash schemes

- Identity theft schemes

- Internet and computer schemes

- Money laundering

Slide 7 Is the "COSO Internal Control 2012" relevant to your Company?

- Depending on the specifics of the national legislation "The COSO 2012" relates to the activities of many organizations that are required to assess and report on internal control in accordance with their applicable laws.

- Managements of small nonpublic businesses or nongovernmental organizations may also find the guidance useful when designing and evaluating internals controls, including anti-fraud programs and controls.

Slides 8-9 The Five Components of Internal Control - COSO 2012

1. Control Environment

2. Risk Assessment - fraud risk assessment!

3. Control Activities

4. Information and Communication

5. Monitoring

Slide 10 Assessing Fraud Risk and Selecting Mitigating Controls

- Principle No 8 Fraud Risk Assessment
- Identification and Recognition of Fraud Risks
- Analyzing the Fraud Risks
- Response to Fraud Risks

Slides 11-12 The Focus of This Presentation

- 3D Fraud Risk Assessment Model
- 3 Dimensions: Functional, Methodological and Timing
- Risk and Chance
- Fraud Risk Appetite and Fraud Risk Tolerance
- Dinev's Fraud Resistance Cube

Slides 13-14 Types of Fraud Risks Affecting Your Organization

- Theft or embezzlement of tangible or intangible assets
- Conflict of interests and non competent personnel
- Recording transactions in the wrong period, amount, or account
- Failing to gather relevant information when developing time sheets
- Inappropriately use of spreadsheets for applying formulas or calculations
- Recording transactions that do not exist or did not occur
- "Ghosts" employees
- More

Slides 15-16 The Principles Related to 3D Fraud Risk Assessment Model

- Fraud Resistance Strategy (Dinev's Fraud Resistance Cube)
- Fraud Risk Assessment as a part of Fraud Resistance Strategy
- "Zero" Fraud Risk Tolerance
- "Zero" Fraud Risk Appetite

Slides 17-20 Methodology for Accomplishing the 3D FRAM

- Fraud Types and Fraud Risks
- Fraud Risk Assessment Terminology

- Functional Dimension - What?
- Methodological Dimension - How?
- Timing Dimension - How long?

Slides 21-23 Attributes Related to the 3D Fraud Risk Assessment Model

- Stand-alone engagement
- Integral Part of Risk Assessment
- Motives, Incentives and Pressures
- Fraud Risk Factors
- Fraud Risk Scenarios

Slide 24 Approaches for Performing the Fraud Risk Assessment

- Understand potential fraud indicators, including incentives, pressures, opportunities, attitudes, and rationalizations
- Conduct regular fraud risk assessments
- Conduct fraud risk evaluations based on the whole organizational strategy for resistance to fraud

Slide 25 Risk Assessment Example for Bribery

- Using quantitative factors, numerical thresholds are established to define what constitutes significant risk.
- Using qualitative factors, risk is evaluated as significant based on each factor's attributes and importance to the expert team and/or the client
- After evaluating each factor, an overall assessment is made for defining the fraud risk significance.

Slides 26-28 Quantitative and Qualitative Factors Affecting Risk Assessment

- Quantitative Impact on the Financial Statements
- Qualitative Impact on Account Characteristics
- Impact on the Reputation
- Internal Entity-level Factors
- Other Qualitative Factors

Slide 29 Developing Risk Ratings

- Inherent, Significant and Residual Risks

- Ten Rates according the 3D FRAM functions
- The Total Score is 100
- From 0 to 100
- From 100 to 0

Slide 30 Achieving Effective Resistance to Fraud

- The Main Goal of 3D FRAM - To Develop and/or Increase the Resistance to Fraud
- Preventive, Detective, and Compensating Controls
- Effective Control Activities - What Does it Mean?
- Dinev's Fraud Resistance Cube - Ethics, Compliance, Fraud Risk Assessment, Fraud Detection, Fraud Investigation, Legal Prosecution!

Slide 31 Concluding Comments

- Fraud is a Crime!
- Fraud Risk Assessment is a Very Delicate and Difficult for Performing Engagement!
- "COSO 2012" is the next brick in the anti-fraud walls of the organization
- Professional Anti-Fraud Society makes real attempts to develop and to increase the organizational resistance to fraud
- 3D FRAM is an original methodology created to make it possible further researches and developments

Slide 32 Any Questions?

Thank you for your attention!

This presentation should be performed before the client or to his/her representative before as to provide the awareness of what is going on next!

Let's continue with the Planning Procedures now!

5.2.5. Conducting Planning Procedures

Before starting the establishment of the planning procedures the expert team should consider the steps below which summarize how a company/organization's fraud health check is usually performed:

- Understand the risks of fraud and corruption, document them in a fraud and corruption profile and then identify what sort of footprint would be left behind if each method was used.
- Decide where to collect data and information and build a model.

- Select which tests to apply, run the tests and summarize the results in the form of a diagnostic report.

- Interpret and understand the diagnostics report and run further tests if deemed necessary.

- Perform preliminary research into the findings, evaluate them and decide on the next steps.

Just as with any form of fraud health check, a wide range of equipment, tools and techniques can be used and shown in Part 4. However it is wise to be selective, as the more tools used the greater the volume of information generated, not to mention the cost. If you have a good idea what you are looking for, the scope and extent of the company/organization's health check can be much narrower. A well developed fraud and corruption profile is the key to knowing what to test for.

Although planning continues throughout the engagement, the objectives of this initial phase are to gain an understanding of the entity; to understand its environment, processes, relationships, including anti-fraud internal controls; to identify significant fraud risk areas for assessment; and to design and use efficient fraud risk assessment techniques. To accomplish this, the methodology includes guidance in

- establishing an understanding about the 3D FRAM with the client, entity management, and those charged with governance;

- understanding the entity's operations and its environment, including its organization, management style, anti-fraud internal controls, and internal and external factors influencing its operating environment;

- performing procedures for brainstorming with the expert team members as to assist in planning the engagement;

- identifying significant accounts, accounting applications, and financial management systems; important budget restrictions; significant provisions of laws and regulations; and relevant internal controls;

- determining the likelihood of effective information system (IS) controls;

- identifying assertions and using them in planning the fraud risk assessment;

- determining materiality for the financial statements including tolerable misstatement (formerly test materiality) for accounts and related assertions;

- performing a preliminary risk assessment to determine the risk of material misstatement, whether by error or fraud; and

- developing the fraud risk assessment strategy and fraud risk assessment plan, including entity field locations to visit.

Based on data obtained throughout the the fraud risk assessment, the expert team should monitor and revise, if needed, preliminary assessments made during the planning phase for significant fraud risk of corruption, misappropriation of assets and/or misstatement and the likelihood of control ineffectiveness.

The notification letter maybe used by some expert teams to notify the client about the new engagement. This letter may include:

- source of work (request or mandate);
- objective(s) of the fraud risk assessment;
- organizational units and locations to be contacted;
- estimated start date;
- estimated date of entrance conference;
- expert team performing the fraud risk assessment;
- expert team manager contact name, phone numbers, and e-mail addresses; and
- other information.

During the discussions with the client, the expert team could give particular emphasis to the susceptibility of the entity's activities to malpractices and misstatements due to corruption and fraud as discussed earlier.

The fraud risk assessment team could discuss critical issues, such as

- areas of significant risk of corruption and/or fraud;
- areas where the management could override of controls;
- unusual operational and/or accounting procedures used by the organization;
- important anti-fraud controls;
- impact of possible fraud and corruption at the financial status and reputation of the organization;
- how fraud significance will be used to determine the extent of response;
- the application of national legislation to the entity's facts and circumstances; and
- the requirement that the expert team should plan and perform the fraud risk assessment engagement with an attitude of professional ethics.

This should include emphasizing the need to exercise professional skepticism throughout the engagement, being alert for information or other conditions that indicate that the management could try to influence the methodology as to obtain a favorable for them opinion about whether the fraud risk is significant or not.

Understanding the Client's Industry and Operations. It is impossible to perform a fraud risk assessment in a professionally manner without a thorough understanding of the industry in which the client operates as well as all the operations. Such an understanding enables the expert team to place the engagement into proper perspective and to develop a proper assessment of fraud risk and planning risk significance.

Included in the expert team's set of information with respect to the client's industry and operations could be the following:

- General economic conditions of the nation and the geographic region in which the client is located (its status in the international financial crisis, for example)

- Governmental and for example, European Union regulations that might affect the industry and operations.

- Changes in technology and the industry's sensitivity to those changes

- Technologies, including IT used for the activities

- Accounting practices that might be common or unique to the industry.

- Competitive conditions prevalent in the industry

- Financial and economy trends that prevail in the industry

Reliance on the Work of Internal and External Auditors

As explained earlier in Part I, the objective of the expert team regarding the reliance on the work of internal and external expert should be define as very important one.

The reasons are that 1) internal audit differs significantly from that of the external or independent audit. Internal experts perform usually a number of high-level consulting and monitoring services for top management, including a continuing and evaluation of internal control and detection of possible fraud indicators. Beyond that, they typically review operating practices of the client in order to promote increased efficiency and economy, and make inquiries of operating departments at management's direction.

Although the client's internal audit staff may have complete organizational autonomy, it must be remembered that they are still client employees. Therefore, they do not have the level of independence required to render an independent audit opinion on the client's activities and especially on the possible fraud risks associated with the owner(s) and/or the management.

The expert team could also evaluate the opinions and work of the external independent auditors as to identify any errors, irregularities, fraud patterns and/or adjustments made by them. Don't forget the rule, that in a case of the external auditors the business law very often says: "The client is always right!"

The expert team could consider the following attributes of the client's internal audit staff in deciding the extent to which their work can be replied upon:

- The purpose served by the internal audit function in the organization
- The professional competency of the internal audit staff
- The objectivity and level of ethics of the internal audit staff
- The work and recommendations of the internal audit staff

If it is decided that the work of the internal audit staff can or can not be relied upon, the expert team's activities may be affected in either or both of the following ways:

1. Increase the rate of fraud risk significance, and/or

2. Decrease he rate of fraud risk significance.

3D FRAM proposes the independent expert team NOT actually to use the client's internal audit staff to perform certain techniques and surveys using interviews and questionnaires.

5.2.6. Performing The Interviews

The model of the interview will differ for different companies and/or organizations but the common elements could be seen at the Fig. 5-1 below.

Planning the interviews. Planning your interviews will efficiently produce the amount and quality of information you need for answering the question posed by your fraud risk assessment objective.

The information needed. It is important to know first what information you need to obtain to answer your fraud risk assessment objectives, and to answer your specific fraud risk assessment step. Make a list of the things you need to know regarding the fraud risk assessment objectives.

Why to use interview for such Information. Determine whether that information can and should be obtained by interviewing and cannot be obtained through other research methods. It is possible to use ashore information and interviews to corroborate it.

Accountability stages. The cognizant managers and employees at the lowest levels of accountability and everyone above that position in the chain of command should be able to provide certain information that no others can provide.

Staff positions. Line positions are managers and some employees in the chain of command such as first-line supervisors, middle managers and executives and staff positions are people who are not in the chain of command but who influence the process.

Specialists. Specialists who can provide you important information about the fraud risk factors include consultants, contractors, vendors and experts in a given field.

Time for interview. Carefully plan the sequence and length of your interviews for maximum results. Interviewing people in a logical sequence will provide your best interview results.

Planning
The information needed
Why to use
Interview the employees
Time for interview
Time limits
Logical questions
Place for interview
Open-ended questions
Understandable questions
Interview owners /directors
Closed questions

Performing Interviews

Fig. 5-1 Performing Interview procedures

Consultants and Specialists. Interview consultants and specialists first. They can give you background, overviews and explanations that will help you understand the activity you're assessed.

Interview directors and managers. The directors and top managers can give you an overall view of how the decision makers are managing the whole organization and they can reveal how information is flowing in the organization.

Interview the employees. Work subordinates are doing should be consistent with the organization's mission. If not, there is a focus problem. Answers from subordinates should be consistent with answers from managers and executives. If not, there's a communication problem. Everyone in the line should be familiar with pertinent objectives, policies attitude and/or morale problem.

Directors and managers again. You could ask the knowledgeable officials you interviewed previously about answers you received and problems you found from your interviews. If the cognizant directors and managers are not aware of those problems, that's a problem. If executives dismiss problems that you believe are serious, that's a problem.

Place for interview. Choosing the best interview location will help maximize the quantity and quality of information you gain. Generally, a convenient, private, comfortable setting with good acoustics will provide the best results. Some locations are always better for interviewing than others.

Limit the interview time. Limit your interviewing time for maximum productivity and efficiency. Interview during mornings or afternoons, if you can, whichever works best for you. Schedule different durations for different types of people.

How to conduct the interview. The manner in which you interview your subjects will contribute to the quality of information you get. Affirm in advance that you will conduct your interviews in an orderly manner, and plan them accordingly.

In your message, be sure to state (1) the specific fraud risk assessment engagement for which the interview is being scheduled, (2) this fraud risk assessment's general purpose and specific objectives and (3) the name of the persons who will conduct the interview and (4) where and when they will conduct it.

Ask questions in a logical manner. Ask questions in a logical manner and order. Pose generalized questions first and build on those answers. Ask simple questions, then build toward tougher ones. You could lay foundations with elementary questions, then ask questions that expound on those answers.

Ask open-ended questions. Use as many open-ended questions as possible. Open-ended questions ask for extensive information such as descriptions and explanations. Consider the following examples.

"Could you tell me about . . . ."

"How do you proceed with . . . ."

"How did you learn about corrupt practices?"

"Please explain when and this could happen."

"Why were these documents altered like this?"

"Why are you thinking this way?"

With each of these questions, the interviewee will be compelled to provide more than a simple "yes" or "no." Although "yes/no" questions have their value, they are useless for obtaining extensive information.

Ask understandable questions. Ask questions that will be needed for obtaining information needed to answer the questions posed by your fraud risk assessment objectives. Do not waste your time or your interviewee's time asking "phony" questions that have no relevance to your fraud risk assessment objectives.

Ask and closed questions. Ask "closed" questions that will produce simple, straight answers when you need specific information. The following examples are typical.

"How many people work in your company?"

"Who is your manger?"

"How long have you worked here?"

Qualify your interviewee. You could ask questions that qualify your interviewee so you can be confident that the information you will receive is credible, accurate and therefore useful.

5.2.7. Performing Fraud Risk Factors Assessment

Performing the fraud risk factors assessment includes inquiries, reviews, observations and examples for them are presented below.

Inquiries of Management and Others

- Are any inquiries made of management, the audit committee (or equivalent), internal experts, and other employees about the risks of fraud?

- Are you able to identify the owner(s) and/or appropriate members of management to interview?

- Do you regularly corroborate representations of management through other ways?

- If the client does not have an audit committee, are you able to identify any other stakeholders when they exists?

- Are you allowed to identify appropriate employees to interview?

- Do you consider the effect of service organizations on the company's internal control when gathering information and conducting fraud related inquiries?

- Do interviewers prepare for their interviews by reviewing documentation of the engagement team discussion or other appropriate information?

- Do you combine your inquiries about fraud with inquiries made for other planning purposes?

- Do interviewers avoid reading from a list of prepared questions?

- Do interviewers ask appropriate follow-up questions?

- Are additional inquiries made to resolve inconsistencies between responses?

- Do interviewers avoid sophisticated fraud risk terminology and accounting jargon and speak in terms the interviewee can understand?

- Are interviews conducted one -on-one?

- Is the responsibility for conducting interviews not assigned to inexperienced staff?

- Do interviewers avoid excessive note taking, or have a second staff member take notes, and focus their attention on the conversation?

- Do you consider explaining to interviewees the reasons for your fraud related questions?

- Are members of the engagement team performing interviews skilled at effective interviewing techniques?

- Do interviewers ask primarily open-ended questions?
- Do interviewers routinely ask each person they interview whether they are aware or suspect that fraud is occurring, and whether they have committed any fraud against the company?
- Do interviewers routinely conclude the interview by asking if there is anything else the employee would like to add or anyone else the expert should talk to?
- Are interviewers alert to employees' verbal and nonverbal clues that they are being evasive or deceptive?
- Do you ensure that all information from your inquiries that is relevant to the identification of fraud risks is documented for further consideration in the risk assessment process?

Considering Fraud Risk Factors

- Do you consider the presence of fraud risk factors in each fraud risk assessment engagement?
- Do you consider the size of the entity when evaluating fraud risk factors?
- Do you consider the ownership characteristics of the entity when evaluating fraud risk factors?
- Do you consider unique operating or industry conditions related to the entity when evaluating fraud risk factors?
- Do you consider the presence of fraud risk factors only after completing other planning procedures, including the engagement team discussion and client inquiries?
- Do you evaluate fraud risk factors without considering significance or mitigating controls?
- Do you avoid disposing of individual fraud risk factors without considering how they relate to other risk factors as well as other information gathered during fraud risk assessment planning?
- Are you able to determine which fraud risk factors are present and whether they should be considered in identifying significant risks of misstatements due to corruption and fraud?
- Do you sufficiently document the consideration of risk factors and avoid excessive documentation?
- Do you ensure that all information about fraud risk factors that is relevant to the identification of fraud risks is documented for further consideration in the fraud risk assessment process?

Direct Inquiries to All Employees

- Do you know of anyone who is stealing from the company?
- Do you suspect that anyone is stealing from the company?

- Do you know of anyone in the company who is manipulating the accounts or records?
- How could someone steal from the company without getting caught?
- How would you describe the company's (and/or management's) values and ethics?
- Are you upset with the company for any reason? Do you know of anyone who is?
- Have you ever been asked to ignore or override a policy or procedure that is part of your job? Who asked you?
- Have you ever seen another employee circumventing company policies, procedures, or controls? What explanation did they give?
- Have you noticed any unusual changes in the behavior or lifestyle of management or any other employees?
- Do you know of any employees who are under pressure to make ends meet financially?
- How do you think this company compares with others in terms of the honesty of its employees?
- Do you think your co-workers are honest?
- Has anyone you work with ever asked you to do anything you thought was illegal or unethical? What would you do if someone asked you?
- Have you ever been asked to enter false information in the (sales/ purchasing/inventory/ personnel) system or records?
- Has anyone you work with ever asked you to withhold information from the experts or alter documents or records?
- Is there any activity in the company you are uncomfortable with or consider unusual, or that warrants further inquiries?
- Do you feel comfortable raising issues without fear of retribution?
- Is there anything else you would like to add, or anyone else we should talk to?
- Have you yourself done anything against the company that was illegal or unethical?

Direct Inquiries to Management

- What factors (such as market competition or changes in technology) may threaten the company's ability to stay in business or earn a profit?
- How would reporting improved financial results help the company?
- What pressure is put on employees to achieve the company's financial goals, and by whom?
- Have there been any recent changes in sales policies or terms offered to customers?

- Were any large or unusual sales agreements entered into at or near the end of the year?

- What types of customer complaints do you typically receive?

- How is management and/or the board compensated?

- How are financial targets used to determine employees' pay or benefits?

- For example, do bonuses depend on sales or reported earnings?

- Has there been any significant turnover in personnel? In what departments?

- Are there any recent or planned layoffs or changes in pay rates or benefit plans that have or could upset the workforce?

- Have recent bonuses, raises, and promotions met employee expectations? Is there anything planned in those areas that could cause resentment among employees?

- How much help or supervision do you receive from your owners/executives?

- If you could change anything about the company's systems or procedures, what would it be?

- Do any of the company's accounting policies seem unusual or overly aggressive?

- Does management always tend to favor amounts that are on the high (low) side when booking entries, such as estimated liabilities and valuation accounts?

- Does management often use materiality to justify questionable accounting practices?

- Does it ever seem like the method of accounting for a transaction is more important than the transaction itself? Can you give me an example?

- Does the owner/manager run personal expenses through the business?

- What aspect of the company's performance is management most concerned about?

- Are there any changes in procedures or improvements in controls that could easily be made, but management has chosen not to?

- Have there been any unusual changes in the way transactions are processed?

- Are there any people outside the company who have expectations about (or a stake in) the company's performance? What are their needs or expectations?

- Have you ever been asked to record any journal entries that seemed unusual or lacked support?

- Have you ever been asked to make false entries in the accounting records?

- Has the company's relationship with particular suppliers significantly changed (improved or deteriorated) in the past year?

- What types of vendor complaints do you typically receive?

- Is there any inventory you have been told not to count?

- Has there been any unusual movement of goods at or near year end?

- Have there been any unusual changes in the way customer shipments are handled?

Ask about their guidance. Ask questions about their understanding of their guidance (your fraud risk assessment terminology). This information will tell you about how well the guidance has been implemented and about the ability of the fraud risk assessment's team to carry out the guidance and/or requirements.

"Tell me what your manual calls for in this area?"

"Explain your understanding of the regulations."

Look for motive. A person should have a reason for doing things correctly, doing them incorrectly or not doing what they should be doing. The answers will lead to your finding's causes.

"Why do you do things this way?"

"Is this how your manual prescribes the procedure?"

"Has anybody explained this policy to you?"

Look for Opportunity. For anybody to do anything wrong (whether willful or not, whether fraudulent or not), they must have an opportunity to do it. Opportunity is also necessary for establishing the intent.

Always ask for more information. Ask them to tell or show you where you can find additional information, and ask them to send you information that they might have at the office but not with them. Also ask them to send you information that you discussed during the interview, such as reports, brochures, press releases and copies of letters and memos.

Irrelevant questions. Do not ask questions that have no relationship to your fraud risk assessment objective. It's a waste of your time and theirs. Icebreakers and courtesies are excepted, of course, but more and more people are expressing sensitivity to personal questions even when asked as icebreakers.

Inadequate answers. Don't ask questions that will return answers other than you need. For example, asking questions that can be correctly answered without giving you the information you seek will risk getting the wrong information or no information.

Answer-suggesting questions. Answer-suggesting questions give your interviewees hints at what their answers should be.

Accusatory. Don't ask questions that directly or indirectly accuse anybody, even if you believe they are guilty.

"Where have you been getting your money since you stopped using the petty-cash fund?"

Such questions can taint your entire interview, skew your results, and limit your reporting. They also reflect a bias that no expert should have.

Moreover, they infringe on people's rights to due process and trample on the presumption of innocence.

Sensitive and Personal. Do not about sensitive and personal subjects such the following unless you indisputably need the information to help you answer the question posed by your fraud risk assessment objective.

- Physical features such as size, weight, race/ethnicity, hair/eye/skin color, unique markings (birthmarks, tatoos)
- Disabilities such as limps and stuttering
- Age (young, old, middle)
- Sexual orientation
- Religion
- Political philosophies, party affiliations
- Marital, family status
- Outside interests, hobbies, clubs

Questions about these subjects sometimes have a strong relationship to typical fraud risk assessment objectives, so chances are you will sometimes be justified in asking them. Some of these questions might be appropriate to ask in potential fraud cases, but those decisions should be determined separately for each case.

Inquiries of Owner(s)/Management and Personnel

Inquire of the owner(s)/management about the risks of fraud and how the entity addresses them.

You could ask them about the following:

- Their knowledge of any actual fraud or suspicions of fraud affecting the entity.
- Their awareness of any patterns of fraud or suspected fraud affecting the entity.
- Their understanding of the risks of corruption and fraud within the entity, including any specific fraud risks the entity has identified or account balances or transaction classes that may be susceptible to fraud.

- How they communicate to their employees the importance of ethical behavior and appropriate business practices.
- Activities and controls the organization has implemented to address identified fraud and corruption risks or otherwise help prevent, deter, and detect fraud, and how those activities and anti-fraud controls are monitored.
- The nature and extent of monitoring multiple locations or business segments and whether any of them have a higher level of fraud risk.
- If necessary, whether they have reported to the audit committee (or its equivalent) about how the entity's internal control serves to prevent, deter, and detect material misstatements due to fraud and corruption.
- The entity's (a) ethics policies, (b) compliance with laws and regulations, (c) policies relative to the prevention of illegal acts, and (d) use of directives (for example, a code of conduct) and periodic representations obtained from management level employees related to compliance with laws and regulations.

Because management or the owner/manager is often in the best position to perpetrate and conceal corruption and/or fraud, the need for professional skepticism in making the expert's inquiries of management cannot be overemphasized. Generally, it is necessary to corroborate responses, especially those of management or the owner/manager.

The experts should obtain additional fraud risk assessment data to resolve any inconsistencies among responses between management and employees.

The approaches applied during the inquires of owner(s)/management are depicted at Fig. 5-1.

Fig. 5-1 Approaches during the inquiries of owner(s)/management

The following fraud risk factors relate to misstatements arising from fraudulent financial reporting:

Incentives/Pressures

1. Be aware whether information you have gathered about the entity, its operations, and its industry indicates incentives or pressures for management or the owner/manager to intentionally

misstate the information presented in the financial statements. In doing so, consider risk factors such as the following:

a. The situations that indicate the financial instability or profitability of the company may be affected by current financial crisis or other economic, industry, or operating conditions, such as:

b. The situations that indicate strong pressure on management or the owner/manager to meet the requirements or expectations of third parties, such as:

c. The events that indicate management's or the owner/manager's personal gains may be threatened by the company's financial performance, such as:

(1) The owner or management has a significant financial interest in the company that could be threatened by potentially adverse company financial performance.

(2) When there is an absentee owner, a significant portion of management's compensation depends on bonuses, or other incentives, the value of which is dependent on the company meeting aggressive performance targets.

(3) The company is experiencing a weak or deteriorating financial condition and management or the owner/manager has personally guaranteed significant debts of the company.

d. The owner or management puts excessive pressure on operating personnel to meet financial targets, such as sales or profitability incentive goals (for example, for sales personnel).

e. The management or the owner/manager has a strong interest by in minimizing reported earnings for tax motivated reasons.

f. There is a significant interest by management or the owner/manager in hiding or minimizing reported results or assets for other reasons (for example, to minimize the apparent value of the company in a dispute with a co owner, divorcing spouse, etc.).

g. Other:

Opportunities

2. Be aware whether information you have gathered about the entity, its operations, and its industry indicates opportunities for management or the owner/manager to intentionally misstate the financial statements. In doing so, consider risk factors such as the following:

a. Events related to the nature of the company's industry or operations that provide opportunities to engage in corruptive and/or fraudulent activities, such as:

(1) The client's company participates in significant related party transactions not in the ordinary course of business.

(2) The client's company has a strong financial presence or ability to dominate an industry sector that allows it to dictate terms or conditions to suppliers or customers that may result in inappropriate or non arm's length transactions.

(3) The client's company has assets, liabilities, revenues, or expenses based on significant estimates that involve subjective judgments or uncertainties that are difficult to corroborate.

(4) The client's company has significant, unusual, or highly complex transactions that are difficult to assess.

(5) The client's company has significant operations located or conducted in foreign countries where differing business environments and cultures exist.

(6) The client's company has bank accounts (or subsidiary or branch operations) in tax haven jurisdictions for which there does not appear to be a clear business justification.

b. There is no monitoring of management as a result of circumstances such as the following:

(1) When the company is not owner managed, management is dominated by a single individual or small group without compensating controls.

(2) When the company is not owner managed, there is ineffective oversight over financial reporting and internal control by the owner, board of directors, or fraud risk assessment committee.

c. Conditions that indicate a fraud risk because of complex or unstable organizational structure, such as:

(1) It is impossible to determine the unit or individual(s) that control the company.

(2) The client's company has an overly complex organizational structure involving unusual legal entities or lines of managerial authority.

(3) There has been a high turnover in management level employees, counsel, or board members.

d. There are deficiencies in internal control components as a result of circumstances such as the following:

(1) Management or the owner/manager fails to adequately monitor internal controls over the financial reporting process.

(2) There have been high turnover rates or management or the owner/manager continues to employ ineffective accounting or information technology (IT) personnel.

(3) The owner/manager or the management or the continues to employ ineffective accounting systems, especially those with significant known deficiencies in internal control.

Attitudes/Rationalizations

3. Be aware of whether information you have gathered about the entity, its operations, and its industry indicates attitudes/rationalizations on the part of management or the owner/manager to

intentionally misstate the financial statements. In doing so, consider risk factors such as the following:

a. Events that indicate attitudes/rationalizations on the part of management or the owner/manager to engage in or justify fraudulent financial reporting, such as:

(1) The owner/manager or the management fails to effectively define, communicate, implement, support, or enforce the company's values or ethics.

(2) The owner/manager or the management communicates inappropriate values or ethics.

(3) Operational management or personnel excessively participate in (or demonstrate an excessive preoccupation with) the determination of significant estimates or selection of accounting principles.

(4) The client's company has a known history of violations of laws and regulations.

(5) The client's company has a known history of claims against the company, management or the owner/manager, or board members alleging fraud or violations of laws and regulations.

(6) The client's company applies for EU funding and there is an excessive interest by management or the owner/manager in maintaining or increasing the company's earnings trend.

(7) The owner/manager or the management routinely commits to third parties to achieve aggressive or unrealistic forecasts.

(8) The owner/manager or the management fails to correct known significant deficiencies in internal control on a timely basis.

(9) There is an interest by management or the owner/manager in employing inappropriate means to minimize reported earnings for tax motivated reasons.

(10) Management or the owner/manager continually attempts to justify marginal or inappropriate accounting on the basis of materiality.

(11) There is a significant interest by management or the owner/manager in minimizing reported earnings or assets for other reasons (for example, to minimize the apparent value of the company in a dispute with a co owner, divorcing spouse, etc.).

b. Situations indicating a strained relationship between management or the owner/manager and the current or predecessor expert, such as:

(1) Frequent disputes on accounting, audit, fraud risk assessment, or reporting matters.

(2) Limits (formal or informal) that inappropriately hamper access to people or information (or inappropriately restrict communication with the board of directors or audit committee, if the company has one).

(3) Unreasonable demands, such as unreasonable time constraints on completion of the fraud risk assessment.

(4) Unacceptable behavior by management or the owner/manager, especially involving attempts to influence the scope of the expert's work or the selection of personnel assigned to the fraud risk assessment team.

(5) Other situations indicating a strained relationship between management or the owner/manager.

c. Other:

Misappropriation of Assets

The described below fraud risk factors relate to misstatements arising from misappropriation of assets. The extent to which the expert teams considers the risk factors related to incentives/pressures, opportunities arising from control deficiencies, and attitudes/rationalizations is influenced by the degree to which assets susceptible to misappropriation are present. In addition, some of the risk factors related to fraudulent financial reporting may also be present with misappropriation.

Incentives/Pressures

4. Be aware of whether information you have gathered about the entity, its operations, and its industry indicates incentives or pressures for management or employees to misappropriate assets. In doing so, consider risk factors such as the following:

a. What kind of personal financial obligations (such as obligations arising from addictions or abuse related to different vices) create pressure on management or employees, with access to assets susceptible to misappropriation, to misappropriate those assets.

b. Events that indicate adverse relationships between the company and its employees with access to assets susceptible to misappropriation, such as:

(1) Known or prospective future employee layoffs.

(2) Undesired recent or anticipated changes in employee compensation or benefit plans.

(3) Rejection to receive promotions or other expected rewards.

c. Other:

Opportunities

5. Be aware of whether information you have gathered about the entity, its operations, and its industry indicates opportunities for management or employees to misappropriate assets. In doing so, consider risk factors such as the following:

a. Events that indicate an increased susceptibility of assets to misappropriation (including unauthorized disbursements or unauthorized trading in securities), such as:

(1) The client company maintains or processes large amounts of cash.

(2) The client company's inventory is easily susceptible to misappropriation (for example, due to small size, high value, or high demand.)

(3) The client's company has assets that are easily convertible to cash (such as traveler checks and precious metals or stones).

(4) The client's company has valuable fixed assets that are easily susceptible to misappropriation (for example, due to small size, portability, marketability, or lack of ownership identification).

b. Events that indicate possible deficiencies in the company's internal controls over assets susceptible to misappropriation, such as:

(1) There is a lack of appropriate segregation of duties that is not mitigated by other factors (such as effective owner/manager oversight).

(2) There is a inappropriate segregation of duties that makes it easy overriding the controls by the owner/manager or the management.

(3) There is a lack of management or owner/manager oversight of assets susceptible to misappropriation (for example, inadequate supervision of remote locations).

(4) The company lacks job applicant screening procedures when hiring employees with access to assets susceptible to misappropriation.

(5) The company has inadequate accounting oversight over assets susceptible to misappropriation.

(6) The company lacks an appropriate system for authorizing and approving transactions (for example, in purchasing or payroll disbursements.

(7) The company lacks an appropriate system for authorizing and approving the use of company procurement.

(8) There are weak physical safeguards over assets susceptible to misappropriation (for example, inventory not stored in a secured area, cash or investments kept in unlocked drawers, or unprotected passwords).

(9) There is a lack of timely and appropriate documentation of transactions affecting assets susceptible to misappropriation (for example, processing of credits for inventory returns).

(10) Management or the owner/manager has an inadequate understanding of IT that enables IT employees to perpetrate misappropriation.

(11) The client's company fails to conduct inventory counts on a timely basis.

(12) There is a lack of adequate access control over automated records, including controls over and review of computer systems event logs (for example, the audit trail functionality of standardized accounting software packages is not used or can be turned off by employees).

(13) Vacations for employees in key control functions are not mandatory.

c. Other:

Attitudes/Rationalizations

6. Do you know whether information you have gathered about the entity, its operations, and its industry indicates attitudes/rationalizations on the part of management or employees to misappropriate assets. In doing so, consider fraud risk factors such as the following:

a. Events that indicate attitudes/rationalizations on the part of management or employees to engage in or justify misappropriation of assets:

(1) Managers or employees with access to assets susceptible to misappropriation disregard the need to adequately monitor and safeguard assets.

(2) Managers or employees with access to assets susceptible to misappropriation disregard internal controls designed to prevent or detect misappropriation, for example, by overriding controls or failing to correct known deficiencies in controls.

(3) Managers or employees with access to assets susceptible to misappropriation are dissatisfied with the company.

(4) The expert team has observed unusual changes in behavior or lifestyle that may indicate assets have been misappropriated to support this behavior or lifestyle.

b. Other:

Diagnostic Checklist Gathering Information Needed to Identify Fraud and Corruption Risks

The expert team may perform a diagnostic analysis of their process for gathering information needed to identify fraud and corruption risks. The questions are structured to encourage concise answers while, at the same time, providing a broad overview of the information gathering process.

A negative response indicates a potentially troublesome area that may need improvement. Firms may consider additional training, procedural changes, or revisions to firm policies as ways to improve problem areas.

Discussion among Engagement Team Members

- What kind of an engagement team discussion has been held during the planning phase of each fraud risk assessment engagement?

- During the meeting, does the engagement partner remind the fraud risk assessment team about the importance of exercising professional ethics?

- Was the discussion itself conducted with an attitude of professional ethics?
- What kind of an adequate understanding of specific fraud schemes and the characteristics that make assets/accounts susceptible to manipulation did the engagement team members have?
- Are known incentives/pressures, opportunities, and attitudes/rationalizations considered during the engagement team discussion?
- When discussing the potential for fraudulent financial reporting, does the engagement team consider the reasons the company has an fraud risk assessment and the users of the financial statements?
- Does the discussion include an open exchange of ideas, or brainstorming?
- Have you avoided the tendency for discussions to become stale or boilerplate from engagement to engagement?
- Are fraud risk assessment engagement team discussions held in person, rather than by phone or email?
- Who of the managers of the engagement expert team facilitates the discussion?
- How was set a reasonable time limit for the brainstorming portion of the meeting?
- Are you allowed to sufficient time to engage in a well developed discussion?
- Does the meeting take place in a relaxed atmosphere with seating arranged to encourage discussion?
- Do you engage an individual to take notes during the meeting?
- How are engagement team members prepared to participate in the discussion?
- Who outlines the objectives and desired outcome of the meeting?
- Does the facilitator review the ground rules for effective brainstorming?
- Does the engagement team use what if scenarios when discussing fraud risks?
- Do participants refrain from critical discussion and evaluation of ideas generated while brainstorming?
- Do you separate the discussion and analysis of ideas from the brainstorming aspects of the meeting?
- Before leaving the engagement team discussion, does the engagement team reach a consensus on the information that should be considered further when identifying fraud risks?

- Does documentation of the ideas generated at the meeting focus on matters relevant to the identification of risks of material misstatement due to fraud, and is over documentation avoided?
- Do senior staff members refrain from advocating their own ideas in a manner that discourages lower level staff from contributing to the discussion?
- Is the facilitator effective in sustaining the flow of ideas and keeping the energy of the group at a high level?
- Is the timing of the meeting (in relation to the performance of other planning procedures) appropriate for both continuing engagements and newer clients?
- Do all key members of the engagement team, including specialists with an ongoing role in the engagement, attend the meeting?
- If someone is unable to attend the meeting, do you communicate the results of the discussion to that individual?
- As a sole practitioner, are you successful in complying with the spirit of the engagement team discussion requirement?
- Does communication about the risks of fraud continue throughout the engagement?
- Do you ensure that all information from the discussion that is relevant to the identification of fraud risks is documented for further consideration in the risk assessment process?

Considering Fraud Risk Factors
- Do you consider the presence of fraud risk factors in each fraud risk assessment engagement?
- Do you consider the size of the entity when evaluating fraud risk factors?
- How do you consider the owner/manager relationships in the company when evaluating fraud risk factors?
- Are there any unique operating or financial conditions related to the entity when evaluating fraud risk factors?
- How do you consider the fraud risk factors after completing other performance procedures, including the engagement team discussion and client inquiries?
- Are you identify fraud risk factors without considering their significance or anti-fraud controls?
- Do you consider individual fraud risk factors and how they relate to other risk factors as well as other information gathered during fraud risk assessment process?

- How will you be able to determine which fraud risk factors are present and whether they should be considered in identifying fraud and corruption risks?

- How do you document the collected data about risk factors and avoid excessive documentation?

- Are you sure that the collected information about fraud risk factors that is relevant to the identification of fraud risks is documented for further consideration in the risk assessment process?

Considering the Results of Data Collection Methods

- How do you consider unusual or unexpected relationships from initial inquiries if identifying fraud and/or corruption patterns?

- How do you perform data mining procedures related to expenses and their capitalization to identify unusual or unexpected relationships that may indicate fraudulent financial statements?

- Do you obtain an understanding of the company and industry before accepting the fraud risk assessment engagement?

- When performing analytical procedures related to revenue to identify indications of fraudulent financial reporting, do you do more than a simple comparison of current and prior period account balances?

- After evaluating the results of fraud risk analysis procedures, do you consider both the presence of suspected fraud relationships and the absence of expected relationships?

- After analyzing the personal relationships between the owner, management and/or the employees, do you use bases that would be expected to have a reasonable opinion about possible corrupted or fraudulent practices which could be easily perpetrated by the owner or the management?

- How do you analyze trends in the components of revenue and expenses accounts or transaction types?

- After performing ratio analysis related to expenses, do you analyze ratios that use information management generally is unable to manipulate, such as overbilling.

- Do you update your data mining procedures related to early data obtained during the final review stage of the fraud risk assessment?

- How do you document fraud risk analysis procedures related to ranging methodology applied?

- Do you ensure that relevant information from fraud risk analysis procedures is considered when ranging fraud risks?

Considering Other Information

- Do you consider information from client acceptance and continuance procedures when identifying fraud risks?
- Do you consider inherent and residual risks when identifying fraud risks?
- Do you consider information from reviews or compilations of interim financial statements when identifying fraud risks?
- Do you consider the results of inquiries of predecessor experts when identifying fraud risks?
- Do you review the documentation of your understanding of the client, its internal control, and its fraud risk assessment risk factors when identifying fraud risks?
- Do you consider your understanding of accounting procedures and records and the authority, duties, and responsibilities of lower level employees to evaluate where fraud schemes could be conducted and concealed?
- When obtaining an understanding of internal control, do you attempt to determine how accounting and control procedures are actually performed rather than how they are supposed to be performed?
- Do you ensure that relevant information is considered when identifying fraud risks?

Finally, the application of our 3D Fraud Risk Assessment Model in all of its dimensions has been focusing on a preparation of a professional opinion about the likelihood of fraud occurrence and on the more important outcome - to develop or enhance the whole organizational resistance to fraud.

5.2.8. Making Conclusions and Recommendations

Before making the final conclusions and preparing the recommendations the expert team could answer the questions presented below:

- How do you avoid the temptation to use of pieces of information individually, without considering them in the context of all of the information gathered?
- How do you avoid considering fraud significance too early in the process?
- How do you avoid considering anti-fraud controls too early in the process?
- Is all information relevant to the identification of fraud risks assessed and evaluated together?
- Do you synthesize the information to evaluate how seemingly unrelated information might indicate a potential corruption and/fraud risk?
- Do you consider the type of fraud risk that may exist (i.e., corruption, misappropriation of assets or fraudulent financial reporting)?

- When identifying whether a fraud risk could impact the company's image, do you consider the significance or magnitude of the risk?
- Do you consider both quantitative and qualitative factors when evaluating the significance of a potential fraud risk?
- When identifying whether a risk could result in a material misstatement, do you consider the likelihood of the fraud resulting in a material misstatement?
- Do you consider whether the potential risk is pervasive or whether it relates to a specific account balance?
- Do you consider the information in relation to fraud conditions (i.e., incentives/pressures, opportunities, and attitudes/rationalization)?
- When identifying whether a fraud risk could result in a significant quantitative impact, do you consider the extent to which fraud conditions have been observed?
- How do you identify fraud and corruption risks even when only one fraud pattern has been observed?
- Do you articulate fraud risks in terms of their possible impacts on the company's financial stability?
- How do you consider whether it is necessary to identify fraud risks relating to specific operating locations as well as to the company as a whole?
- Does your description of fraud risks indicate, where possible, the processes, people and accounts affected, how they may be affected (that is, interruption, loss), and the type of risk?
- What-If you lack an affirmative reason to overcome the presumption or have observed the presence of fraud patterns related to improper revenue or expenses recognition, do you evaluate the information with a heightened awareness of the need to identify improper revenue or expenses recognition as a fraud risk?
- What-If you do not identify improper capitalizing of expenses as a fraud risk, do you document the reasons supporting your conclusion?
- Do you document identified significant risks of financial and nonfinancial misstatements due to fraud?

Finally, 3D FRAM proposes the risk reduction process to include the following steps:

- The client's owner/management should reach a consensus on the definition of risks levels, likelihood and impact categories discussed in the draft fraud and corruption profile. For example, what would be considered a catastrophic impact as opposed to a severe impact.

- The methods and quick fixes applicable to each unit should be extracted from the quick fix document and given to the relevant managers, who should evaluate and decide which fixes can be implemented. They should report back to the owner/management within a specified time period.

- A workshop could be held where owner(s)/managers re-evaluate and adjust risk levels accordingly and revise the fraud and corruption profile.

- A decision should be made as to the management response to each fraud risk level.

- Legal procedures could be initiated regarding fraud investigation and legal prosecution.

This approach differs from the situation in most empowered organizations with autonomous business units where fraud and corruption are managed solely at the business unit level – because line managers have no effective means of identifying levels of risk or representing them to top management, while owner(s) and/or top management is not sufficiently aware of the potentially catastrophic consequences of certain fraud exposures.

Top management should also be proactively evaluating major exposures, and in a fraud resistant organization they will be aware of the risks and consider them in their decisionmaking process.

Conclusions about Fraud Risk Assessment Process using 3D Fraud Risk Assessment Model

The final fraud risk assessment results could be presented as follows:

• There is a small likelihood (risk) of corruption and fraud occurrence in the organization-client at the moment - the proactive approach has been applied by the owners and management.

• There is a significant likelihood (risk) of corruption and fraud occurrence in the organization-client at the moment - there are urgent measures to be undertaken as like as a fraud detection, fraud investigation, legal prosecution and fraud prevention

• The corruption and fraud risk could be reduced and/or minimized applying quantitative and qualitative measures

The ranging shown above concerns the situation at the moment of making such conclusions and the period of time used for fraud risk assessment process. This 2 ranges type is applied because of the specifics of the type of the risk - the risks of corruption and fraud.

We want just to remind you about the example used in Part 2 where you are one of the two partners in your company and you have received an anonymous e-mail. Reading the text you understand that the other partner embezzles company money with the accomplice - accountant.

You won't calculate the risk as low, middle to high, will you? Just one dollar or euro embezzled by people closed to you will urge you immediately to take adequate measures without waiting the loss for you to be increased enormously.

Following 3D FRAM approaches for risk assessment, evaluation and management, they can first identify those fraud risks which have a less impact and which could not be eliminated. They can then identify options for treating the residual risks, including:

- avoiding the fraud risk,
- reducing the likelihood or impact of the risk by implementing preventive and detective controls
- treating fraud risk appetite as a nonsense
- accepting fraud risk tolerance to be ZERO
- enhancing the whole organizational resistance to fraud with its 6 elements (see in the glossary of terms "Dinev's Fraud Resistance Cube")

The main reason 3D FRAM to apply only 2 rates for the corruption and fraud risks - small (inherent) and significant is these risks are impossible to be compared with and treated as other traditional types of risk. After taking adequate and timely measures the fraud risk could be minimized and categorized as a residual fraud risk.

In other words, the risk of corruption and fraud should be separately assessed and not treated as "specific", "part do the strategic or operational risk", "inherent risk" etc.

Fraud and corruption risks should also regularly be reassessed and reevaluated whenever major change initiatives are introduced; for example, new managers promoted or new employees hired.

Up to this point we proposed and presented you our 3D Fraud Risk Assessment Model as a stand-alone engagement, which could be used not only as a part of the whole Enterprise Risk Management (ERM) of the company/organization but as a part do a financial statement audit and especially as a responsibility consider International Standard on Auditing 240 and the applied in the USA - SAS 99, which follows.

Part VI: 3D FRAM as a Part of Auditors' Responsibilities following the ISA 240 and SAS 99

In this part:

- The Characteristics of the ISA 240 about the Auditors' Responsibility regarding Fraud during a Financial Statement Audit
- The Characteristics of the SAS 99 considering Fraud during a Financial Statement Audit
- Final Comments

6.1. THE CHARACTERISTICS OF THE ISA 240 ABOUT THE AUDITORS' RESPONSIBILITY REGARDING FRAUD DURING A FINANCIAL STATEMENT AUDIT

There is no news that the external (independent) auditors all around the world have the responsibility to comply with the International Standard on Auditing 240 titled INTERNATIONAL STANDARD ON AUDITING 240 THE AUDITOR'S RESPONSIBILITIES RELATING TO FRAUD IN AN AUDIT OF FINANCIAL STATEMENTS, which defines their professional responsibility regarding the risk assessment during a financial statement audit.

And what is the situation in the USA - maybe somebody will ask us immediately? In the USA their Certified Public Accountants (CPA) comply with their own native standard called SAS No. 99 "Consideration of Fraud in a Financial Statement Audit" which highlights the specifics in the audit activities and the federal legislation.

The cited above standards are similar in content but we will discuss them only in the light of the opportunity 3D FRAM to be applied as a part of the financial statement audit too.

Just form the beginning of this part we could insist that the external (independent and governmental) could quite easily apply the 3D FRAM described above as a stand-alone consulting engagement and the compliance with ISA 240 or SAS 99 will be performed in the context of the compliance of all set of standards concerning the financial statement audit.

We provide you shortly with some references of ISA 240 and SAS 99 which will be discussed below:

"INTERNATIONAL STANDARD ON AUDITING 240 THE AUDITOR'S RESPONSIBILITIES RELATING TO FRAUD IN AN AUDIT OF FINANCIAL STATEMENTS

Introduction
Scope of this ISA
1. This International Standard on Auditing (ISA) deals with the expert's responsibilities relating to fraud in an audit of financial statements. Specifically, it expands on how ISA 3151 and ISA 3302 are to be applied in relation to risks of material misstatement due to fraud.

Characteristics of Fraud
2. Misstatements in the financial statements can arise from either fraud or error.
The distinguishing factor between fraud and error is whether the underlying action that results in the misstatement of the financial statements is intentional or unintentional.
3. Although fraud is a broad legal concept, for the purposes of the ISAs, the expert is concerned with fraud that causes a material misstatement in the financial statements. Two types of intentional misstatements are relevant to the expert – misstatements resulting from fraudulent financial reporting and misstatements resulting from misappropriation of assets. Although the expert may suspect or, in rare cases, identify the occurrence of fraud, the expert does not make legal determinations of whether fraud has actually occurred. (Ref: Para. A1–A6)
Responsibility for the Prevention and Detection of Fraud
4. The primary responsibility for the prevention and detection of fraud rests with both those charged with governance of the entity and management. It is important that management, with the oversight of those charged with governance, place a strong emphasis on fraud prevention, which may reduce opportunities for fraud to take place, and fraud deterrence, which could persuade individuals not to commit fraud because of the likelihood of detection and punishment. This involves a commitment to creating a culture of honesty and ethical behavior which can be reinforced by an active oversight by those charged with governance. Oversight by those charged with governance includes considering the potential for override of controls or other inappropriate influence over the financial reporting process, such as efforts by management to manage earnings in order to influence the perceptions of analysts as to the entity's performance and profitability.

Responsibilities of the Expert
5. An expert conducting an audit in accordance with ISAs is responsible for obtaining reasonable assurance that the financial statements taken as a whole are free from material misstatement, whether caused by fraud or error. Owing to the inherent limitations of an audit, there is an

unavoidable risk that some material misstatements of the financial statements may not be detected, even though the audit is properly planned and performed in accordance with the ISAs.3

6. As described in ISA 200,4 the potential effects of inherent limitations are particularly significant in the case of misstatement resulting from fraud. The risk of not detecting a material misstatement resulting from fraud is higher than the risk of not detecting one resulting from error. This is because fraud may involve sophisticated and carefully organized schemes designed to conceal it, such as forgery, deliberate failure to record transactions, or intentional misrepresentations being made to the expert. Such attempts at concealment may be even more difficult to detect when accompanied by collusion.

Collusion may cause the expert to believe that audit evidence is persuasive when it is, in fact, false. The expert's ability to detect a fraud depends on factors such as the skillfulness of the perpetrator, the frequency and extent of manipulation, the degree of collusion involved, the relative size of individual amounts manipulated, and the seniority of those individuals involved. While the expert may be able to identify potential opportunities for fraud to be perpetrated, it is difficult for the expert to determine whether misstatements in judgment areas such as accounting estimates are caused by fraud or error.

7. Furthermore, the risk of the expert not detecting a material misstatement resulting from management fraud is greater than for employee fraud, because management is frequently in a position to directly or indirectly manipulate accounting records, present fraudulent financial information or override control procedures designed to prevent similar frauds by other employees.

8. When obtaining reasonable assurance, the expert is responsible for maintaining professional skepticism throughout the audit, considering the potential for management override of controls and recognizing the fact that audit procedures that are effective for detecting error may not be effective in detecting fraud. The requirements in this ISA are designed to assist the expert in identifying and assessing the risks of material misstatement due to fraud and in designing procedures to detect such misstatement.

Effective Date

9. This ISA is effective for audits of financial statements for periods beginning on or after December 15, 2009.

Objectives

10. The objectives of the expert are:

(a) To identify and assess the risks of material misstatement of the financial statements due to fraud;

(b) To obtain sufficient appropriate audit evidence regarding the assessed risks of material misstatement due to fraud, through designing and implementing appropriate responses; and

(c) To respond appropriately to fraud or suspected fraud identified during the audit.

Definitions

11. For purposes of the ISAs, the following terms have the meanings attributed below:

(a) Fraud – An intentional act by one or more individuals among management, those charged with governance, employees, or third parties, involving the use of deception to obtain an unjust or illegal advantage.

(b) Fraud risk factors – Events or conditions that indicate an incentive or pressure to commit fraud or provide an opportunity to commit fraud...."

You maybe already notice that in the cited part of the ISA 240 the auditors' responsibility is limited to two types of intentional misstatements - misstatements in result of fraudulent reporting and misstatements which are the sequence of misappropriation of assets. There is no word about corruption and off-books fraud. No books, no fraud!

Beside this limitations, such accounting/auditing definition for fraud usually differs regarding the fraud definitions applied in the national legislations all around the world. There is nothing mentioned about the bribes and kickback, illegal gifts, conflict of interest, insider trading will all of is facets, bid rigging, economic extortion etc. The former sequence forms the compound term of the very and wide know word of "corruption"!

Let's hope that our analysis will help for changing of this ISA 240 in the near future! In fact, the updated version of "COSO 2012 Internal Control - Integrated Framework" highlights such expectations!

However, the approach for the risk assessment for misstatement because of fraud following ISA 240, cited before, could be described as follows:

"...18. The auditor shall make inquiries of management, and others within the entity as appropriate, to determine whether they have knowledge of any actual, suspected or alleged fraud affecting the entity. (Ref: Para. A15–A17)

19. For those entities that have an internal audit function, the auditor shall make inquiries of internal audit to determine whether it has knowledge of any actual, suspected or alleged fraud affecting the entity, and to obtain its views about the risks of fraud. (Ref: Para. A18)

Those Charged with Governance

20. Unless all of those charged with governance are involved in managing the entity,8 the auditor shall obtain an understanding of how those charged with governance exercise oversight of management's processes for identifying and responding to the risks of fraud in the entity and the internal control that management has established to mitigate these risks. (Ref: Para. A19–A21)

21. Unless all of those charged with governance are involved in managing the entity, the auditor shall make inquiries of those charged with governance to determine whether they have knowledge of any actual, suspected or alleged fraud affecting the entity. These inquiries are made in part to corroborate the responses to the inquiries of management.

Unusual or Unexpected Relationships Identified

22. The auditor shall evaluate whether unusual or unexpected relationships that have been identified in performing analytical procedures, including those related to revenue accounts, may indicate risks of material misstatement due to fraud.

Other Information

23. The auditor shall consider whether other information obtained by the auditor indicates risks of material misstatement due to fraud. (Ref: Para. A22)

Evaluation of Fraud Risk Factors

24. The auditor shall evaluate whether the information obtained from the other risk assessment procedures and related activities performed indicates that one or more fraud risk factors are present. While fraud risk factors may not necessarily indicate the existence of fraud, they have often been present in circumstances where frauds have occurred and therefore may indicate risks of material misstatement due to fraud. (Ref: Para. A23–A27)

Identification and Assessment of the Risks of Material Misstatement Due to Fraud

25. In accordance with ISA 315, the auditor shall identify and assess the risks of material misstatement due to fraud at the financial statement level, and at the assertion level for classes of transactions, account balances and disclosures.

26. When identifying and assessing the risks of material misstatement due to fraud, the auditor shall, based on a presumption that there are risks of fraud in revenue recognition, evaluate which types of revenue, revenue transactions or assertions give rise to such risks. Paragraph 47 specifies the documentation required where the auditor concludes that the presumption is not applicable in the circumstances of the engagement and, accordingly, has not identified revenue recognition as a risk of material misstatement due to fraud. (Ref: Para. A28–A30)

27. The auditor shall treat those assessed risks of material misstatement due to fraud as significant risks and accordingly, to the extent not already done so, the auditor shall obtain an understanding of the entity's related controls, including control activities, relevant to such risks. (Ref: Para. A31–A32)

Responses to the Assessed Risks of Material Misstatement Due to Fraud

Overall Responses

28. In accordance with ISA 330, the auditor shall determine overall responses to address the assessed risks of material misstatement due to fraud at the financial statement level.10 (Ref: Para. A33)

29. In determining overall responses to address the assessed risks of material misstatement due to fraud at the financial statement level, the auditor shall:

(a) Assign and supervise personnel taking account of the knowledge, skill and ability of the individuals to be given significant engagement responsibilities and the auditor's assessment of the risks of material misstatement due to fraud for the engagement; (Ref: Para. A34–A35)

(b) Evaluate whether the selection and application of accounting policies by the entity, particularly those related to subjective measurements and complex transactions, may be indicative of fraudulent financial reporting resulting from management's effort to manage earnings; and

(c) Incorporate an element of unpredictability in the selection of the nature, recognition, evaluate which types of revenue, revenue transactions or assertions give rise to such risks. Paragraph 47 specifies the documentation required where the auditor concludes that the presumption is not applicable in the circumstances of the engagement and, accordingly, has not identified revenue recognition as a risk of material misstatement due to fraud. (Ref: Para. A28–A30)

27. The auditor shall treat those assessed risks of material misstatement due to fraud as significant risks and accordingly, to the extent not already done so, the auditor shall obtain an understanding of the entity's related controls, including control activities, relevant to such risks. (Ref: Para. A31–A32)…"

From here the comparison of the similarities and differences between the approaches applied by the 3D FRAM and the cited parts of the ISA 240 could serve as an addition to the big picture of the fraud risk assessment process.

The similarities between the risk assessment of the misstatements in financial statements because of fraud and the 3D FRAM could be summarized in the following manner:

• The basic steps of the financial statements audit are planning, sampling, testing and reporting

• Developing an audit program for performing audit procedures, for testing the internal controls and the statements made int the financial statements

• Inspecting the documentation and records as to formulate opinions

• Preparing a report with an opinion based on the financial statement audit goals.

The differences between our 3D FRAM and the risk assessment during the financial statement audit following ISA 240 could be defined as follows:

• The fraud risk assessment program in 3D FRAM is developed as to identify the likelihood of fraud occurrence and not to provide the reasonable assurance about the the effectiveness of the internal controls or about the opinion for fair and true presentations of the financial situation of the organization using the financial statements.

• The phases of the fraud risk assessment in the traditional audit are based on the link between the internal controls and the risk of fraud. 3D FRAM uses data mining and the prospects for possible and/or expected events.

• 3D FRAM uses the discovery sampling - ISA 240 uses the random selected sampling.

• The fraud risk assessment in 3D FRAM focuses on the authenticity of the presented statements and documents and not on the recorded and documented data for every one statement.

• 3D FRAM uses data collected and/obtained mostly from external sources but the traditional audit usually relies mostly on the internally generated data.

• The opinion using 3D FRAM is prepared using reliable data with regard of the intent associated with the possible specific fraud scenarios for the organization.

In addition to the requirements of ISA 240 described above the auditor should perform other specific procedures during the whole audit duration, namely:

• Assessment of the audit evidence trough:

  • Assessment of the risk of a material misstatement because of fraud during the whole performance of the audit.

  • Assessment of whether the analytical procedures, performed as detail tests or during the whole review draw the attention to unrecognized risk of material misstatement because of fraud

  • Assessment of the risk of material misstatement because of fraud at or near the end of the field work procedures

• Taking measures regarding misstatements which could be in a result of fraud

• Performing meeting with the management, audit committee etc. considering possible fraud.

Level of assurance

The level of assurance considering the fraud risk assessment will depend on the level of concealment complexity and on (in)ability to access to the the accounting books and records.

In a case of on-books fraud scheme and non complicate the auditor will be able to obtain a high level of assurance about the fraud scenario occurrence.

In other case of off-books fraud scheme and a high level of complexity, the auditor won't obtain the same level of assurance about certain fraud scenario occurrence.

Reliable evidence

The concept of reliability encompasses both quantitative and qualitative aspects of the audit evidence associated with the fraud scenario. Practically, after the event is identified, the question will be about whether sufficient and reliable evidence is available as to adequate and necessary measures to be taken.

Sufficient competence and capacity

The sufficient capacity and competency concern the ability of obtaining data from external sources and this external source to be informed that the auditor requires such data.

There is a tendency recently many companies to require contract clause for performing their own audit during their business with construction or maintenance companies with expensive and long-term projects.

Test procedures

There are two fundamental test procedures considering the fraud risk assessment:

a) test procedures of fraud scenarios, and

б) test procedures of the controls, developed for deterrence of external and internal fraud.

Both types of test procedures could be modified according the specific of the organization and where there are no any anti-fraud controls, promptly to be created adequate controls.

6.2. THE CHARACTERISTICS OF THE SAS 99 "CONSIDERING FRAUD DURING A FINANCIAL STATEMENT AUDIT"

You could use the reference of the SAS 99 "Considering Fraud during Financial Statement Audi" applied in USA as a comparison to ISA 240 as to see the similarities and differences between them!

"AU 316"[19]

Consideration of Fraud in a Financial Statement Audit
(Supersedes SAS No. 82.) Source: SAS No. 99; SAS No. 113.
Effective for audits of financial statements for periods beginning on or after December 15, 2002, unless otherwise indicated.

Introduction and Overview
.01 Section 110, Responsibilities and Functions of the Independent Expert, paragraph .02, states, "The expert has a responsibility to plan and perform the audit to obtain reasonable assurance about whether the financial statements are free of material misstatement, whether caused by error or fraud.[footnote omitted]"1 This section establishes standards and provides guidance to experts in fulfilling that responsibility, as it relates to fraud, in an audit of financial statements conducted in accordance with generally accepted auditing standards (GAAS).2
.02 The following is an overview of the organization and content of this section:
• Description and characteristics of fraud. This section describes fraud and its characteristics. (See paragraphs .05 through .12.)
• The importance of exercising professional skepticism. This section discusses the need for experts to exercise professional skepticism when considering the possibility that a material misstatement due to fraud could be present. (See paragraph .13.)
• Discussion among engagement personnel regarding the risks of material misstatement due to fraud. This section requires, as part of planning the audit, that there be a discussion among the audit team members to consider how and where the entity's financial statements might be

susceptible to material misstatement due to fraud and to reinforce the importance of adopting an appropriate mindset of professional skepticism. (See paragraphs .14 through .18.)

• Obtaining the information needed to identify risks of material misstatement due to fraud. This section requires the expert to gather information necessary to identify risks of material misstatement due to fraud, by

a. Inquiring of management and others within the entity about the risks of fraud. (See paragraphs .20 through .27.)

b. Considering the results of the analytical procedures performed in planning the audit. (See paragraphs .28 through .30.)

c. Considering fraud risk factors. (See paragraphs .31 through .33, and the Appendix, "Examples of Fraud Risk Factors" [paragraph .85].)

d. Considering certain other information. (See paragraph .34.)

• Identifying risks that may result in a material misstatement due to fraud. This section requires the expert to use the information gathered to identify risks that may result in a material misstatement due to fraud. (See paragraphs .35 through .42.)

• Assessing the identified risks after taking into account an evaluation of the entity's programs and controls. This section requires the expert to evaluate the entity's programs and controls that address the identified risks of material misstatement due to fraud, and to assess the risks taking into account this evaluation. (See paragraphs .43 through .45.)

• Responding to the results of the assessment. This section emphasizes that the expert's response to the risks of material misstatement due to fraud involves the application of professional skepticism when gathering and evaluating audit evidence. (See paragraph .46 through .49.) The section requires the expert to respond to the results of the risk assessment in three ways:

a. A response that has an overall effect on how the audit is conducted, that is, a response involving more general considerations apart from the specific procedures otherwise planned. (See paragraph .50.)

b. A response to identified risks that involves the nature, timing, and extent of the auditing procedures to be performed. (See paragraphs.51 through .56.)

c. A response involving the performance of certain procedures to further address the risk of material misstatement due to fraud involving management override of controls. (See paragraphs . 57 through .67.)

• Evaluating audit evidence. This section requires the expert to assess the risks of material misstatement due to fraud throughout the audit and to evaluate at the completion of the audit whether the accumulated results of auditing procedures and other observations affect the assessment. (See paragraphs .68 through .74.) It also requires the expert to consider whether identified misstatements may be indicative of fraud and, if so, directs the expert to evaluate their implications.

(See paragraphs .75 through .78.)

• Communicating about fraud to management, those charged with governance, and others. This section provides guidance regarding the expert's communications about fraud to management, those charged with governance, and others. (See paragraphs .79 through .82.)

• Documenting the expert's consideration of fraud. This section describes related documentation requirements. (See paragraph .83.)

[Revised, April 2007, to reflect conforming changes necessary due to the issuance of Statement on Auditing Standards No. 114.]…"

So, we hope that the fraud risk assessment process, described by our 3D Fraud Risk Assessment Model and applying ISA 240 and SAS 99 will gage the interest of other experts, academicians and researchers who will want to make a step ahead in this so important and significant for all societies areas.

FINAL COMMENTS

The news in the first edition of Dinev's SMARGuide could be summarized as follows:

3D Fraud Risk Assessment Model (3D FRAM) concentrates the experts' efforts to the integration of three dimensions: functional, methodological and timing.

3D FRAM provides a new business opportunity as a stand-alone engagement which could be performed as a part of the traditional financial statement audit or enterprise fraud risk management.

3D FRAM heavily supports the updated "COSO 2012 Internal Control - Integrated Framework" especially in the part of assessing fraud risk in the companies.

You alone could make your own conclusions about the advantages and disadvantaged of our 3D FRAM and could send your comments using our email addressL info@iepinet.eu.

And our advise is: After reading this "paper" in its e-formats - .pdf or .ePub, turn back and read it again! This 3D FRAM is proposed not to be a fiction for only a holiday but to serve you as very time when you feel you need it!

This is the first version of 3D FRAM and it will be updated regularly for free for all who supported our efforts and bought it till 2013!

What's next! The detailed description of the model "Dinev's Compass for Fraud Detection" will be presented soon! Look at http://iepinet.eu/IEPIUSA/NEWS.html

See you soon!

IEPI Ltd.

April 18, 2012

[1] Managing the Business Risk of Fraud: A Practical Guide, AICPA, ACFE, IIA, 2008, p. 5

[2] ACFE, 2010 Report to The Nations On Occupational Fraud and Abuse, p. 6

[3] ACFE, 2010 Report to The Nations On Occupational Fraud and Abuse, p. 7

[4] Zabihollah Rezaee, Richard Riley, Financial Statement Fraud: Prevention and Detection", 2nd ed.,Wiley, 2010, p. 5-6

[5] Website: www.cifas.org.uk

[6] http://www.homeoffice.gov.uk/agencies-public-bodies/nfa/, Last visited on April 18, 2012

[7] Managing the Business Risk of Fraud: A Practical Guide, AICPA, ACFE, IIA, 2008, p. 20

[8] http://en.wikipedia.org/w/index.php?search=fraud+scheme&title=Special%3ASearch last visited last on16 March 2012

[9] http://en.wikipedia.org/wiki/Phishing, Last visited on April 15, 2012

[10] http://www.oversightsystems.com/resources/industry_research.php, Last visited on April 17, 2012

[11] Managing the Business Risk of Fraud: A Practical Guide, IIA, AICPA, ACFE, 2008, p.24

[12] http://en.wikipedia.org/wiki/Data_mining, Last visited on April 17, 2012

[13] http://customsolutionsofmaryland.50megs.com/, Last visited on April 18, 2012

[14] **Stephan Spenser, Google Power Search, 2011, O'Reilly Media Inc., p. 1**

[15] **Stephan Spenser, Google Power Search, 2011, O'Reilly Media Inc., p. 7**

[16] Look at http://goo.gl/TWbX5, Last visited on April 1, 2012

[17] http://en.wikipedia.org/wiki/Cost_benefit_analysis Last visited on April 18, 2012

[18] http://en.wikipedia.org/wiki/Sensitivity_analysis, Last visited on April 18, 2012

[19] http://www.aicpa.org/Research/Standards/AuditAttest/Pages/SAS.aspx#SAS84 Last visited on April 17, 2012

www.ingramcontent.com/pod-product-compliance
Lightning Source LLC
Chambersburg PA
CBHW042147220326
41599CB00003BB/12